Since 1981, Michael Wiese Productions has been dedicated to providing novice and seasoned filmmakers with vital information on all aspects of filmmaking and videomaking. We have published more than 50 books, used in over 500 film schools worldwide.

Our authors are successful industry professionals — they believe that the more knowledge and experience they share with others, the more high-quality films will be made. That's why they spend countless hours writing about the hard stuff: budgeting, financing, directing, marketing, and distribution. Many of our authors, including myself, are often invited to conduct filmmaking seminars around the world.

We truly hope that our publications, seminars, and consulting services will empower you to create enduring films that will last for generations to come.

We're here to help. Let us hear from you.

Sincerely,

Michael Wiese
Publisher, Filmmaker

SOUND DESIGN

The Expressive Power of Music, Voice, and Sound Effects in Cinema

by
David Sonnenschein

Published by Michael Wiese Productions
11288 Ventura Blvd., Suite 621
Studio City, CA 91604
tel. (818) 379-8799
fax (818) 986-3408
mw@mwp.com
www.mwp.com

Cover Design: Alexander Arkadin
Book Layout: Gina Mansfield

Printed by McNaughton & Gunn, Inc., Saline, Michigan
Manufactured in the United States of America

ISBN 0-941188-26-4

Library of Congress Cataloging-in-Publication Data

Sonnenschein, David
Sound design: the expressive power of music, voice, and sound effects in cinema/ by David Sonnenschein.
p. cm.
Includes bibliographical references.
ISBN 0-941188-26-4
1. Sound motion pictures. 2. Sound—Recording and reproducing.
3. Motion pictures—Sound effects. I. Title.

TR897 .S66 2001
778.5'344—dc21

2001035804
CIP

TABLE OF CONTENTS

ACKNOWLEDGMENTS .... **xiii**

FOREWORD .... **xv**

PREFACE .... **xvii**

THE CREATION OF A SOUND DESIGNER xvii

INTRODUCTION .... **xix**

HOW TO USE THIS BOOK xx

NOTATIONAL SYSTEMS xxi

SOUND ENERGY TRANSFORMATION xxii

CHAPTER 1 CREATING THE SOUND DESIGN STEP-BY-STEP **1**

THE FIRST SCRIPT READING 2

WHAT TO LISTEN FOR 2

Objects, actions, environments, emotions, and transitions 2

Explicit sounds 3

Environments 5

Clues to the emotions 6

Physical or dramatic transition 9

GROUPING THE VOICES 10

DRAWING VISUAL MAPS 12

MEETING WITH THE DIRECTOR 15

THE SOUND MAP — DRAFT 1 18

CONSULTING BEFORE AND DURING THE SHOOT 23

ACCOMPANYING THE PICTURE EDIT 25

ANALYZING THE FINAL PICTURE EDIT 26

THE SOUND MAP — DRAFT 2 31

DEFINING VOICE SOURCES AND MODIFICATIONS 32

DEFINING SOUND EFFECTS AND AMBIENCE SOURCES 35

COORDINATING WITH THE MUSIC SCORE 43

EXPERIMENTATION AND OPEN OPTIONS 45

EXHIBITION CONSIDERATIONS 46

THE SOUND MAP — DRAFT 3 49

PRE-MIX DECISIONS 50

THE FINAL MIX AND PRINT MASTER 52

CHAPTER 2 EXPANDING CREATIVITY **53**

TAPPING INTO THE DREAMSCAPE 55

IMAGINATION TOOLS 56

INVENTING ORIGINAL SOUNDS 57
Cartoon and foley 57
Musique concrète 58
Recording techniques 60
Sound shaping 60
Emotional impact 61

CHAPTER 3 FROM VIBRATION TO SENSATION **63**
THE SOURCE 63
THE MEDIUM 64
SOUND QUALITIES 65
Rhythm 65
Intensity 66
Pitch 67
Timbre 67
Speed 68
Shape 68
Organization 70
PHYSICAL EFFECTS OF SOUND 70
THE EAR 72
Hearing development 72
Outer ear (pinna/ear canal) 73
Middle ear (ear drum/ossicles) 73
Inner ear (cochlea) 74
Sensitivity 74
Masking 75

CHAPTER 4 FROM SENSATION TO PERCEPTION **77**
LISTENING MODES 77
Reduced 77
Causal 78
Semantic 78
Referential 78
Less is more 79
GESTALT PRINCIPLES AND ILLUSION 79
Figure and ground 80
Completeness, good continuation, and closure 81
Proximity and similarity 81
Common fate and belongingness 82
Illusion 83

SPACE 83
Size, distance, and perspective 84
Echo and reverberation 85
Directionality 85
Subjective/emotional space 86
Movement 87
TIME 89
Temporal resolution and integration 89
Speed 89
Subjective time 90
TONE 91
Frequency perception 91
Loudness 92
Recognition 93
Habituation and hearing loss 94
Tonal center 95
Out-of-tune and beat phenomena 96
Historical perspective 96
ENTRAINMENT 97
CHAPTER 5 MUSIC TO OUR EARS **101**
ORIGINS OF MUSIC 102
FEELINGS VS. ORDER 103
EMOTIONAL SIGNIFIER 104
Openness 104
Insights 105
Groups 106
Emotional inventory 107
GENRES 109
STRUCTURE AND FUNCTION 110
World music 111
Feminine form 113
Violating form 113
THE CASE OF THE SONATA 114
RHYTHM AND ANTICIPATION 115
Rhythm of the body 115
Meter and phrasing 116
Repetitiveness 116
Perception of rhythm 116
Anticipation 117

MELODY 119
HARMONY AND DISSONANCE 120
TONAL CENTER 123
SILENCE 124
CONTRAST 128

CHAPTER 6 THE HUMAN VOICE 131
THE VOCAL INSTRUMENT 131
DEVELOPMENT OF SPEECH 132
SPEECH RECOGNITION AND VERBAL UNDERSTANDING 134
MEANING VS. FEELING 137
PROSODY — VOCAL MELODY AND EMOTION 138
MANTRAS, NONSENSE, AND BEYOND 142
VOICE PERSONALITIES 144
ALIEN LANGUAGE 146

CHAPTER 7 SOUND AND IMAGE 151
EYES AND EARS 151
ON SCREEN, OFF SCREEN, AND OUTSIDE THE STORY WORLD... 152
***On screen* 153**
***Off screen* 153**
***Nondiegetic* 154**
MUSIC IN FILM 155
***Emotional signifier* 155**
***Continuity* 155**
***Narrative cueing* 155**
***Narrative unity* 155**
***Programmatic music* 156**
***Anempathetic music* 156**
DIALOGUE IN FILM 156
***Theatrical speech* 156**
***Textual speech* 157**
***Emanation speech* 157**
***Elimination* 157**
***Ad libs and proliferation* 158**
***Multilingualism and foreign language* 158**
***Dialogue recording and postproduction* 159**
SPATIAL DIMENSIONS 159
***3-D space* 160**
***Hi-fi vs. low-fi perspective* 161**
***Size* 162**

Point of audition 163
Sensation and texture 164
TEMPORAL DIMENSIONS 164
Rhythm of life 164
Linearity 164
Narrative cueing 165
BRIDGING AND BREAKS 165
SYNCHRONIZATION 166
Point of synchronization 167
ADDED VALUE AND MULTIPLE MEANINGS 168
CHAPTER 8 SOUND AND NARRATIVE **173**
NARRATIVE ANALYSIS 173
MUSIC AND STORY 175
CHARACTER IDENTIFICATION 176
Objective audience perspective 177
Subjective character experience 177
Nonliteral sound 178
Emotional associations 179
PRIMARY AND SECONDARY EMOTIONS 181
ENVIRONMENTS AND THE “SOUNDSCAPE” 182
INVENTING SOUND OBJECTS 190
Impact 190
Firearms 191
Vehicles 192
Fire 193
More ideas and techniques 193
AUDITORY HIERARCHY 195
DRAMATIC EVOLUTION 198
Earthquake effect 200
PRODUCTION DESIGN AND IMAGE ANALYSIS 201
PERFORMANCE ANALYSIS 203
SOUND REFERENCES 205
Universal 205
Cultural 206
Historical 209
Film specific 210
PLEASANTVILLE — CASE STUDY INTEGRATING STORY AND MUSIC 212

CHAPTER 9 THE FUTURE OF SOUND DESIGN **215**
A WORD ON SOUND POLITICS — WHEN CAN WE START? 215
INTERNET AND INTERACTIVE MEDIA 217
APPENDIX **219**
CLASSIFICATION OF SOUNDS 219
FILMOGRAPHY **225**
BIBLIOGRAPHY **227**
INDEX **233**
DAVID SONNENSCHEIN **245**

ACKNOWLEDGEMENTS

This book is the fruit of influence from many masters in many disciplines. I have been fortunate to be able to apply their knowledge and creativity in the area of film sound. Some of the industry's most innovative and prolific sound designers who contributed actively by sharing their experiences with me were Gary Rydstrom, Dane Davis, George Watters II, Ben Burtt, and Frank Serafine, while Walter Murch has served as a longtime inspiration through his teachings, writings, and groundbreaking films. The Brazilian musical genius Hermeto Pascoal showed me how to create symphonies with baby toys, a swimming pool, and the voice of the Pope — mixing these unexpectedly with his folklore, classical, and jazz traditions. John Cage certainly deserves high honors in this area of avant garde sound composition as well, inspiring a whole generation. Pioneers in sound healing, music therapy, and the influence of sound on our well-being, Dr. Mitchell Gaynor, Don Campbell, Dr. Alfred A. Tomatis, Robert Jourdain, Dr. Peter Ostwald, and Joachim-Ernst Berendt have shown how we can expand our human potential with the use of sound. Michel Chion and Claudia Gorbman have been instrumental in codifying the use of sound and music in film, so that we may have a theoretical language to share, study, and create in the audiovisual form. I am grateful as well to those who have encouraged me directly and offered feedback during the years of preparation of this book, including Anna Penido, Steve Capellini, Marcelo Taranto, Richard Ollis, Midge Costin, and Ralph Sonnenschein, and finally to Michael Wiese and Ken Lee, who recognized the value of this book since its early stages of gestation.

FOREWORD

I first knew of David Sonnenschein when we were both graduate students at USC School of Cinema-Television and his thesis film won the MPSE (Motion Picture Sound Editors) Golden Reel Award for Best Sound. It was almost twenty years later that we crossed paths and I found myself having an enlightening and spirited discussion about the creative potential of sound in visual media. In the intervening years, David had developed a career as writer, producer, and director of films, and I had become a sound editor in Hollywood (*Crimson Tide*, *The Rock*, *Armageddon*) and head of the sound department at USC. I am thrilled that David has written down his wonderfully creative practices and eclectic theories on sound. Both the serious student and professionals alike can benefit from David's personal experience as musician and filmmaker, as well as his extensive research in the areas of psychoacoustics, the human voice, and Gestalt psychology.

As a feature film sound editor I have had the good fortune of working on one of the best sound editing crews in Hollywood. However, my frustration grew as I became painfully aware of how infrequently sound is used to its full creative potential. When USC approached me to teach, I jumped at the chance. Here was an opportunity to teach future directors, producers, writers, etc., how to use sound well. At the School of Cinema-Television we provide cutting-edge technology and facilities for the students and set them on the course of "learning by doing." Anyone can pick up a piece of equipment or a manual to learn "how to." So the most important resource is in fact the faculty with their experience in the field and their ability to tap into the students' creative skills. Many of the best sound designers in film today are graduates of USC: Walter Murch, Ben Burtt, Gary Rydstrom, to mention a few. They attribute their success to being encouraged to explore, experiment, and create by the then faculty head, Ken Miura.

Students come to me all the time with a script or copy of their film in hand, asking how to begin thinking about sound. This is where David's book comes into play. It leads the reader down the path of creativity and experimentation with sound in a way no other text has done before. To me, it's a cross between Michael Chion's work and *The Artists Way* for sound. *Sound Design* really leads the reader into the exploration of sound in a narrative approach, giving a way to create a soundtrack which is specifically designed for his or her film.

David's step-by-step methods of creating a sound design are somewhat outside the norm for the film industry, but that's what makes them so fresh and creative. One of the parts I found most enjoyable and enlightening were the interviews of sound designers I know and respect. I discovered I had marked the pages for most of those interviews so I could pass the information on to my students. So dive in and start creating and designing!

Midge Costin, MPSE
Associate Professor/Head of the Sound Department
USC School of Cinema-Television

PREFACE

The creation of a sound designer

What attracts someone to become a sound designer? Musicians fascinated by the potential of playing with images... cartoon "*whiz-bangs*" affecting a tender young mind... a solitary techie finding a creative outlet.... The routes are many, and each brings its own fertile seeds of expression.

My story may shed some light on how different experiences meld into a synergy toward sound design. I began studying clarinet at eight, performing in symphony orchestras and chamber groups, then took up the flute with the conscious choice *not* to read music, but to *jam*, developing my ear's sensitivity and spontaneity.

As a neurobiology undergraduate at UC San Diego, my interests in physiology, psychology, and dreams were united by research in a sleep laboratory. Fascinated by the mind-body interface, I published several studies relating brainwaves to mental states and biorhythms, and developed insight into the physiological and perceptual processes that serve as foundations for the creation of sound design.

My musical exploration continued when I lived in Indonesia and Thailand, listening to, collecting, and playing local instruments made of bamboo, palm fronds, and gourds. Returning to the U.S. to direct "Little Red Riding Hood: A Balinese-Oregon Adaptation," I mirrored the form of the Balinese mask dance, playing bamboo instruments with the clarinet and flute, and composing a nonverbal soundtrack by assigning to each character a theme and instrument in the style of Prokofiev's "Peter and the Wolf."

In the M.F.A. program at USC Cinema School I found a healthy atmosphere to continue exploring sound design, inspired by guest lecturers like master sound designer Walter Murch. My thesis film *The Owl's Flight* utilized sounds of Pre-Columbian ceramic instruments, animal calls, Tijuana marketplace atmosphere, and a variety of fire effects to construct the right mood for a story about a Mexican Indian shaman and the battle over his sacred healing mask, which garnered an award from the Motion Picture Sound Editors (MPSE).

Relocating to Rio de Janeiro, I directed the feature *Super Xuxa*, a *Wizard of Oz*–like fantasy starring Xuxa Meneghel, the popular kids' TV show host and singer. This gave me the opportunity to introduce a sound design concept to an industry which in the past has not paid much attention to audio quality, collaborating with Brazilian producers and directors to develop their soundtracks while administering workshops throughout Brazil and Cuba. Finding a gap in the literature regarding the narrative use of the soundtrack, and recognizing that my sound design methodology is quite unique, spurred me to write this book.

With digital technology upon us, I am also exploring the expanding possibilities of sound design for interactive media and have formed Sonic Strategies — a company dedicated to education, consultation, and development in this growing arena. The concepts presented within this book are fundamental to all audiovisual work, and so are beneficial to New Media developers, as well as filmmakers. As you read, I hope you become as inspired as I have.

INTRODUCTION

Giving meaning to noise, sound becomes communication. Humans have used sound for eons to alert one another, organize activities, exchange messages, entertain, love, and battle. Through sound we can trace the evolution of religion, music, language, weaponry, medicine, architecture, and psychology, not to mention cinema.

The ancients attributed acoustic phenomena to divine origins as a sort of powerful and indestructible substance animating everything that moves. For them the thud of a spear piercing an animal contained a death-dealing power, and the roar of a waterfall caused the earth to tremble. Egyptian generals excited their men with trumpet calls and drumbeats to improve their morale and stimulate greed for combat. During the Renaissance, sounds were devised to deceive authorities with hidden meanings inside chromatic intervals, a secret communication of contraband ideas and religious controversy.

Storytelling has used sound to invoke myth, suspend reality, and create emotion since the times of fire circles in protective caves. Sound designers in the 21st century have the same job — to combine sight and sound for enrapturing their audiences. Both the shaman of old and the sound designer of today must develop their perceptive ability, meaning the two sides of creative intelligence: impression and expression. Vocal reproduction of either sound effects (compare a shovel digging into sand, gravel, clay, then snow) or human voices (impersonating friends or famous people) can enhance our ability to hear what is happening and know that it is indeed registering in the brain.

The true sound designer must be immersed in the story, characters, emotions, environments, and genre of the film. With their contribution the audience will be led down the path in an integrated, yet most often subconscious manner toward an experience that is authentic and human, a metaphor for the life experience itself. Using all the tools of music, psychology, acoustics, and drama, the art of orchestration comes into play, selecting the right sound for the right moment. The sound designer performs a balancing act between making the best aesthetic choices and the technical parameters of completing the film on time, in budget, and with the tools and personnel at hand.

But for all the rules offered in this book or anywhere else, storytelling should always come first. Yes, learn the basics, then you can know when to break the rules. Mistakes can also become the genius of error, so have no hesitation about trying things out. If it works, use it! Rather than consistently following a formula, experimentation within form is a way that art, energy, and drama can be created. It may seem like an exalted goal, but the path from sound "janitor" to sound designer can evolve from being a "techie," to an "artiste," and finally a storyteller.

How to use this book

This book pulls together theory and background on sound generation, psychoacoustics, music, voice, image, and narrative. The sources are wide and sometimes very technical or esoteric, but the purpose of this text is to be user-friendly and practical. If you want to get more in-depth, many resources are listed in the Appendix, and can offer you remarkable journeys in themselves.

Screen the film examples listed if you can, as there are usually many more incredible moments of sound than have been cited here. Even if you've seen them before, it is likely that you didn't focus all your attention on the sound elements. The creativity of each of those sound designers can inspire your own ideas, so don't be shy about saturating yourself with the inspiration of your peers.

When I say **TRY THIS**, go for it! The root of all your creativity is in having experience and sharing it. Get all that theory, file it where it belongs; then get into doing the act of listening and making sounds. The incubation period is necessary as you study and receive explanation of purpose to all the structure. Then first-hand observation of the real world is invaluable, learning to separate and distinguish elements, and you will be able to more keenly recognize relationships both between sounds and between environments. By sensing psychoacoustic phenomena directly, you will be more prepared to manipulate the sonic elements according to your personal world view of the real world of sound, not just repeat what others have done inside films. You will discover what you like or dislike, and how open you are to new experiences which you can then share with the audience. You'll also find where your personal strengths lie (physical, psychological, creative, technical) and what you might want to develop further to become a master sound designer.

Go listen, record, and make sounds where no one has gone before. The suggestions in this book are the tip of the iceberg, only the beginning of where you might venture. Experiment, explore, and report back to the audience with your creative voice.

With the audiovisual world moving into interactivity and the Internet, this is also the perfect medium for us to create a forum of ideas with sound design. I encourage you to be in contact with me directly with any questions, discoveries, or fascinating insights which can then be shared with all through a Web site that will be developed. Keep in touch through my email: *dsonn@charter.net* (if there are any changes in email, please check with the publisher at *www.mwp.com*).

I'm looking forward to hearing from you. Have a fantastic journey.

Notational systems

The tools and language for the sound designer require notational systems to be able to communicate to oneself and others while developing the orchestration of the soundtrack. Some useful ones that are covered in detail in this book include:

1) **Chronological** — what activities and focus are needed to create each stage of the sound design (see Chapter 1, **Creating the Sound Design Step-by-Step**)
2) **Acoustic** — the mechanical properties of sound as can be measured (e.g., duration, frequency, intensity, rhythm, reverb, etc.) (see Chapter 3, **From Vibration to Sensation**)
3) **Perceptual** — how the human ear and brain absorb and interpret sound (see Chapter 4, **From Sensation to Perception**)
4) **Musical** — representation of any sounds that possess "musical" features (see Chapter 5, **Music to Our Ears**)

5) **Phonetic** — human speech that gives meaning to vocal sounds (see Chapter 6, **The Human Voice**)
6) **Audiovisual** — film theory involving perception and the use of sound with visual information (see Chapter 7, **Sound and Image**)
7) **Emotional** — how a sound affects the interpretation of a character's emotional state, or the audience's reaction (see Chapter 8, **Sound and Narrative**)
8) **Descriptive** — categorization of sound effects, objects, animals, ambiences, etc. (see **Appendix**, ***Classification of sounds***)

Sound energy transformation

Another perspective on how sound works is based on looking at the relationship between the film, the theater, and the audience. In other words, what sounds are coming from where, how are they transmitted, and what effect do they have upon sensation and perception? (These three sequential stages are uni-directional in the traditional movie theater, but within the new interactive media there will be a bi-directional flow blossoming more and more.)

Then we have the different parallel levels of what qualities the sound is transmitting to the audience:

1) **Physical** — the mechanical, electronic, technical aspects interacting with our bodily, biological functions
2) **Emotional** — story, emotional identification with the characters and their goals, creating empathetic reactions (like laughing or crying)
3) **Intellectual** — structural, aesthetic considerations that are most often conveyed verbally in the context of human interaction
4) **Moral** — ethical or spiritual perspectives and dilemmas, alerting us to possible choices beyond our own personal fulfillment or survival

These all provide parameters to help define the function of the sound design in telling the story of the film. As characters and the audience are transformed, so is the sound. In this relationship, there exists a kind of resonance that makes the film work on many levels. This book explores all these levels throughout each chapter.

SOUND ENERGY TRANSFORMATION — CHART

Sequential STAGES	FILM →	SCREENING →	AUDIENCE
Parallel LEVELS			
PHYSICAL technical, mechanical, biological	sound sources, acoustic environment, recording, editing, mixing, transfers	sound playback system, theater space, theater audience presence	auditory system, neurological functions
EMOTIONAL psychological, dramatic	story, characters, goals, conflicts, tone of voice, music, rhythm	external audience reaction (e.g., laughter, screams, crying)	laughter, tears, heart-beat, empathy for characters' emotions
INTELLECTUAL structural, aesthetic	music composition, verbal ideas	(not applicable)	heightened awareness, confusion, mystery, suspense, humor
MORAL spiritual, ethical	unresolved dilemmas, ambiguous relation-ships, search for resolution/unity	(not applicable)	choice of identification, inner questioning

CHAPTER 1

CREATING THE SOUND DESIGN STEP-BY-STEP

With an eye and ear on practical applications, this chapter starts right off with the nuts and bolts of developing the soundtrack from script to final mix. These are the stages:

- ***The first script reading***
- ***What to listen for — objects, actions, environments, emotions, transitions***
- ***Grouping the voices***
- ***Drawing visual maps***
- ***Meeting with the director***
- ***The sound map — draft 1***
- ***Consulting before and during the shoot***
- ***Accompanying the picture edit***
- ***Analyzing the final picture edit***
- ***The sound map — draft 2***
- ***Defining voice sources and modifications***
- ***Defining sound effects and ambience sources***
- ***Coordinating with the music score***
- ***Experimentation and open options***
- ***Exhibition considerations***
- ***The sound map — draft 3***
- ***Pre-mix decisions***
- ***The final mix and print master***

The order of steps in the design of the soundtrack proposed here is a likely scenario that allows your greatest participation in the creative process, but you may not always have control of the scheduling. Each production will have its own circumstances: the moment when you are contracted, with whom you will be meeting, what elements you will have at hand or what really works for your personal style, as well as that of your principal collaborators — the director, sound editor, and music composer.

Remember that none of these techniques, nor the order in which they may be applied, are absolutes. Each person will have strengths in perception and imagination (i.e., perceiving without an outside stimulus) that may emphasize the verbal, visual, aural, logical, emotional, or kinesthetic capacities of brain processing. So the techniques and exercises suggested throughout this book should serve as guides for you to find and utilize the most effective methods that tap into your own expanded awareness and creativity.

The first script reading

The written script should be the first "listening" you will have of your soundtrack. Even if the film has been shot, or edited, don't let your eagerness to jump into the visuals spoil this unique opportunity. Regardless of the difference between the writer's words and what has been shot, read the script first. Your impressions of what will transmit the story through sound will be virgin, and may very well draw more upon your inner ear if the input is from the page rather than the filmed image. Once you've seen the image, it is almost impossible to go back to the more primary stage without being influenced by the impression that the visual will have made.

When reading the script for the first time, you'll get a lot more out of it if you do this from beginning to end with no interruption, and at a pace as close as possible to the final film pace (usually a minute per page). If you can do this, you'll get a more accurate feeling of the storytelling pace and the rhythms inherent in the drama, and it will be your *only* opportunity to get it like a first-time viewer. After this reading you'll be digging into individual elements, pulling things apart and putting them back together while consciously searching for creative solutions. So close the door, turn off the phone, and get into it for a few hours nonstop, as if you were sitting in the movie theater. But leave the lights on and have a pencil in hand. You will use the pencil like a conductor's baton, nimbly marking the script as your eyes dance down the lines.

What to listen for

Objects, actions, environments, emotions, and transitions
On the first reading you'll be looking for key words and ideas that immediately impress you. In subsequent readings, especially after meeting

with the director and other creative colleagues, these same ideas and more key words should be tracked down in much greater detail, while you note the development and transformation of these sounds throughout the story. Techniques for clarifying the developmental lines for the sounds will be given below.

There are several different "voices" to listen for within the following categories:

1) sounds linked to **people, objects,** and **actions** on screen that are **explicitly described**
2) **environments** that can be fleshed out with sonic ambiance
3) key words in both scene description and dialogue that give **clues to the emotions** of the scene (both of the character and of the spectator)
4) moments of **physical or dramatic transition**

When you notice these on the page, circle, use checkmarks or any other rapid notation to mark the word or phrase. If you feel the urge to write an observation, economize by using a word or two at most, just enough to later cue the memory of your entire thought. You can invent a code (e.g., "ew" for *eerie wind*), marking the repetition or development of a certain sound or theme that carries throughout the film. But keep moving forward without losing the pace of the story, and don't worry about getting it all marked out on the first read-through.

Explicit sounds

Scriptwriting convention pays a certain homage to the power of audio by requesting that each sound be capitalized in the body of the scene description:

```
The oncoming truck's HORN BLASTS as the out-of-con-
trol car swerves violently, its WHEELS SCREECHING.
```

It makes for a bit more exciting reading — and a good writer can create a visual rhythm on the page that can aid in establishing rhythm on the screen — but the major purpose is to help the production manager identify, schedule, and budget the production of these sounds. In fact, after the sound designer has completed the script analysis and created the sound map, the production manager will have a much more accurate document for basing his budgeting.

The sound designer's development of the audio track is more extensive and subtle than the screenwriter's, and for good reason. The page simply should not and cannot hold the depth of information that will be on the audio track, as similarly a script should not detail camera angles nor all production design elements.

But within every **character**, **object**, and **action** on screen there can be generated a potential sound that may give further dramatic impact to the scene and story, and this sonic coloring is the challenge for you to reveal.

```
The little boy tiptoes along the spiky tops of the
rotten picket fence, trying in vain to ignore the
menacing bulldog chained just below him.  As the
mad dog lunges against its restraints, the boy's
hands spastically flap to maintain balance, his
sneaker losing grip.
```

So here we see two **characters**, a protagonist and antagonist, the boy and the dog. What kind of sounds would each be eliciting in this circumstance? The boy would try to be as silent and invisible as possible, but he can't avoid breathing, which might very well be irregular, forced, and audible due to his stress in holding everything else so controllably, especially when he slips. It seems that the dog would be growling at the very least, perhaps in a crescendo toward an aggressive bark.

The **objects** include a chain, which holds double intent in the scene. The wild clinking forms part of the aural attack against the boy, but as it clangs taut it serves as the only thing protecting him. (Notice how this audio analysis could contribute to the storyboarding and blocking of the action if done before the shoot.) The contact of the boy's shoes with the untrustworthy fence could surely generate nerve-racking, splintering creaks, and the slip itself may be accentuated with the weakness of a slippery rubber sole.

Both characters and objects are linked to the **action** verbs, which create an emotional context to the scene. Find motion, directionality, and moments of impact. Sound qualities that might accent each of the verbs in the above scene could be: "tiptoes" — dainty tap-tap-tapping; "lunges" — attacking, explosive, growing closer; and "spastically flap" — arrhythmic whooshing.

Environments

Information about the environment first appears in the scene headings, which are as succinct as possible to help the production manager do the breakdown, and which denote three items: EXTERIOR or INTERIOR, LOCATION (with perhaps HISTORICAL PERIOD) and TIME OF DAY. Then there usually is a modest amount of detail given in the first paragraph of scene description, appearing something like this:

```
EXT. CORNFIELD - NIGHT

The rows of cornstalks bathe motionlessly in the
moonlight. In the middle of the field, a single stalk
begins to shake, slowly at first, then possessed with
a nervous energy that spreads contagiously to its
neighbors.
```

Part of your job will be to create the reality of these explicit locations and times, but for now you should look for the subtext that these environments may lend to the development of the story and characters. The above scene could belong to a terror or comedy film, and may mix the genres to have an even greater impact at the moment of tension and turning point in the narrative. Let's assume this is a pure terror film, introducing since the beginning of the script (with an appropriate title) a supernatural, malevolent force.

The words "Night," "motionlessly," and "moonlight" tell us this would be a quiet place, but what might be the type of silence that would contrast well with the first break of that silence by the rustling of the cornstalk? To best hear the cornstalk's shaking, which will be a random mixture of fairly high frequencies, the contrasting background "silence" could be a single frog croaking in a lower register with a defined periodicity.

Attention will be heightened when the sounds of "silence" noncompetitively fill in the tonal and rhythmic spectrums, with our brains more readily registering the aural contrast.

The distance or intimacy of the sounds can transmit a dramatic intent by telling us where we are and what might be a threatening noise to be noticed. We can decrease the frog's immediacy by filtering out the higher frequencies in its croak and giving a tiny reverb to lend a sense of calmness, distance, and surrounding space. By accenting the high frequencies of the cornstalk shaking we create a greater presence. If we choose to make the environment claustrophobically collapse, the frog croak can gain on the high frequencies, while we multiply the croaks to have frogs surround us from all sides. Or we can do the opposite, as the cornstalks' movement spreads menacingly, by adding reverb and increasing the volume to the point of filling up the whole environment, and thus our subjective head space as well.

Clues to the emotions

Adjectives and adverbs give flavor to the scene descriptions, hinting to the director, actors, production designer, DP (director of photography) and sound designer what feeling should prevail. One can imagine a thousand kinds of "LIVING ROOM — DAY" if no emotional detail is given to the scene description and only blocking of the actors' movement is indicated (which is pretty bad screenwriting technique, since this aspect should be left mostly for the director and actors to determine during rehearsals). But if a word or two of colorful portrayal is interjected, it thrusts our eyes and ears into a specific reality: *abandoned, rainbow-colored, marble-columned, blood-stained, cold neon,* etc.

You may see a word that seems so out of context with the rest of the description that it could serve as a sound clue. Mark it for special attention. For example, the location could be a very dark alley, with sinister tension built into the movement and dialogue. If suddenly there appears a "luminous ethereal ball," the contrast should be made that much greater by characterizing the environment's negative, antagonistic feeling with a sonic ambiance that will allow the arrival of the good-guy ball in the most opposite of sounds to those of the threatening alley. You can most effectively use pitch, timbre, and attack in counterpoint.

Description of a scene can give you a sense of energy and direction of emotion. During a horse race, for example, bettors have gambled not only their money but their hopes, and these can be exposed through the action and reaction in the soundtrack. It can also give hints to the characters' personalities and what we can expect to accentuate in the audio during their dramatic journey throughout the film.

```
The chanting crowd rises to its feet as the horses
head into the home stretch.

Hooves pound.  Frank's horse Supper Time nudges
ahead of Peter's horse Zip Drive.

Frank bounces like a superball, HOOTING like a
hyena.

Peter GROWLS like a bear, punching the air in swift
hooks.
```

Assuming these two fellows will be competing not only at the racetrack but throughout the story, their forms of communication and temperament will have nuances in acting style, costume, camera angle, and sound. The sound treatment will start with the use of voice (each actor's interpretation), how it is recorded (type and placement of microphone, location, or studio recording) and postproduction sweetening (filters, multitracking). Then the conditions of the ambient sounds and music will be added to reflect, support, and/or contrast with each character, following the principles of psychoacoustics (outlined in the later chapters). It all begins with the emotion that jumps off the page.

In the above case, what the two characters are feeling at that moment is considered a primary emotion, in contrast to a scene description that generates a reaction from the audience (or reader), which is denoted as a secondary emotion. An example of this is clear in a scene in which the character is trembling with anxiety, but the audience is rolling in laughter:

```
Hanging over the bubbling industrial cooking pots,
Harold tries for the third time to lift the slippery
```

```
hard-boiled egg between his two big toes.  As he
holds on for dear life to the drooping coat hang-
er, he manages to pinch the egg with his extra long
toenails.  Slowly, slowly, he raises the egged toes to
his mouth... But slowly, slowly the egg begins to
crack and disintegrate...
```

In a scene that has a contrast between primary and secondary emotions, we have a choice to employ the sound purely with one emotion, or to use spatial or temporal counterpoint to heighten the tension. In the following examples, I am taking liberty to use my own definitions for the various types of comedy and the rules they may follow — for the sake of showing the kinds of choices that can be made in sound design.

A satire would most likely carry us into Harold's world as the chosen point of view, focusing on the primary emotion by exaggerating the seriousness of his plight. This could be done by exploiting the cliché sounds of an action thriller, i.e., threatening low frequencies in the boiling vats below, nerve-racking dissonant metal bending of the coat hanger, Harold's audible irregular breathing, and the ominous cracking of the egg reverberating in the tiled kitchen.

In a slapstick comedy, the tone would also be exaggerated and even less subtle, with a silliness in recognition that we are the delighted observers participating in the secondary emotion, prodding us directly to the point with a more cartoonish style of sounds. The bubbles would sound with more melodic poppings, sliding the tones in a circus-organ-like clown dance. The bending hanger would be a springy *doowing-doowing*. Harold's breath would probably not be heard at all, so as to help focus us on our own laughing breath even more. The cracking of the egg would have a stuttering but intelligent rhythm, a kind of tease to draw out the tension to the fullest extent.

In a comedy that alternates between the primary and secondary emotions, we have the opportunity for a sophistication of shifting point of view and pulling the audience off-guard more than they expect from either a pure satire or a slapstick comedy. By mixing the conventions, a new rhythm can be established, a kind of "beat frequency" phenomenon between the two points of view, primary and secondary, that tickles the audience's fancy so that they feel like their own heads are being tossed around on an emotional rollercoaster. Intersecting planes of reality conspire to heighten the humor, and in this case the sounds can be selected from both points of view to make this counterpoint. For example, the threatening volcanic-like bubbles from below will contrast greatly with the cartoonish springy hanger from above. Harold's struggling breath could be heard in hyper-closeness, then completely disappear when the egg cracking is cued to enter in full attention-getting intensity.

Physical or dramatic transition

The flow of drama leads us to turning points in the story that evoke shifts in physical space, intent, emotion, and in general a new direction for the characters and plot. When reading the script, note where these occur, as they will serve as signposts for changes in the soundtrack as well.

The most obvious shifts of physical space occur at the change from one scene location to another. Certainly this is motivation to change the ambient sounds to help orient the audience to the new space, but rarely is this change a dramatic turning point in itself. More likely you will have to dig for the psychological transition that can be escorted with a shift in the audio.

Still on the physical plane, a common transition element is a door. This can be leading the character into a new space, unknown adventure, or surprise twist. In thrillers the cliché of an attack upon the entering character continues to elicit anxiety, often accentuated with the low-volume sound that suddenly is broken by the loud, contrasting thrust of the intruder. There are also moments of a sudden, unexpected entry into a room by a foreign element that is accompanied by a definite shift in the ambiance. Imagine, for example, a dog kennel late at night when a cat somehow sneaks in through a window crack, wakening the snuffling hounds into a barking fervor. So a window, drawer, cabinet, closet, chimney, drain, manhole, elevator, car trunk, cave, swimming pool surface, ocean wave, and shadow can all serve as "doors" into other realities.

Ask yourself about the predominant feeling before and after this transition. What would the characters be hearing because their attention would be more prone to one aspect of the environment than to another? How would the audience participate more in the world of a character with respect to a shift of sounds? Some bipolar extremes could be:

- closed-open
- loud-soft
- dry-echo
- low pitch-high pitch
- near-far
- empty-full
- harmony-dissonance
- friendly-menacing

The choices made should be based on an analysis of the arcs and dramatic turning points of the characters and plot, consciously emphasizing, suggesting, or even contradicting what is occurring in the subtext of the script.

Looking beyond the physical cues, there are usually many moments that exhibit profound transitions indicated by either a character's action or dialogue. One example in *As Good As It Gets* occurs in the restaurant scene when Jack Nicholson is courting Helen Hunt in his very ungainly fashion. As he is drawing towards a decisive revelation and shift in his character, the natural sounds of the restaurant (murmur of other diners, silverware, glasses, etc.) fade away, leaving a kind of magical vacuum for the two characters to sink into with their emotional teeth and hearts. When the scene tension is resolved with a humorous shift, the sounds of the restaurant return to their previous levels. The magic moment has passed.

Grouping the voices

Upon completing your first reading of the script and having marked the different "voices" that struck you as significant, take a rapid rereading and note these words on a separate page. Find a logic to group them by type: action, object, emotion, etc. Now skim over each group and let the words begin to take sides. Do you find very similar words? Opposing words? What is the opposition that is being created? Is there a similar opposition in the different groups of words?

If the film is fairly simple in structure, it may have only one bipolar contrast. But most films have at least two levels of storytelling — the more consciously obvious goal and conflict, and the more subconscious subtext. Be aware that the list of bipolar pairs may need to be separated into more than one thematic conflict.

An example of this kind of separation is illustrated with the script analysis of a Brazilian film called *Negociação Mortal* (*Deadly Negotiation*) for which I created the sound design. Two distinct bipolar lists were derived from the script, which included development of musical aspects such as rhythm and frequencies that followed these bipolarities.

DEATH	**LIFE**
mechanical	organic
clock (high pitch, constant)	heart (low pitch, speed up-slow down)
4/4 rhythm	3/4 rhythm
scream of death	scream of orgasm
inhale cigarette, cocaine	breathing
man — real life	woman — real life
woman — "Death"	man — little boy
money	love

POWER	**WEAKNESS**
winner	loser
conqueror	conquered
man	woman
Death	man
armed	handcuffed
power of words	insecurity

Figure 1-1 bipolar sound lists for *Negociação Mortal*

As is the case with any film that is multilayered in its tones, symbols, and characters, this film has exceptions to these bipolarities, which can serve for rich counterpoints and unexpected plot twists. So be aware of the relative nature of such charts; they are guidelines, not necessarily eternal truths (even for the two hours of the film).

There may be tripolar relationships as well. These can fall into basically two types:

1) **Left-Center-Right**, a linear relationship in which the "left" and "right" are two extremes (bipolarities) with a neutral, combination, or half-way element that is distinct from either extreme. This usually encompasses a smaller spectrum of all the flow possibilities than the 3-way Pie (described below) can obtain. Examples of this might be: yellow-green-blue, child-teenager-adult, hunger-satisfaction-nausea, nervous-attentive-bored.
2) **3-way Pie Division**, a triangular relationship in which the three elements are all equally weighted and each shares boundaries and relationships with the other two, with a maximum of flow possibilities encompassing a complete cycle or spectrum. Examples of this would be: red-blue-yellow, life-death-rebirth, seed-tree-flower, intellectual-emotional-physical.

If the screenplay you are working on begs to be supported by three themes or elements, this can be a useful paradigm to apply to the sound design as well, extrapolating the same tools as used with the bipolar relationships.

Drawing visual maps

Now with this understanding of the deeper resonating elements of the script, you can look for patterns that will give you clues for building the sound design structure. Take a piece of paper and draw a line down the middle in the long direction. Mark points along the line representing the significant plot points, moments of transition and heightened conflict. If there are certain repeated elements or scenes that are important to the story, give them some graphic symbol where they appear along the chronological line you have drawn. If you have drawn in pencil it would be helpful to ink over after you've got everything laid out, or make a photocopy, so that when you begin the next phase of drawing you can erase the overlaying design without disturbing the basic structure.

Refer back to the bipolar charts that you made of your "voices" and select the two most representative words for each bipolarity, e.g., death-life, power-weakness, success-failure, male-female, rational-intuitive, money-love, etc. Looking at the dramatically high points of the story, ask yourself what is happening in the bipolar conflict? Most stories have a central character who will be experiencing these conflicts, so put yourself in that character's shoes and see what he or she is feeling at this moment.

Let's take the example of death-life to illustrate this technique. In *Negociação Mortal* the main character, Mario, meets a mysterious woman who later is revealed to be Death, the grim reaper in a seductive form. She predicts his death in seven years' time, leaving him to invest his energies as he wishes until then. As the story leaps forward to the fateful date, Mario finds that his world of successful but ruthless business is suddenly thrown out of his control when he is kidnapped, hooded, handcuffed, and whisked off to an isolated cabin. The events unfold as Death reveals herself in the cabin and begins a final seduction to climax the film. The major bipolar contrast revolves around Mario's attempt to control all that is living around him and his inability to control his ultimate destiny with Death. A graphic representation of the time line and bipolar units (usually done with an erasable colored pencil) would look like this:

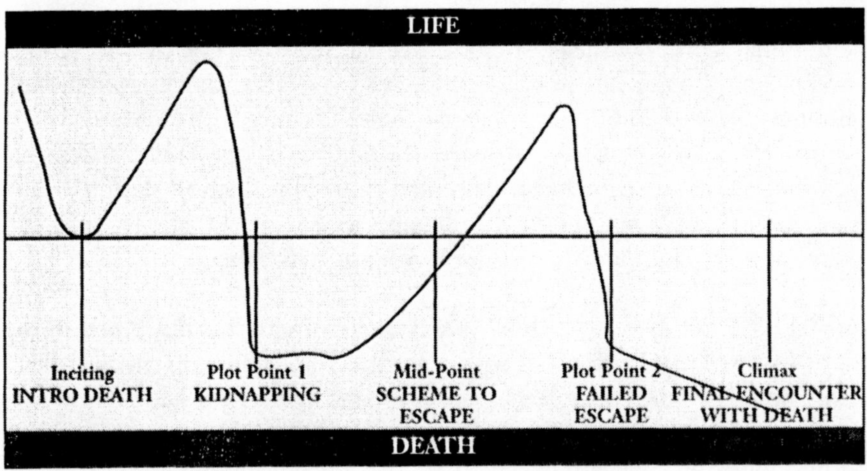

Figure 1-2 visual map A

A second bipolar unit of power-weakness overlaid on the same time line will have a different curve than the first (done with a different colored pencil), at moments crossing, counterpointing, and finally resolving to a mutual climax, like this:

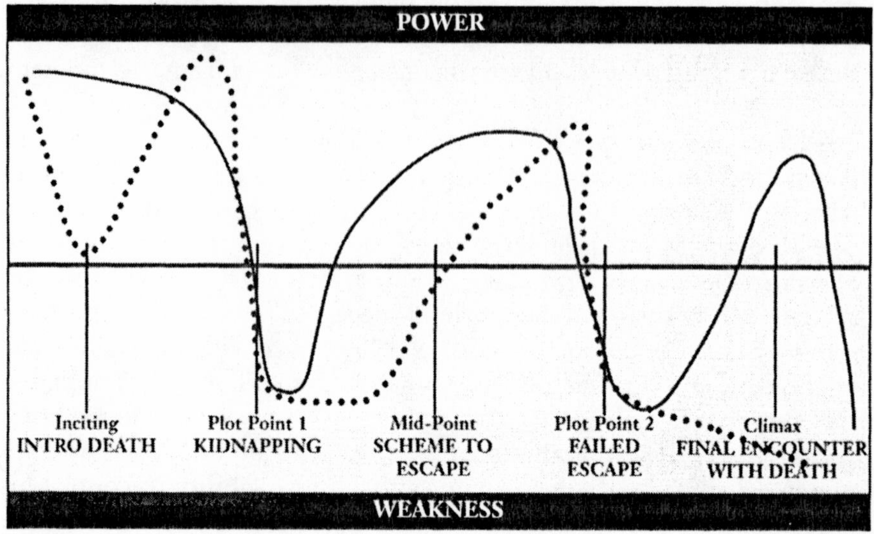

Figure 1-3 visual map B

What do these graphics reveal for the sound design? As the basic dramatic elements are put into opposition, we can visualize a kind of emotional scoring of the entire film. We can see when one theme emerges and becomes dominant or suppressed, as well as how the multiple themes bounce off one another. Each of these themes will continue to be expanded in the treatment of voice, sound effects, ambiance, and music (as they may have also been expressed in the production design). Any associations with sounds in the diegesis (story world of the film) can serve as a starting point to give direction to these themes.

In the example here, Death is linked to a clock that is described in the script — ticking, with a high-pitched, mechanically constant 4/4 beat. Nowhere is a heart or heartbeat described in the script, but I found it as an intuitive opposite to the clock in the death-life bipolarity, generating other opposites such as a low-pitched, organically varying 3/4 beat that is sensed as the natural rhythm of the heartbeat. (In fact, the physiological beat lies between 3/4 and 4/4 rhythms.) These elements then spawn parameters for two of the musical themes that will counterpoint throughout the film, based on the overall graphic line that was drawn on the visual map.

Meeting with the director

Assuming that you are not the director doing your own sound design (in which case you might try some of the following approaches with your sound editor and music composer), all of what you have created up to this point must be shared with the director. Depending on both of your personalities and experiences, there will be a greater or lesser degree of collaboration on the specific steps of the sound design process. But it remains absolutely imperative that the director hears your ideas and absorbs what you have to offer, and that you *listen to the director*, who will probably be the only one to have a complete vision of the characters and story.

Creating sounds that are best for the film requires sonic, structural, and emotional information to flow through you in two directions, both listening and speaking. Walter Murch refers to this as "dreaming in pairs," where each takes turns proposing alternate scenarios to the other that provoke the dream imagery or subconscious creativity in the listener. The memory or intuition of the listener rises to its own defense when it hears itself being challenged, revealing the hidden intent and appropriate selection of sound.

While making the visual maps, you may choose to do this side by side with the director, and find that this process becomes more like a dance, jam session, and/or communal art piece. Ideas flow spontaneously like a four-handed piano improvisation. The real-time aspect can generate unexpected rhythms on the page. For example, if one of you draws in a more architectural blueprint style — very rhythmic, exacting, and measured — this can create a very surprising counterpoint to another style that is more anatomically based — with curves, ovals, branchings, and threadings. Where do they intersect? What third forms result from the synergy? What dialogue of ideas, links, and new insights surfaces from your intuitive and logical processes?

If you find yourselves stuck on a particular point, try handing over the colored pencil to the other person to do the drawing, or if you've both been doing it, try exchanging colored pencils and themes.

If the director is not sure about your suggestion or just plain doesn't like it, explore this opportunity and ask about exactly what aspect does not fit in. Is it that the director already has a sound in mind and can't get used to a different idea, or is there something intrinsically out of place with your proposal? Finding what is out of balance can very well reveal what is needed to put things in balance, just as a string on a guitar blares out when it needs tuning up or down; and you should hope that your director will have the perspective with which to judge this.

Most likely you have been hired as a sound designer because the director understands the benefits and is eager to collaborate with you. Even so, you may have a director who is tremendously ignorant of the full potential, language, and process of sound designing. In this case, you should have a little chat as to what extent you will be given the authority and decision-making powers in creating the sound design. Some directors may feel uncomfortable with their lack of experience in this area, and you have to watch out for the trap of taking advantage of this by becoming a one-man band. That is not what film production is about (unless this is an **auteur** film, which means that the director would probably be doing the sound design anyway), and you may be jeopardizing the final movie if you don't make the effort to become as intimate with the director's views as the director is with yours. You very well may have to seek different communication techniques to become the most effective with each individual director, just as you might with different students, lovers, or bosses. If one analytic style or graphic exercise worked with one director, but doesn't seem to generate a rapport with another, rather than being insistent, experiment with a new modality. Some will prefer hours of dialoguing with you; others may like written words, or charts, or diagrams; and others will want to hear the sounds themselves before commenting. Find out what is the best language for communication with your director, and translate your own fluency and style in a way that will resonate with the director's.

You may receive from the director very specific indications of how to hear the film, or a certain song or instrumental recording that the director either wants to incorporate as is or to use as a guide for an original composition.

Sound designer Dane Davis has had a very close collaboration with his directors:

"The directors of *The Matrix* were watching dailies, or in talks with me, and would be unconsciously making vocal noises like *kung-kung* or *tchurr-tchurr* and sometimes it was very key to the scene. One example is in a scene with a baby in a pod and it's filling up, and it's horrifying, oh my God! There was a valve that was sealing up, and in the dailies when that shot came up, one of the directors made a *ka-chonk* sound, and it stuck in my head. No matter what I did with hydraulic air releases, valves, rubber things, sections of pipe, tires, reverse tire hits and stuff to make this machine work, I knew that ultimately it would still have to go *ka-chonk* under all the other textures and music. I knew they would love it and they did. They would rarely define sounds in that movie with examples of realistic sounds, which some other directors might do. They would say they wanted it to be 'electrical' and 'drippy and wet' and 'digital,' kind of contradictory, but very cool and something for me to work out. I added that it should have a respiratory system, a circulatory system, and a heartbeat, and they liked that. Also that it should be made of spare parts. That was the only discussion we had, because I had a really good intuitive lock on what they were looking for."

If this suggestion fits like a glove with your own ideas for the soundtrack, this will be easy to integrate. But the challenge comes when the idea seems (at least at first) quite outside your imagined design. If you don't understand why, or don't feel attracted to what the director has selected, ask about the motivation, emotional links, or other references. Do this in a curious, nonthreatening way, like an investigative reporter seeking the inside story, rather than as a prosecuting attorney looking to win a case in point. In this dialogue you may find some of the richest fruits of collaboration, because there lies the possibility of a truly new idea being generated through the paradigm of thesis-antithesis-synthesis.

A director once played for me a very haunting, melancholic piano solo as a suggestion for the main theme, but my initial reaction (which I kept internal) was that this had nothing to do with either the main character's personality or goals (which were narcissistic, ruthless, and power-hungry). I questioned the director as to how he heard this music in the film and found that he sensed an urge to pull out from the character something that was indeed covert and really counterpoint to his external appearances. Now employing this notion, we developed a sound design that worked specifically on the dissonance and counterpoint between these two aspects of his character, the overt-external and the covert-internal. The final result was much more rewardingly ambiguous and allowed for many variations on a theme as the film progressed through the different stages of the character's confrontation with his inner fears and longings.

The sound map — draft 1

Traditionally, a sound map, known as a cue sheet, is generated by the sound editor at the end of his editing job as a guide for the rerecording mixer to follow the different tracks of dialogue, effects, and music, indicated along a time frame of minutes and seconds, with image landmarks and cues for entrances, dissolves, fades, etc. What I'm referring to as the first draft of the sound map is a rough sketch of what the editor and mixer will eventually use, but based on a time frame of dramatic sequences with notations of sonic elements that may enhance the storytelling aspects of the film, with no regard for the physical or electronic track separation of closely occurring sounds that must take place before the mix.

Although the film can always benefit from having a preliminary sound map before shooting, in most cases the sound designer is called onto the picture only after the film has been shot. For the sake of representing the ideal, I will describe here the first draft of the sound map as if it were to be done before shooting. In fact, the end result will be similar to a map initiated after viewing either the dailies or a first cut of the film, when the input will come also from the images shot, as well as from the script and the director's vision.

The sound map has two axes, vertical for time, horizontal for sound elements. The time axis should be separated into sequences with certain binding dramatic, physical, and temporal elements. Most often this will be denoted by the slugline in the script, with interior or exterior, name of location, and time of day. However, it may be more useful to join several scenes into a sequence (e.g., `EXT. PARKING LOT + INT. CAR + EXT. STREET + EXT. SIDEWALK`) or even to separate a single long scene into more than one sequence, if several different plot twists or mood changes occur in the same location that may require punctuation and modulation in the soundtrack. The nomenclature of these sequences should be coordinated by the director or producer so as to remain consistent with the other production departments' breakdowns.

The headings on the horizontal axis at this stage are a much more subjective choice than the customary division between dialogue, effects, and music; you may separate and label the types of sounds in many ways. I like using the following discriminations: **concrete sounds**, **musical sounds**, **music**, and **voice.** Once again, this categorizing is flexible, as one particular sound may fit into more than one possible division or may fall between the cracks. Your choice should be based on what helps you create the overall design and transmit this to the director, sound editor, and music composer, since ultimately the audience will have an undivided sonic experience with no labeling whatsoever.

At the first draft stage, it is not necessary to get every single sound written on the map, and in fact too much detail will clutter it up. But the essence of the scene can also be reflected in some of the most mundane sound events, if properly placed. So look for what helps tell the story, referring to the sonic events that you discovered in your initial analysis (as mentioned earlier in this chapter under ***What to listen for***).

The map can look something like this:

SEQ. 23 RACE TRACK			
concrete sounds gates clang open horses breathing hooves pounding	**musical sounds** clock ticking	**music** mechanical rhythm 4/4 beat	**voice** crowd roar
SEQ. 24 STOCK MARKET FLOOR			
concrete sounds phones ringing agitated footsteps	**musical sounds** clock ticking	**music** mechanical rhythm 4/4 beat	**voice** aggressive shouting

Figure 1-4 sound map

I have denoted **concrete sounds** as those that appear to be connected with the image. In general, these would be considered to belong to the diegesis, pertaining to the reality within the film and the environment of the characters, whose point of view would incorporate these sounds. More often these would fall into the category of sound effects, rather than ambient sounds. Examples (when they appear on screen with a corresponding image or induce a reaction from a character) would be: door SLAM, audience APPLAUSE, telephone RING, horse GALLOP, ax CHOP, paper TEAR, clock TICK, gun FIRE, tire SCREECH, balloon BURST, baby CRY.

Any of the above sounds might also fall into the category of **musical sounds** if they become dissociated from the diegesis and turn into a kind of sensorial or emotional element independent from the characters' space-time reality within the story. For example, the sound of ticking when we see a clock in the room or on someone's wrist remains a concrete sound, but as soon as this same sound that is now unlinked to the image pervades a scene with its emotional effect of urgency or relentlessness as the underlying tone, it then falls into the area of musical sounds. Ambient sounds can also be considered in this division, especially when they are not creating a reaction in the characters, but rather setting a general mood. Examples would be: WHISTLING WIND, air conditioner HUM, distant HOWLING COYOTES, POUNDING SURF, playground LAUGHTER, echoing SONAR BEEPS, CRACKLING FIRE.

Any sound that might serve as inspiration for the music composer should be noted here. For example, a rhythm like a heartbeat is broken naturally by its valve-pumping action into triplets (almost, but not exactly with a real heart), with an accent on the first two beats: **1-2-3-1-2-3-1-2-3**. This, along with its muffled, low-frequency pitch, can generate the basis for a musical theme that will be linked through a dramatic element by association with the character's heart.

The category of **music** I use for both noting diegetic music (singers or musicians on screen, radio, record player, etc.), and making suggestions to the music composer, which include structural ideas (like the triplets of the heartbeat), emotional parameters, orchestration possibilities, and the development of motifs. The visual map that you made earlier serves now for inspiration to spot relationships, patterns, and macrorhythms in the whole film to help line up the musical motifs. Taking advantage of the psychoacoustic principle of our brain's ability to better discern simultaneous sounds when there exists a separation of frequencies, your observations can indicate what range of pitch will be most appropriate to use in conjunction with the other sounds occurring in the same scene.

I like to use the word **voice** rather than dialogue because this encompasses all sounds emitted through the mouth, including some very telling expressions: `uncontrollable YAWN, wet SNEEZE, unexpected HICCUP, BLOWS cigarette smoke, SMACKS a kiss, hoarse COUGH, angry BOOING, derisive LAUGH, embarrassed GIGGLE.` Dialogue may also be noted if there will be either special treatment by the actor (whispering, drunk, foreign accent) or some kind of postproduction manipulation (echo, increase of bass frequencies, telephone voice). Although it will be essential to hear the dialogue clearly in the final mix, this is not the moment to worry about the content of the words (beyond how they serve as guideposts for your creativity). What you should be looking for are the nonverbal elements that can contribute to the storytelling and emotional aspects of the soundtrack, while generating further motifs and links with the other audio categories on the sound map.

At this stage of filling in the details of the sound map, let yourself dwell on each sequence, saturating your consciousness with several readings if necessary, and viewing the sequence again in your mind with all the sounds that are suggested in the script and that emanate from your inner ear. Write them down on a big piece of scratch paper. You can close your eyes, if you find this helps stimulate your auditory sense. Don't censure any seemingly bizarre or out-of-context sound that occurs to you. You can always cross it off later, but it may also lead to a valuable connection that you haven't yet perceived.

The time you'll need to do this sequence-by-sequence development with care will undoubtedly be longer than the running time of the film itself, that is, more than the customary one minute per feature formatted screenplay page. You don't need to do this all at one sitting; in fact

TRY THIS

A listening meditation

If your mind is wandering or it just seems very silent inside your virtual auditorium, try listening to a piece of music that you feel has some connection to the tone or genre of the story. Instrumental music has the advantage of keeping you in a more intuitive, nonverbal state, while lyrics may give you some cultural inspiration, or awaken a memory or unexpected word synchrony. You can do this as a little break from your concentration, relaxing with your eyes closed, or you can try it with the script and sound map in front of you, allowing the story to interact directly with the rhythms, melodies, harmonies, and emotions of the music. If a more obvious musical genre doesn't bring anything new to the inner images, you may be surprised to find out how a classical piece of Beethoven, Debussy, or Bartok may counterpoint a very urban setting and characters, or how jazz or rock may infuse a period piece with new sonic insights that you had never before considered.

you might find that on different days or times of day you may have different inspirations. Be aware of your own rhythm of focus and daydreaming states, as there usually exists an ultradian cycle of approximately 90–120 minutes within your attention span. Let this be as saturating a process as the production schedule will allow.

When you reach the end of the sound map, take a breather in another environment, even if it's for only a few minutes. You will be switching gears into another process and it helps to make a clean break out of this detail-oriented thinking.

Now go back to the results of your work with ***Grouping the voices*** and ***Drawing visual maps*** and refamiliarize yourself with the patterns that you discovered. Skim over them quickly and note what can readily be superimposed over the detailed work you did on the sound map. Line up all the pages of the sound map on a long table or the floor so that there is a single time line from top to bottom, just as there is in your visual maps. Take the same colored pencils that you used on the visual map, and circle or underline the sounds you have listed on the sound map that correspond to those colored themes on your visual map.

Look for the patterns emerging on the sound map as well. Are there places that do not correspond between the visual and the sound maps? If so, this may be an indication for the need to insert a sound that would not necessarily be in the diegesis (a **concrete sound** in my nomenclature), but would work very well as a subjective, nondiegetic addition to the track (a **musical sound**). Or it may be a hint for the composer to return to a certain theme or variation of a theme at this point in the drama. In a more unusual case, this lack of synchrony between the two maps may motivate you to *remove* certain sounds that would normally play in the scene, using the forced or unnatural silence as a connecting emotional fiber.

■ ■ ■ ■ ■ ■ ■ ■ ■ ■ ■ ■

To review the steps up to this point:

- ***The first script reading*** — Immerse yourself in the written description of the scenes and let your inner ear come alive.
- ***What to listen for*** — **objects, actions, environments, emotions,** and **transitions** — Key words and ideas will serve as basic elements to construct the sound design.
- ***Grouping the voices*** — Find the polarities between these elements to develop balance and counterpoint.
- ***Drawing visual maps*** — Use graphic representation of the flow of the story with the sonic structure to reveal an overall composition for the sound design.
- ***Meeting with the director*** — Present your work-in-progress to confirm the style, tone, and choices, listening carefully for feedback and global perspective.
- ***The sound map — draft 1*** — Separate the script into sequences and list the sounds in categories of **concrete sounds, musical sounds, music,** and **voice**.

Consulting before and during the shoot

Ideas for sound that arise from the script can help the producer lower production costs and ensure more consistency with the narrative direction of the film. The sound designer will seldom be hired before postproduction, but if the opportunity arises early enough in preproduction, you can offer extremely beneficial advice to the producer, director, and production sound recordist.

Possible helpful hints and economies can be found in:

- **Reducing or removing shots** that might be expensive or time-consuming, by substituting with sounds. This requires creative analysis of what dramatic elements are needed to move the story forward and develop character.
- Assisting in **selection of locations** by considering acoustic factors. The most beautiful spot for a 19th-century period piece could be totally inadequate because of unnoticed traffic sounds that cannot be removed from the production track without costly dubbing.
- Indicating **proper equipment and materials** for specific sound recording situations. Extra microphones and an adequate mixer might be needed for a complex dialogue sequence, or sound-absorbent materials like foam or blankets could help eliminate unwanted reverb in a hard-walled location.
- Planning to **record wild sounds on a location shoot** can save time and money in postproduction. Scheduling must be done conscientiously so as not to slow down the rest of the crew, preferably recording before or after the shooting hours.

During the shoot try to take a look at the dailies, which may raise some creative suggestions for recording isolated wild sounds in that particular location. Through observation of what is already happening on screen you may imagine an **additional useful close-up** of a sound-making object or action not originally planned in the shot list, but that could successfully reinforce an aural theme. This is particularly applicable if any montage sequence is anticipated that can break free from a strictly linear, dialogue-driven script. Sounds and images can have a subjective, dreamlike connection to the emotional or intellectual line; frequently the ideas echo between sounds and images, each generating a reflection or variation in the other. Pickup shots after principle photography are another possibly less-expensive solution, but it might be more cost-effective to get these newly inspired inserts immediately, before moving away from a hard-to-get-to location.

George Watters, supervising sound editor on* Star Trek II, III, *and* VI, *has some advice about set construction:

"On the sets of the Enterprise, the plywood was creaking every time Commander Kirk walked by. That was one of my big gripes in *Star Trek VI*. When sets are built, they should make sure they are solid so there is no creaking from plywood, because we then have that noise under all the voices on the production tracks, and you have to bring the actors back for looping. It will cost more to get the actors back to fix it than it would to build it right in the first place. You don't want to replace close-up dialogue, and many directors object as they would rather live with the noise in order to save the original dialogue."

Accompanying the picture edit

If you are fortunate enough to be brought onto the film before or while the picture is being edited, you will have the opportunity to interact with the director and picture editor in their decision-making process. Your thematic ideas and specific suggestions can influence the style and rhythm of the image cut in various ways.

A scene or shot may play longer if there is sufficient information in the audio to warrant a slower pace. Off-screen sounds can help motivate the characters' thought processes and actions. If the director or editor is concerned about a dead moment on screen, but doesn't want to cut away perhaps because of lack of coverage or some other reason, you have an opportunity to help the scene play by coloring with off-screen dialogue, a transformation in the ambiance, or a motivated noise like a car horn, glass breaking or baby crying. In *The Godfather*, a train that is never on screen is used very effectively in the restaurant scene when Al Pacino shoots a man for the first time.

A scene may play shorter if you decide to overlap the dialogue or diegetic sound effects between two scenes, compacting information. This technique is very common, but you may have some special insights on the alchemy of seemingly incongruent sound and image juxtapositions, and on when this can serve to propel the audience into the next scene with a greater sense of anxiety, curiosity, or humor.

Sometimes a sound will hold more power than an image; you might experiment during editing to find that the scene will have more impact or suspense by not revealing the audio source. If this style works well in one scene, you and the editor might look for other crucial moments where it may be applied in the film, establishing a certain structural, emotional motif. Usually this type of image-sound dynamic is suggested in the script, but you should be daring and imaginative at the editing stage as well, looking for some real nuggets of audio storytelling energy to emerge at just the right moments.

The picture editor may wish to take advantage of other techniques that can lead to creative sound design. Try cutting without sound to get the visual rhythm by itself, adding sound later. This can lead to discoveries of asynchronous uses of sound and image that may convey more power than the sync to which we are all accustomed. Also, try watching the film at different speeds (high and low) as well as in reverse. Like a painter looking at his work upside down or in a mirror, it frees you of the content to look at the pure structure, which in turn can evoke new sensitivities toward the sound.

Analyzing the final picture edit

If you have been hired after the image has been cut, you will have the choice to watch the film in real time as your first exposure to the story or to take advantage of the script (even if it isn't exactly what ended up being shot) as your first resource. If you find that your strength of audio imagination comes more from the words on a page, read the script first, but if you know that you will respond maximally with the image as your first stimulus, then you may choose to disregard the script entirely, or use it simply as a structural reference for your sound map.

Once you are ready to watch the film, try to do it in one sitting, for the same reasons as it is best to read the script for the first time with no interruptions. Whether you are watching it on video, computer, flatbed, or screening room, request that there be as few comments as possible from others present, other than brief remarks regarding scripted but unheard audio elements that are essential to understanding the scene. This first viewing should allow you the luxury of being the receptive audience — letting you enjoy, question, laugh, cry, and otherwise be totally reactive and involved in the characters' drama. You may keep a pad and pen available for noting your first impressions, but avoid any extensive writing that could distract from your full attention to the unfolding story. Note key words of your initial feeling for the scenes, like *crystalline*, *damp*, or *funny*, rather than literal sounds which you will surely insert later anyway.

After this first screening, an in-depth conversation with the director should clarify both his or her intentions with the story, characters, and scenes, confirming whether or not your first impressions as a viewer of the film are close to the director's intentions. Unless you have worked before with the director and have considerable background in common, you might want to save up your creative ideas for sharing until after you have had plenty of time to develop them to their full potential. This really depends on the chemistry of your two personalities, as the exchange might be necessary for the desires of the director to be articulated. If the director wants some specific feedback this would be a good starting point for dialogue. If there are aspects of the film that you did not like or understand, try to bring these up in as constructive a manner as possible by asking questions, probing for solutions to the weak points you might perceive. On the other hand, if you have positive feedback, by all means let the director feel your excitement about the beginning of your collaboration.

Your next step is to watch the film again, with or without the director, editor, and music composer, this time in control of the "pause" button while you "spot" the film. As each scene goes by, you should stop to note detailed ideas in all four areas of your sound map — **concrete sounds**, **musical sounds**, **music**, and **voice**.

Concrete sounds associated directly with the image, and most likely in sync with some kind of action, can be derived from visual elements like **movement**, **weight**, **size**, **solidity**, **resistance**, **contact**, **texture**, **temperature**, **impact**, **release**, etc. Depending on the film genre and style, the degree of realism can vary. If the tone is dramatic, the sounds should not be noticed as anything separate from the event, even though they may very well be artificially inserted, replacing the production track and sweetened in the mix. This work is invisible in the end, a mostly unrecognized craft that intends to make the diegesis seamless and believable.

On the other extreme, a film like *Who Framed Roger Rabbit?* depends tremendously on the creation of a physical cartoon character plunked in the middle of a live action set with human actors. Roger comes to life through sounds that give him the texture and weight of an inflatable, plastic, stretchy body that can do things that normal folks can't manage without being tortured to death. His believability is consummated by the concrete sounds synced with his visual contortions.

Often an action on screen will not be able to generate the desired sound effect that should accompany it. Replacing dirty backgrounds, wrong timbre, or weak sounds recorded during production is extremely common, and the solutions are often very surprising. (This will be explored later in this chapter in more detail in ***Defining voice sources and modifications.***) At this moment, be attentive to what is needed to complete the reality on screen.

Review the areas that were mentioned earlier in this chapter in the section ***What to listen for*** during script analysis — objects, actions, environments, emotions, transitions — as these continue to provide directions for your analysis of the picture as well. You will now have the choice to emphasize specific elements on screen, depending on their importance to the diegesis, characters' point of view, and emotions.

Musical sounds may be insinuated from the concrete sounds and their corresponding sync images, as the border between these categories can be indistinct at times. For instance, if a car passes through a shot in the background, we can suppose that the motor (a concrete sound) will continue to be heard after it passes out of frame. But what about the other cars, trucks, horns, sirens, etc. that might be in action off screen interacting with the visually linked car? This will depend on the kind of neighborhood, time of day, and most importantly the link that the characters have to their environment. Is the city friendly, hostile, speedy, lazy, distant, suffocating?

Look for two or three elements to personalize each environment, as these will allow you a certain variety within the scene to accent certain moments, create transitions, or contrast different moments during the story in the same setting. If you have several dramatic scenes between a couple in a bedroom, for example, perhaps a clock ticking could stress the nervousness or uncertainty, thunder from the storm outside might accompany moments of suppressed anger, and plumbing gurgles may anticipate lust welling up (or humor, if overplayed). Constant ambient sounds like the clock may be laid on the track for the entire scene and the volume modulated during the mix for emphasizing the proper tone. A sound event like thunder or pipe gurgling needs to be selected for its specific attack, tone, and timbre and placed appropriately to the accompanying action, dialogue, and intent of the moment.

A single part of a multitracked ambiance may serve to carry from one scene to the next. The sound may have been an off-screen ambiance whose source becomes revealed with the transition to the new setting. This helps create a sense of continuity in geography; it also glues the storytelling with a kind of question-and-answer structure in the audiovisual framework. It is particularly effective in comedy or drama — when the sound is indicated to be one thing but turns out to be another upon revelation of the true source of the image.

While watching the scene, what seems to be the predominant emotion experienced by the characters? Is this the same emotion that you feel while watching the scene? If there is a difference, be aware of the psychological space created between the primary (character) and secondary (audience) emotions. When designing the musical sounds for the scenes that have these simultaneous yet distinctly different impacts, you should usually play each audio element to support just one emotion at a time. An exception would be with an aural double entendre, in which there can be construed two meanings for the same sound event, one for the character, one for the audience.

Your notations on **music** for the scene should include reference to pitch, rhythm, and relationships to repeated or developing scenes, characters, themes, and emotions. Observe what will help integrate the music with the other audio elements of voice, effects, and ambiance. Even if you are not musically trained, your contributions to creating the audio narrative can serve as valuable guidelines to the composer, who has many artistic and technical tools at hand to complete the soundtrack.

The effect of contrast in pitch can be indicated, as in the use of low musical frequencies with high voice frequencies to help keep the dialogue clear, or the opposite effect can be produced, i.e., making the voice purposely less intelligible by masking with a musical pitch in the same frequency range.

Musical rhythm can establish a driving force to a scene that may be generated by visual rhythms (e.g., windshield wipers, wings flapping, shaking head), picture editing rhythm, or subjective pacing where there is no apparent visual movement to motivate a beat. A musical sound with definite periodicity like a dripping faucet or squeaky hamster wheel may lead into a specific beat for the music, as was done with the sound of coins clinking and cash registers opening in Pink Floyd's classic song "Money."

Characters, settings, and emotional motifs are often benefited by musical themes, so you may note appropriate moments for these various developments. Look for the transitions: When the tone shifts, the hero is thwarted, or the treasure is found. Your insights can help the composer create the most effective accompaniment to the drama, while orchestrating in harmony with the overall sound design.

Besides the verbal content passed through the dialogue, what is the voice communicating? If you couldn't understand English (or whatever language the film is shot in), what would you understand by the sounds emitted by the actors? The nonverbal voice melody and rhythm (**prosody**) can transmit all sorts of information — urgency, anger, nausea, snootiness, playfulness, seduction, falseness, etc. You can hear it in the musicality of the voice, as well as in the breathing and spaces between words.

A cough, sneeze, snore, tongue click, cigarette puff, whistle, swallow, hiccup, or kiss can serve as part of a nonverbal vocabulary for a character, especially if there is some recurrence or transformation of this sound throughout the film. For example, if a character's arc takes him or her from being healthy to sick, a slight cough might build to a deep wheezing; if this is not yet fully exploited in the production track, the sound design could emphasize this in post with added sounds. They may be easily inserted either by avoiding lip sync, putting the sound off screen, or adding it when the character's back is to the audience.

Recognizing what tone is established by the character's voice intonation is a strong hint for which direction to take the sound design of a scene. Is the speech percussive, suggesting a syncopated beat that could be extended to the music and environmental sounds? Is it slurred and barely intelligible so that the same might hold for an unseen, off-screen couple arguing in the apartment down the hall? Are there pauses that could be accented with a sonic commentary like a wolf howl, fart, or key clacking in the door?

The voice may call for a counterpoint ambiance to help lift it into more definition, such as a puppy barking against the miserly growl of a gruff old man. In *The Elephant Man*, after the deformed main character has been chased into a corner by a dozen pursuers, he wails in agony "I... am... a... man...," then slumps to the ground while an indistinct, high-pitched animal cry is heard in the distance, as if its heart is being ruthlessly torn out.

The sound map — draft 2

Following the format and procedures cited earlier in building the first draft of the sound map, you now have at hand full narrative details and the image stimulus to fill in all the sound elements with relation to the time line of sequences. As you complete this map, refer to the visual map (or create one now if you have not already) to check on the flow of your aural themes. If a scene appears to be extremely congested with sonic information, look for the dramatic purpose and dominant emotion to help select the most important sounds. When in doubt, leave the sounds on the map to be edited and then selected during the pre- or final mix with the director's feedback.

In general, the audience will be able to absorb at the most two separate audio elements at any one moment, and these must have a good separation of pitch, timbre, and/or rhythm. If more elements are added, or if the acoustic characteristics are too similar, the sounds will begin to blend, creating a single information pattern for the brain to interpret. Often the varying volume of the tracks during the mix will create a psychoacoustic space between potentially fusing sounds, allowing each to command attention for its moment on stage. An extreme example of this occurs in a sequence in *Air Force One* during the confrontation between the tied-up President Harrison Ford and the Russian terrorist Gary Oldman. In the span of a few seconds as the President cuts himself loose and counterattacks, the focus shifts back and forth between two musical themes (the Russian and the American), explosive dialogue, melodramatic screams and groans, body slamming, machine gunning — and it all works because of the extremely agile fingers and discriminating ears of the rerecording mixer.

But more often when the tracks have simultaneous heavy doses of attention-getting sound, something is dumped in the final mix. You can make the mixer's job easier and your sound design cleaner by keeping this in mind when creating the sound map.

Defining voice sources and modifications

As with many of the functions explored up to this point, there exists a traditional crew position for cleaning up the voices — the dialogue editor. Whether you do this work yourself, or coordinate a larger crew in specialized areas, the same principles and tasks apply.

The most important point to accomplish in recording and editing the dialogue is to make sure that the voices are understood (unless they are intentionally meant to be ambiguous or unintelligible, which will be dealt with later in this chapter), and secondarily that the quality of the voice and accompanying ambience should not be distracting from the intention of the scene. What kinds of production problems may cause these faults?

- The **recording volume** is too low or high, resulting in lack of presence, tape hiss, or distortion.
- The location **background sounds** remain unforgivably imposing and are incapable of being cleaned away from the voice.
- The **performance** has a problem with overlapping dialogue, swallowed words, or incorrect pronunciation or emphasis.

Various solutions exist:

- **On-location dubbing, wild track**
- **Alternative production take**
- **Postproduction dubbing**

If the problem is detected *during production* but there is no chance of shooting another take, try to record another **wild** audio take with the actors close to the time, emotional state, perspective, and background ambience of the rest of the scene. With two tape recorders available, you can let the actors hear their recorded voices while simultaneously doing the on-location dubbing session. This method can even be done using a single recorder with a tape change (preferably DAT cassette) and drawing upon the actors' audio memory, as well as your own.

Find **another production audio take** that does not have the problem, which can be synchronized with the chosen image take. You will very likely have to expand or contract the pauses between words and phrases to line it up for lip sync. This substitution technique is more commonly employed when the line is off-screen, which may influence the picture edit if this option presents itself at an early enough stage.

Postproduction dubbing (also known as **looping** or **ADR** — automated dialogue replacement) is the most common method, done in a studio with the original image and sound screened repeatedly so that the actor is able to rehearse the rhythm and intonation. There are advantages with the controlled atmosphere of the ADR room, but technical and artistic considerations must be observed.

To avoid the feeling that the voice perspective doesn't fit with the image perspective, place the microphone at a distance similar to where it would be placed during the production recording. Volume adjustments alone will not replicate the sense of distance, since the acoustics modify in terms of frequency range, audible voice components, and secondary sound waves. When the voice is close, we hear effects of breathing, lip and tongue movements, and enhanced high frequencies that give greater presence. At a distance, these close-up effects lessen and an increase may appear in reverb that can identify the type of space. Filtering can accentuate these parameters, but the microphone placement remains the most essential element in recreating the original reality.

If you will be replacing only a portion of the dialogue and inserting the dubbed voice between production track lines, it is imperative to employ the same kind of microphone used on location so that the sound edit remains seamless. The quality of a studio mike might be "richer" than the shotgun or lavaliere on the set, but it will attract attention if it jumps back and forth, and then you'll spend wasted time trying to equalize it in the mix. If, on the other hand, the whole scene and all the characters' dialogue will be replaced, there is no need for a reference, and you are freer to use whatever mike sounds best.

Actors in the dubbing studio sometimes have difficulty returning to the emotional framework of the scene that is being screened in a small dark room. The fact that they are alone, wearing headphones, watching a film of themselves over and over, and trying to remain perfectly in sync, can stifle their naturalness and spontaneity. If they need some help in recreating their energy level, you might offer to use a boom operator so that the actor can move around freely, rather than be chained to a mike on a stand.

Frank Serafine, an innovator in electronically synthesized sounds for film, has also helped create scenes with background dialogue:

"All the time in foley I have people walk or talk off stage. I have actors subliminally talk about stuff, heavy conversations in the loop groups. But they are really low on the track and you have to be listening. Stuff gets through that's unscripted with the improv groups. They really study, get a cassette of the film, pull books, especially with something like a science fiction movie. Even in a normal movie like at an airport, you've got stuff going on there, like in loading zones, calling taxis. You can bring a film totally to life. People turn their heads, you add new lines. You're in with the actors and it's kind of fun for me."

Modifying the voice in postproduction can lend a very different personality to the character. *THX 1138* was a forerunner in changing a voice to make a robot-like quality, by sending the signal through a ham radio, then rerecording the slightly out-of-tune returning voice. Today there are many computerized filters offered, but it is worth looking for these more unusual solutions if you want a really unique sound.

If there is any dialogue that occurs off screen, you might consider placing this portion of the dialogue on a track that is off center as well. You have to test the effect in the whole sequence to see whether it really works, or becomes a distraction because the voice is popping around in space too much.

Since this book focuses primarily on the narrative aspects of sound, and there are many details to master with respect to microphone choices and placement, room acoustics, filtering, mixing, etc., other more technically oriented texts on postproduction sound should be consulted. A good complementary reference, with a comprehensive step-by-step description of each of the processes and equipment used, is *Sound for Film and Television*, by Tomlinson Holman and Gerald Millerson.

Defining sound effects and ambience sources

One of the most surprising audiovisual phenomenon allows the audience to believe that whatever sound is synchronized to the image is the sound being emitted by that image. Combining this with the fact that some realistic sounds do not play nearly as dramatically as sounds created by totally different sources than seen in the film, foley artists have made careers by punching steaks for a boxing match and squishing cornstarch for walking in snow. The lesson is: Listen for the sound that works, not necessarily looking for an "authentic" source... and have fun with your discoveries!

The sources usually available for creating the sound effects are:

- **production tracks**
- **sound libraries**
- **wild track recordings** on location or in the studio
- **foley**
- **samplers** and **synthesizers**

During the shoot there are likely to be some useful sounds recorded on the **production tracks**. Clothing movement, silverware clatter, car passes, and such may all end up being perfect for the final mix. However, they must all be separated completely from the dialogue track so that you will be able to create a clean music-and-effects track for international dubbed versions. Because so much overlap of dialogue usually occurs with these effects, the common procedure is to replace everything with other sources, especially foley, which also gives you the advantage of being able to control and standardize the quality of each sound.

Ambience from the production tracks is mostly important for creating a seamless sonic landscape, helping to create the illusion that all the cuts of the scene are taking place in a continuum. If one angle has a louder background than another, this can be masked in the mix by using a continuous additional track with the room tone or location ambience, which the sound recordist should have gathered during a couple minutes of forced silence just after the scene is completed. If this was not obtained for whatever reason, a louder nonproduction ambience track using similar frequencies can be added to disguise the sound holes. Rarely, though, does the production ambience go beyond this more mechanical function, and it can't really contribute the right dramatic tone to the scene. You'll have to create this in post with your inner ear and the other sources available.

You can find tens of thousands of options in **sound libraries**, easily searchable on catalogued CDs. Compared to the older selections on tape which has to be wound back and forth, nowadays this process can be extremely agile — using a digital sampler to store preliminary options, and even testing against the image immediately, if you are working electronically. But for all its slickness, there remains the danger of becoming lazy with a prerecorded sound that seems "okay," and moving on to the next with the speed of lightning. Because time crunches dictate so many productions, there may be no other option than to keep moving forward, but if possible use the library sounds in a more creative manner by:

- adding two or more sounds together to create a new sound
- changing the duration and/or pitch
- looping, inverting, filtering, etc.
- using the sound as a sketch only for creating an original recording

With the advent of the sampler and electronic editing, a recognizable sound can now be converted into thousands of variations, from the vaguely familiar

George Watters focuses on getting accurate location sounds and authentic effects:

"In *The Red Corner*, to record the motorcycles, I diagrammed in detail their movements in the street scenes. The recording was done in the exact location prior to breaking down the set. This allowed us to get the same reverberation from the walls of the buildings, the natural sounds in the alleys, etc. Often these things may be artificially handled in the mix. It is not possible to record like this during shooting because everyone is crammed for time.

"In *Gone in Sixty Seconds*, we found a real '67 Shelby 6500 GT 500 to record, because the production cars used in shooting, while looking great, were unsafe to drive at high speeds. We recorded the real GT 500 prior to the completion of principal photography, utilizing the transportation crew to truck the car to a race track. For two days we simulated the movie script from previously diagrammed moves, including horns, door slams, hoods, even the alarms, and I did all the driving myself. It is so much easier cutting long car sequences when you have accurate sounds reflecting specifically what is on screen."

to one completely obliterated from the original meaning. If you have the fortune of time to play with an extensive sound library and the abundant computerized tools available, this can be a rewarding experience, but balance the focus with the play. Remember every so often to refer to your sound map and visual map so your journey into foreign sonic lands can bring the treasures back into the narrative context.

The search for and creation of new sounds can be one of the most joyful, surprising, and rewarding activities of sound design. You'll be set for the hunt to make original **wild track recordings** on location or in the studio, with equipment minimums including a variety of high-end mikes (directional is basic, cardiod and stereo are useful); a Nagra, portable DAT, MD, or high-quality cassette recorder (crystal sync or time code aren't necessary for this process); and well-insulated, full-frequency headphones.

In seeking a **constant ambience**, your choices are based on finding a specific environment at a specific time that is generating the desired sonic background for a scene. When the thousands of ambiences offered in the sound libraries don't quite fulfill the need, you will have to explore the physical terrain yourself.

If the scene was shot on location, this may be a good place to return to at different times of day to capture what may have been missed during the production, when hopefully the recordist took a few minutes of background ambience to match the dialogue. If there are particular sounds like birds, frogs, human movement, wind, or machines, almost certainly the time of day will be related to how busy these elements are. Analyze the scene first to know when the fictional world is taking place and at what energy level, so that your ambience will enhance this reality. If there are dramatic transitions that can be accentuated within the scenes, consider recording the environments with several levels of activity or energy, then mix them on separate tracks to accompany the changes of energy in the scene. These variations can also be applied to several scenes in the same location, when the dramatic arc can be enhanced with the change of energy in the ambience track. This will almost certainly be a subliminal suggestion for an audience caught up in a good story; like so many tools in the hands of a sound designer, the contribution is not noticed consciously but adds considerably to the evoked feelings.

With all ambiences there is the question of seeking what best fits the visual; more often than not the same location will not work for both. And if the scene is shot in the studio, you will be required to create this ambience from other sources. Regardless whether the genre is a realistic drama, terror, or comedy, the path to finding the best ambience needs a keen observation of the visual elements on the screen, an understanding of the emotional moment, and the ability to access your own inner ear to create the best sonic landscape for the scene. In Chapter 2, **Expanding Creativity**, you will find experiments to help develop these intuitive powers.

Here is a helpful hint when you are building a loop track for your ambience. Often you will need several minutes' duration to cover the entire scene, and you may have much less than that for an adequate background recording. The solution is to loop the sound, but the point of connection sometimes jumps levels or timbre, making it stand out. If your ambience is very constant with no attacks, peaks, or decay (no bird chirping, horn blowing, etc.), then you can transfer it twice, once normal and once in reverse. When you attach the ends of the normal to the reverse into a loop, there will be no jump at all. (Any peak sounds might register as strange in reverse.)

For finding, creating, and recording **isolated sound effects/events,** you will also need to tap into your inner ear, but the process can be compared more to modern music improvisation, whose forefathers include tribal shamans, John Cage, and the Beatles with "Revolution 9." Your raw materials are unlimited, with thousands of discoveries awaiting you as the composer/performer/editor.

If you are working with portable objects and surfaces for generating sounds, ideally you should be in a soundproof studio to get clean recordings. But if this is not possible for budgetary or logistical reasons, find a space that has as few background sounds as possible, being very attentive to seemingly invisible noises like air conditioners, refrigerators, bird twittering, traffic hum, and so on, which might dirty your track. Often choosing late-night hours helps avoid interruptions of telephones ringing, conversations, and general human movement.

Be aware of any unwanted reverberation from a hard-walled space like a bathroom or kitchen; you can always add it later in the mix if you want, but you can't remove it. A carpeted room will help and you can also hang blankets. Exceptions come up when you are sure that a reverb or echo is exactly what you're looking for, and a particular stairwell or storm drain adds just the right coloring to your recording.

Sometimes a sound cannot easily be created or recorded outside its home environment, like a large factory machine that generates a peculiar thump and whirl that fits perfectly for the movement of some robot in a sci-fi film. If the sound is very loud in relation to the surrounding environment, you may be able to isolate it with digital sculpting of the sound waves in the computer. Another possibility is to request to activate the sound-making devices you wish to record one-by-one during off-hours, getting a clean background.

Everyday materials and objects can be recruited to create an infinite range of timbres, tones, attacks, and decays. The kitchen, tool room, and bathroom are fertile locations to explore. Cooking, cleaning, and construction implements can generate sounds that become totally disassociated from their origin, lending unusual feelings to a scene: chopsticks clacking on a rake, pancake batter dropped slowly into sizzling oil, clanging a pot with water swirling inside, squirting an almost-empty suntan lotion bottle, squeezing a ripe tomato inside a plastic bag. Mix metal, wood, plastic, glass, and organic material and surfaces. Hit, drop, scrape, rub, twang, bounce, twirl, submerge, blow, heat — play with earth, air, fire, water. Experimentation is the name of the game.

If your tape recorder is multispeeded, try varying the velocity to hear the effect immediately, then modify according to what works best for the scene. Otherwise manipulate the sound with your studio equipment to find what speed can be most effective. Sometimes the same sound can be multilayered with different speeds, creating a sense of reality with more weight, as was done in *Terminator 2* in the final scene of the molten metal pool.

Most often speed and frequency factors will be coupled on analogue tape systems (slower speed induces lower pitch, and vice versa), but if you need to work with them independently, you can do so with digital editing systems. This might be the case if the duration of an image is set and you want to adapt a sound effect to fit exactly without changing the frequency; or conversely, the length of the sound effect is correct, but you must change the pitch to avoid or create a masking frequency.

Foley sounds are primarily those created to accompany the noisemaking movement of actors in real time. Even if footsteps, coffee cup clinking, or squeaky leather chairs were recorded during the shoot, the standard practice is to replace them all in the foley room for the sake of uniformity and ability to totally isolate these sounds from the dialogue, to be able to construct not only a realistic sonic presence of the action, but also a complete M&E (music-and-effects) track for future international releases with foreign languages.

Foley artists must have incredible observation powers and rhythm to be able to duplicate an action through sound. Their talent is generally applied in a totally invisible manner, seeking to make something sound as close as possible to the expected natural sound. This belies the necessary creativity required to find unlikely solutions. For example, in a scene of a bicycle crashing into a series of trash cans, the foley artist may record several tracks:

a) a bicycle upside down with its gears spinning
b) a screeching sound from the squeezed neck of an exhaling rubber balloon
c) tossing the bicycle on top of a couple of empty trash cans
d) a ceramic platter shattering
e) a spastic bicycle bell ringing in agony
f) plunking on an out-of-tune kalimba (metal thumb harp) to mimic broken spokes

(A frightened-cat meow from a wild track or library source would also add some flavor to the wreckage.)

The style of the film (especially comedy or terror) may allow exaggeration of the foley sounds. For example, clothing being ripped on camera usually has been prepared by the costumer to release easily in a specific manner, but it provides no usable sound. When the foley artist rips a cotton rag close to the microphone, the effect can be drawn out much more dramatically than it would normally happen even if the clothing were being ripped naturally. Another illustration is the boxing punch — how many wacks, thumps, and splatters have been created by hitting thick beef steaks or crushing melons? Scorcese's *Raging Bull* shows a classic use of the variety of sounds that can be created by one human being violently contacting another human being.

After the collection of raw sounds has been made, **samplers and synthesizers** can be applied as a creative means to an effective narrative end. The use of electronic and computer technology has become so commonplace not only in film postproduction, but also in our daily lives, that the digital sculpting of sounds can be easily embraced. The cost of these tools has dropped drastically in the last few years, so nearly everyone can have access, and the software has become more user-friendly for those who are less technically oriented and more intuitive. The only reason not to exploit this technology would be based on the philosophical position that sounds should not be manipulated in this manner because that would distort the reality presented in the film (as stated in the Danish genre/manifesto *Dogma 95*).

Sampling is a method of selecting a sound or portion of a sound and converting it into digital memory. The sampled sounds can come from:

- **production tracks**
- **wild tracks**
- **studio recordings** (including **foley**)
- **libraries** (both independent collections — tape, CD, or MD — and onboard digital selections)
- **well-known clips** from popular songs, political speeches, or TV programs (remember about acquiring the rights if you plan to commercially exploit others' creations)

Once the sound is digitized, it can be manipulated in a myriad of ways, which will be discussed in more detail in the section on ***Experimentation and open options***.

Synthesized sounds cover a large variety of sound waves that are not originally generated by physical vibration of air molecules, but rather begin as sounds with electronic analog or digital sources. 1950s sci-fi films exploited the earlier analogue synthesizers' other-worldly effects, which worked so well because they obviously were not being produced by anything natural on Earth. Until digital synthesizers became widely available, electronic sounds were applied mostly to the realm of weirdness or as a rock'n'roll cultural symbol based on popular music associations. But the digital revolution swung open the gates for synthesizers to become integrated with the finest-sounding acoustic musical instruments, as well as any voice, ambience, or sound effect. Synthesizing today includes sampling as one of its most exciting sources of electronic information to manipulate. It is an exceptionally useful tool for integrating the areas of sound effects, ambience, and music, and will be further explored in the section ***Coordinating with the music score***.

As this subject deserves an entire book (you can refer to *Sound Synthesis and Sampling* by Martin Russ), the focus here is primarily on the narrative potential within the film soundtrack, rather than the technical details of type and use of equipment or software. Asking the question of what sound works best for the story will serve as a faithful guide during your explorations and experimentation. Refer to the analyses of character and emotion in Chapter 8, **Sound and Narrative**, as well as your visual map and sound map, to anchor your inspirations to the dramatic line.

Coordinating with the music score

All the work you have done in designing the visual and sound maps can be shared with the music composer to help integrate the creation with all other sounds in the film. Depending on your own degree of familiarity with musical theory and nomenclature, and on the experience the composer has with dramatic film scores, the form of communication will vary between the two of you. The director, as mentioned earlier, will contribute the crucial overview for this conversation to result in the most effective soundtrack. Without this exchange, an unfortunately huge amount of brilliant (and sometimes costly) creativity is often thrown away in the mix, given that the sound editor has covered 100% of the film, as has the music composer, and only 50% of each may remain in the final track.

But besides avoiding this wastefulness of time and energy, an integration of music with sound design can be extremely rewarding in conveying a stronger narrative line. An example given in the section on ***Grouping the voices*** illustrates how the two meters of 4/4 and 3/4 in the film *Negociação Mortal* are linked to mechanical/clock and organic/heart themes, respectively. This is a distinct indication to the composer as to which rhythms might best be applied to certain musical themes and where these themes can recur in the story.

The proper choice of frequencies is absolutely essential, noting where the voice ranges are in dialogue, as well as pitches of specific ambiance or sonic events. The music may either counterpoint in frequency, allowing easy perceptual separation of the elements, or may blend closely in pitch so that a musical instrument can emerge subtly from inside a sound effect or voice. Either the music or the effect might be manipulated digitally to prepare for the desired association. The ordered relationship of these sounds with the music will give a sense of rightness rather than arbitrariness, and you and the composer will need to agree.

Dane Davis worked with composer Don Davis in an exceptionally collaborative nature:

"The directors of *The Matrix* laid down the edict that the sound stage was not the place to resolve conflicts between music and sound effects. It was a huge movie, with huge dynamics, but we wanted it to be intense and clear. Don and I made a kind of checkerboard, switching focus between music and sound effects, but neither went completely away. We would separate by frequencies as well, knowing how the dynamics of the spectrum were going to play, so that the music wouldn't have any big bass during a big explosion, or any high violins when there was glass breaking. The sound of the glass was a key thing because Neo still thought that his world was physical, even though we knew it wasn't and you could have put a cat meow on the mirror and it wouldn't have mattered. But Don wanted to introduce a kind of glass harmonic, slightly screechy and dissonant, because that was a key part of Neo being jarred perceptually. Together we had to make it wet and digital, doing a kind of little dance between music and effects at the beginning of the scene. By the end, it gets all messy and overwhelming, tying into the confusion and threat for the character when he finally screams."

As mentioned before, samplers and synthesizers have become common tools for the music composer, so take advantage of the language that you have created in the rest of the soundtrack and offer suggestions for the use of sampled sounds in the music. For example, in a documentary on coal workers in Brazil, their shoveling of the coal created a distinct *ssssh-weeeek* noise. The director requested that the music track be based on the folk music of the region, which includes a gourd shaker with seeds inside that has a very similar timbre to the shoveling sound. With these two sampled sounds, an integration can be made with the visual theme of hard labor and the cultural theme of the folk music.

The integration of on-screen sound effects with the music can also give further depth to the nondiegetic reality. Most film music that is not seen to be played or sung on screen relies on a purely emotional connection to the image, drawing the audience's attention through cultural and psychoacoustic variations with the intent to build a distinct feeling. By linking the screen action and its synchronized sounds directly into the musical composition, the world of the film story can more readily penetrate into the subjective experience of the audience.

For a more theoretical analysis of narrative film music that also traces the development and psychoanalytical functions, read *Unheard Melodies* by Claudia Gorbman. Also look for the excellent documentary on video, *Music for the Movies*, which illustrates how specific dramatic effects have been achieved through many of the master composer's film scores.

Experimentation and open options

Whether you are doing the sound editing, or working with an editor or operator, take advantage of the time before the mix to try out the different possibilities of sound-image you have imagined. Invite the director to see the work in progress to make sure you'll be providing what is hoped for and to test his or her reactions to your inspirations. The more agreement you have at this phase, the smoother the mix will go.

If something doesn't work as expected, you'll have time to search for another sound before discovering its failure during the mix. If a sound works yet seems incomplete, look for a complementary sound. In *Backdraft* the fire effect was composed of rumblings, creakings, cracklings, whooshes, and explosions, but it was the addition of deep-throated, wild cat growls that gave a truly menacing quality to the blooming flames.

To avoid expensive overtime during the mixing sessions, it is wise to try out your sound combinations during the editing phase. You may not have the technical capacity to play them all at once, but if you are creating a single sound event (like the bicycle crash example cited earlier), put the essential components together to make sure they will give the desired effect. You will need to leave the tracks separated until the pre-mix, when you can still do some adjustments with attack/delay, filtering, and volume, but if you are positive that a modification is needed and you have access to the appropriate equipment and software during editing, then you can economize time in the more costly studio mix.

During the sound editing is the time to try manipulating the speed, pitch, timbre, and even direction of the effects. Have fun experimenting with something you've never tried before. Take the ideas in the chapter on **Expanding Creativity** and apply them to the sounds and technical medium as if you are playing a musical instrument, improvising, and getting feedback from your actions. This requires you to become a master (or to be directing a master operator/editor/player) of the equipment and the sound elements. Open up the circuit of energy flowing between your fingers, eyes, ears, and the incoming information. You move it, it moves you, and internal and external stimuli become one with your consciousness.

The moment of creation is not necessarily the moment of judgment, since this may inhibit the adventure of discovering really new sounds. Allow the wonderment to surface, opening up to the sparks of intuition. You may find the judgment comes within seconds or weeks; this is a natural cycle for any artist with a specific goal.

When you have arrived at a point of satisfaction with the modified sound, leave the original sound available on a separate track to be able to mix at the right balance with the new variation, in case neither works best alone.

There may be a specific flaw that must be cleaned up in the sound wave, like crackling static or an unwanted vocal noise; this could be done either in the edit with graphic software by projecting and modifying the shape of the sound wave, or later in the pre-mix with filters and equalizers. The decision as to when to do this depends on the available editing and mixing equipment, software, technicians, and your personal preferences.

Exhibition considerations

Before preparing the tracks for the mix, it is imperative to know what kind of sound exhibition system(s) the film will employ. The current (2001) systems in cinema theaters worldwide are:

- **Dolby SR** and **Ultra-stereo** — 4 tracks, Left – Center – Right – Surround (LCRS)
- **Dolby Digital** and **DTS** — 6 tracks, (also known as 5.1 Surround) Left – Center – Right – Left Surround – Right Surround – Subwoofer

- **Sony's SDDS** — 8 tracks, Left – Left Center – Center – Right Center – Right – Left Surround – Right Surround – Subwoofer

The technology for accomplishing the encoding and reproduction of these different systems is delineated in detail in other texts (refer to Tomlinson Holman's book, *Sound for Film and Television*), but what remains fundamental to the sound design is the understanding of the potential of each of these configurations, and the necessary preparation of the sound map to maximize the potential of this final acoustic stage.

In the LCRS system, the dialogue normally projects from the center with effects and music coming from the left, right, and surround speakers. Ambiance and music can take advantage of the multiple sources to create a space within which the audience can be enveloped. Expansion and contraction can be felt physically when the sound opens and closes in the surround speakers, and this can parallel not only the visual context (outdoors or large enclosed spaces with reverb vs. tight, intimate quarters) but also the psychological sense of freedom vs. claustrophobia, or public/crowded vs. private/alone.

Placement other than center for voice or effects (that are not balanced equally between left and right) can be used for off-screen sonic events, but interestingly it is not necessary to accompany the visual placement of every event because of a strong relationship that occurs in our minds with the sound-image bond. For example, if someone is walking across the screen, the footsteps can be balanced in the center (as they have been on mono TV sets) and we perceive the sound not only in temporal sync, but also in correct spatial placement, as our brains create the bridge to reestablish a normality to the situation. Rather than overstimulate the auditory nervous system with constant unnecessary movement between speakers, choose moments of heightened emotion or physical charge to make this movement evident and impactful.

With the addition of other speakers beyond the basic four LCRS, the variables increase and more discrete placement can be made with the sounds. This can be put to fantastic use in battle scenes, flying, chases, and any highly kinetic scene. The subwoofer offers a greater frequency range for the whole sound design, with powerful impact on low sounds like a buffalo stampede, volcano eruption, or rocket take-off.

One other note on preparing for reproduction in a typical movie theater. Sometimes the intention of the sound design can be destroyed by the physical space and acoustics of the theater. So be aware that if you intend to have a sharp cut from a loud bass sound to immediate silence, this might not happen in a reflective theater that allows the reverberation of the low frequencies to rumble around long after the picture cut.

A decision must be made by the producer, director, distributor, and/or sound designer as to the most effective exhibition sound system to employ in the film release. Three factors will influence your decision:

- the **genre** of the film
- the **system of delivery**
- the **budget**

The film **genre** that you are working in will dictate how much you can or should exploit the multichannel systems. In an intimate drama the focus is on the characters, their interaction and dialogue. There is little need for expanding the space with sound, and this may even be counterproductive to creating a link with the people on screen. A documentary relating strongly to people may also opt for less spreading of the sound, to optimize focus on the characters. At the other extreme, an action film is meant to drive the audience into a participatory ride with a kinesthetic sense of sound movement, and can fully capitalize on the six- or eight-channel systems. There may be a need in the story to build strong contrast between an intimate, closed sequence and an expanded, dynamic sequence, requiring an alternating use of the multichannels.

If you are working in video or 16mm, your exhibition **delivery system** may be in mono, but remember to consider possible high-end home systems (like DVD) and blow-ups to 35mm, which require at least four tracks. If you keep your stems (pre-mixes), you can return at a later date to do a new final mix for a different system, with a bit of reorganization on the addressing of the tracks. This re-mix is not ideal, as you will probably not have the same elements available in a mono mix that you would want for a multichannel mix, so it is helpful to plan for your potentially most sophisticated mix, then simplify if necessary.

The last suggestion depends on your **budget** constraints. Building a sophisticated sound design requires more time (therefore money) than a simple one, and a mono mix is certainly much cheaper than a Dolby Digital mix in terms of time, hourly rates, and licensing fees. So you may have to opt for the simpler design and mix because you have no other choice. Be sure that your economizing will not impede your release potential, which could ultimately reduce the full commercial potential of the film.

The sound map — draft 3

FX1 (Track 1)	FX2 (Track 2)	FOLEY (Track 3)	AMB (Track 4)	AMB (Track 5)
4:20 BABY CRY	4:22 DOOR SQUEAK	4:18 BOOT STEPS	WIND 1	CRICKETS
4:28 HORSE SNORT	4:30 OWL SCREECH	4:27 CLOTHING	V 4:30	V 4:28
4:30 Λ SIREN	4:40 GUNSHOT	4:41 BOOTS RUNNING	4:31 Λ ENGINE ROOM	4:29 Λ WIND 2
V 4:35	4:46 EXPLOSION 1	4:58 SHEETS	V 4:52	V 4:58
4:41 NEON BUZZ	4:51 FLAMES		4:55 Λ FRIG HUM	
4:43 NEON BUZZ	V 4:55			
4:45 NEON BUZZ	5:01 PHONE RING			
4:49 EXPLOSION 2				
4:53 TEA KETTLE				
V 4:55				
4:57 CLOCK TICK				

Figure 1-5 final sound map/cue sheet

The final sound map (cue sheet) details exactly what sounds are on which tracks at exactly what time, and where these sounds will be placed in the theater sound system. Rather than offering thematic expression of the audio, this version is like a musical score to give accurate guidance to the sound editors and mixers. The cleaner, yet more complete, the better.

Notes should include what type of entrances and exits each sound should have, with a fade in or out, cross fade between two sounds, or a straight cut. A common graphic marking of these volume changes consists of an upside-down (fade in) or upright (fade out) V, placed at the beginning or end of the sound transition.

Any anticipated effects with filters, equalization, or effects like reverb, digital voice-manipulation, or pitch changes should also be noted, as well as specific perspectives like telephone voice, room echo, or underwater sounds.

This definitive sound map should group the audio elements similarly to the earlier, more conceptual maps, in this case with respect to the separation of each pre-mix — music, effects, and dialogue.

Pre-mix decisions

There are three basic reasons for dividing the sound elements into pre-mixes:

- The building blocks of individual sounds into sub-groups are more easily handled in **isolation**. Often with very dense tracks it may be necessary to pre-mix on more than one level. For example, an effects track might be broken down into types of sounds, first joining several wind sounds together on one track, then animal sounds on another, and finally the variety of sounds needed for a lance and sword battle scene. These three tracks are then balanced in another pre-mix to form the complete effects track.
- The **origin and treatment** of effects, music, and dialogue are quite distinct (studio, library, production tracks, etc.) and the techniques of maximizing their impact vary. For example, voice pre-mixes generally aim at getting the most intelligibility and reality as possible, striving to smooth out any differences in the original recordings because of background noise, microphone placement, perspective, and location.
- For international sales that will be dubbed into a foreign language, the film will be sold with an **M&E track** (music-and-effects), so these must have a separate mix without the dialogue.

During the pre-mixes you will make your final decisions on the details of filtering, equalizing, effects, and screen placement. The balance between any original production or library sounds and manipulated sounds is determined at this stage. Maximize the dramatic intent of each pre-mix, keeping a clear separation of frequencies. The placement and

George Watters reflects on the loudness factor in the final mix:

"With all the digital formats available today, some directors want to go for a loud mix because they think louder is better. It becomes difficult to convince them to keep levels down. On occasion, we've lowered the mix during the print master without them knowing. Another way to deal with this is to try to get some variation in the peaks and valleys of the sound instead of keeping it at a constant level.

"A good example of this was in the mix for *Pearl Harbor*. With such a continual barrage of airplane sounds, guns, explosions, crashes, etc., we were able to give the audience some breathing room during and in between various action sequences. We lower everything before a plane crash, then pull it down again after, letting it up on a scrape again, then down, so it's not just one ear-screeching noise. You don't want to hurt the audience's ears with prolonged high-pitched sounds; it's too uncomfortable and can wear them out. Variation and contrast is key, not volume."

movement of sounds between speakers may follow your original concept, but once you hear it on screen you might want to adjust them by addressing them to the channels that give the best result.

Certain decisions will be final regarding the balance of sounds within each category. The ambiance tracks, for example, will wed all elements at this stage to create a seamless sonic environment. A rainstorm will be mixed with raindrops, wind, thunder, and banging shutters into its final form. The only change in the last mix stage will be the overall volume with respect to dialogue and music. Likewise, music and dialogue will have their own final balancing and equalizing to complete their respective stems.

An example of how the division of tracks can even affect the dialogue delivery occurs in *Beauty and the Beast*, where Gaston enters the castle and yells for Beast in an operatic tenor. His voice bounces off the walls, created by four separate delays plus reverb. Sending to the LCRS tracks, the voice booms on screen, then trails around the space in the surround channels.

The final mix and print master

With each of your pre-mixes completed, you will have the joy of sitting back and watching your handiwork sewn together for the first time. The mixer will give an improvised level to your tracks and you can jot down what might be modified, or request the change immediately. If the mixing system has a memory of the manual moves, this will facilitate your communication process with the technician.

The dialogue is almost always the priority to be heard, unless your sound design calls for an unusual moment of confusion or secrecy when the words are not meant to be clear.

This last phase requires you to find the best focus of attention to support the story. Hopefully the music and effects have been developed in parallel, so that they support rather than compete with one another. If, however, there is too much happening simultaneously, now is the time to eliminate the least impactful element, even if it is a beautiful sound by itself. Sometimes music composers or sound editors sitting in on the mix will feel betrayed to see their favorite sequences reduced to near silence, but the decision must serve the film as a balanced whole. Your job as a sound designer has been to create this balance from the beginning of the concept through execution, nurturing and profiting from the talents of all your collaborators.

The final say will be with the director (or producer); hopefully your dialogue throughout the entire process has been such that you can easily reach an agreement on what should be heard and when. During the few moments of diverging opinions, listen for what the director's motivation may be and look for other ways to support this different vision. This may mean changing your original position — and if you have built a good rapport so that you don't need lots of valuable time on the sound stage, it could be worthwhile to explore how this change may influence the meaning of the sequence and also reflect throughout the rest of the mix.

CHAPTER 2

EXPANDING CREATIVITY

All the hands-on training and technological know-how in the world are not enough to design an interesting soundtrack. This chapter introduces a powerhouse of hints, tools, and inner journeys to help you gain access to your own inspirational sources. The right-brain hemisphere is generally associated with intuitive, nonverbal abilities, and will be stimulated through various exercises throughout the book, ultimately integrating with the logic-oriented left hemisphere to create a complete application of the task. Some examples of how we can stimulate our creativity:

- Using **guided imagery**, sounds can originate from our own minds, linking to the filmed picture.
- **Animal sounds** can become powerful archetypal elements conveying subtle or intense messages when they are dissociated from their original source.
- The **interaction of eyes with ears** follows a physiological process that can become a consciously played game, resulting in a new perspective on the story and scene.
- Exchanging sounds, experimenting with **new combinations** and **improvisation**, often uncover richly rewarding results.
- By using **your own body and the environment** as vast musical instruments, inventing original sounds for the film can become a unique, magical experience.

The mastery of technical and theoretical aspects is paramount to the full realization of sound design, but what will allow you to truly soar as a professional is the level of creativity you can bring forth. Of course there is that innate talent which each of us carries and has attracted us to make sounds in the first place. There are, however, specific approaches that can maximize our creativity.

The principle of saturating oneself with all elements of a project (script, image, guide tracks, director's indications, research, etc.) allows an internal process to be instigated. In *The Act of Creation* by Arthur

Koestler, the path of creativity is traced in science and art, defining clearly how logical absorption can facilitate tapping into impressionistic, metaphorical connections.

This exploration occurs when we are in a mental state that is other than our normal **beta** brainwave waking alertness. It can be a daydream state or at night in the hypnogogic state — just before falling asleep or waking up. When you sleep there is an opportunity to explore every night; if you keep a dream journal by the side of your bed, those floating fragments may become concrete ideas to apply to the job the next day.

We are wired to perceive the changes in the world through all of our senses. If we remain in an isolation chamber, blacked out, utter silence, odorless, floating in body-temperature water, the only stimulus comes from within. Besides our physiological functions like breathing, heartbeat, digestive system, and even more subtle systems such as the lymphatic and spinal fluid, our mental processes not only continue operating, but generate internal imagery and imaginary sensations to compensate for the lack of external information and change. This phenomenon can be applied to sound design if the direction for the internal thought processes is guided by the purpose of storytelling. What does this mean in practice?

Without an isolation chamber available, you can enter these altered states through meditation, listening to or creating repetitive sounds (mantras, toning), or focusing on geometric forms (mandalas, yantras) or on a white wall for an extended period. To receive something of value within your sound design work, set the intention with a "post-hypnotic suggestion" for what you are seeking before you enter into these quiet places. It may not happen the first or second time, or every time, but by willfully surrendering to the power of your subconscious it will eventually reward you with its full potential.

So often we find time as our enemy to this creative potential, needing to deliver on a deadline. The "blank page" can be very scary and an excuse to fall back on what has worked before. This chapter and the other **TRY THIS** techniques offered in this book give the possibility of breaking through these blocks to help find solutions beyond the banal clichés.

Tapping into the dreamscape

As the narrative in a film represents a state of being for the director, sound designer, character, and audience, it can be explicit (conscious) or implicit (unconscious). The poetic function of sound relates to the meaning of this state of being through allusion, i.e., its indirect significance. Like dreamscapes, the language of sound imagery has parallels to the figures of speech in our verbal tradition.

LANGUAGE OF SOUND IMAGERY	
simile	acoustic similarity of two sounds (scream and siren)
hyperbole	obvious and intentional exaggeration (scream with alarm clock)
metaphor	suggest comparison of an actual sound with an idea (scream with blinking red light)
allegory	representation of abstract through concrete (scream held mysteriously until climax, e.g., in *The Shout*)
irony	contrast of least-expected opposites (scream with smile)
paradox	apparent contradiction that may express inner truth (scream from cigarette)
vivification	manifest living traits in an inanimate object (scream from doormat)

If we happen to be besieged by the threat of chaos, sound will have a different type of influence. For example, a conversation that is mixed with a loud radio talk show and busy ambience can be overwhelming. Our normal filtering process to isolate important sounds can be overridden to emulate what schizophrenics experience.

Unavoidable loud noises have been used in torture prisons with assaulting tapes of human screams, breaking glass, barking dogs, and roaring lions. This type of prolonged auditory harassment can indeed break a person's spirit, and also can be used for creating harrowing passages in film. Be aware that a certain level of habituation may occur, so the intent must be well orchestrated.

The contrast of dream and waking experience inside a film can be emphasized through sound. In *Apocalypse Now* the helicopter rhythm was created synthetically (synchronized to the rhythm of the real helicopter) and presented as an abstract form in a dream, then introduced as the real helicopter in waking reality.

Imagination tools

Beethoven's creative thinking provides an example of nonlinear composition, which can be applied to the process of sound design. In juxtaposing passages by content rather than by order, he escaped the conventionality of the linear mode of creativity. His symphonies were built outward from an abstract deep structure, which had such innovation that originality seeped into every level of composition. The technique of utilizing the sound map in Chapter 1 offers an opportunity to work at this level in designing sound for film.

Jean Cocteau scored some of his films using a principle he called "accidental synchronization," in which he took some parts of recorded music made specifically for his film, but applied them deliberately to the incorrect scenes. Walter Murch has used a similar technique in editing both picture and sound, by ordering his storyboard in columns and discovering leaps of time, asynchronies, and juxtapositions out of context between the columns. The shuffling of the elements opens new possibilities in both cases, and can be applied to the different sound elements and images of any film to reveal unforeseen modes of storytelling.

Sonic imagery can be drawn from memory within a person's experience, inside dreams or stimulated from a film. If a mental archetype is elicited through a word like *mother* or *snake*, the interpretation can be shifted with the synchronization of different images and/or sounds. The words can take on totally different significance, for example, when accompanied by a celestial drone, Sousa march, or heavy metal music.

In *Rush*, a Jimi Hendrix tune was fragmented, sampled, then strung into little out-of-order clips as the character becomes strung out on drugs. As the personality falls apart the music clips turn into sound effects piling on top of themselves, playing at different speeds, pitches, and rhythms, and finally breaking apart like a drug trip.

Gary Rydstrom suggests we look to the not-so-obvious:

"There was a *Seinfield* episode where the character did exactly 180° opposite of what his instincts were and then his life actually went really well. Sometimes in the creativity area like sound, my instincts tell me to do one thing, but I do exactly the opposite and see what happens. For example, if you're designing a scary weird creature, try putting in a high-pitched, low-level sound. Who knows, maybe that will be scarier. Try using no sound. Try focusing on a certain detail that you normally wouldn't think of but might give you an interesting perspective. Both creative processes have merit, going with your gut instinct, and going the opposite of your gut instinct.

"You have to be open to the unexpected. In *Casper* I wanted to make a *wah-oo-wah-oo* sound for the fat ghost and got a timpani for that. I don't know how we discovered this, just by goofing around, a big part of creativity; when we got the timpani I got a big rubber hose and blew into it with the other end on the surface of the timpani, opening up the crack a little bit, and we'd get these air flows over the surface that made whistly ghost vibes for the Casper character himself. We didn't expect to find that. In the same film we found with a revolving door that if we pushed it backwards, it would squeak against the grommet. It sounded like groups of ghosts wailing in the distance. We just kept pushing this revolving door in Bank of America over and over to get these great sounds. For *The Haunting* we needed more realistic, scarier kinds of ghosts. I didn't have any idea and went to get a drink of water, had to replace the 10-gallon bottle and blew across the top. Like blowing over a Coke bottle, but with this deep resonance, which I turned into a whole sound library. You have to be completely open to unexpected things."

Inventing original sounds

Cartoon and foley

There is a rich history of the creation of original sounds since the golden days of animation. With a kaleidoscope of sound effects, film opened up the possibility of combining all sorts of original sounds with images. Overlapping with the domain of the foley artists, the sound effects for cartoons generally were done with acoustic contraptions or even simple kitchen or tool-room paraphernalia, synchronizing to real-time images in the studio. Whether done in the studio or post-synced, this area remains one of the most fertile grounds for inventing new sounds, especially when combining two or more. Some examples of these discoveries include:

- *Indiana Jones* giant boulder rolling down the cave = a Honda Civic station wagon rolling down a gravel slope with the engine off
- *Star Wars* laser saber = long wires under tension, struck with metal
- *Ninja Turtle* punch = cheese grating and wet pillow noises. Compare this to the *Indiana Jones* face punch = slapping a leather jacket onto the hood of an old fire engine, along with the dropping of overly ripe fruit on concrete

A few other techniques for sound generation that can be used:

- fire = cellophane crumpled at different intensities, then dropping the pitch
- rain = salt sprinkled onto paper
- hail = rice sprinkled onto paper
- walking in mud = hands on soggy newspaper
- creek = straw blowing gently into a glass of water

Experimentation is the key here, so don't be closed to the potential of some unexpected sound you may create. As Gary Rydstrom was seeking fire sounds for *Backdraft* while blowtorching a metal pipe, he discovered eerie musical singing sounds. He comments, "There's no excuse for having a mental or creative block in sound. You can just go out and collect things in the real world — they make the sound, not you."

Musique concrète

Parallel to the development of cartoon and foley sound has been the purely audio experimentation by Stockhausen, John Cage, and the *musique concrète* movement which incorporates any and all kinds of sound generation (acoustic, electronic, human, etc.) in the formal settings of concerts and studio recordings.

When it comes to comedy, there are many possibilities for opening up to the unexpected in order to get a laugh. George Watters relates his experience with* Naked Gun*:

"I'd give the Zucker brothers three or four choices on every one of the sounds, because you'd play one and they'd say, 'Eh, that's not very good,' or you'd go to the next and all of them would start cracking up, 'That's great!' Then you know you hit a home run there. It's really subjective. What's funny to one person is not funny to another. Remember that if something funny works in a temp dub, you better save it for the final, because the director will ask for it. On the other hand, if the test audience doesn't laugh at the sound, then the director will tell you to get rid of it, even though they loved it the week before in the temp dub. For comedy, I think that simpler is better. One sound can sell something or make it funnier rather than putting lots of elements in, which may muddy it down, making the audience think too much. An example is getting hit on the head with a baseball bat. It's funnier to not use reality. Leslie Nielson had a dumb George Kennedy as his sidekick. If someone hit Kennedy on the head, I'd use something hollow because I think it is funnier than a regular *clunk*. The audience will think, 'This guy's not too bright because he doesn't have any brains inside.' But I'd always give choices, so we'd use whatever got the biggest laugh."

Many classical musical instruments can be played with "extended techniques" to generate a full range of emotions and surreal effects. The violin and guitar family can create harmonics, screechy noises, vibrato, and a resemblance to the human voice, especially with the cello. Flutes can emulate fantastic wind sounds, and when combined with the player's voice can create beat frequencies. The keyed instruments like the clarinet can perform *clickety-clacking* in a wide range with rhythmic precision and bursts of energy.

Pianos can be prepared unusually with screws, coins, or any other materials fitted between the strings to radically modify the sound. Rubbing the strings directly with a wool sock can make it sound like a howling wind. Beating the lower strings repeatedly will sound like thunder. If you hold the sustain pedal and sing loudly, the strings will resonate those tones in an eerie echo.

Playing different sizes, shapes, and densities of metal, plastic, glass, or wood with percussive mallets (wooden sticks, hammers, hard rubber), a violin bow, or compressed air will produce innumerable types of sounds.

Recording techniques

There are obvious rules to getting clean production tracks — and most of the time any manipulation of these you will want to do in postproduction. However, when you are looking for something unique, try modifying the recording circumstances as well. The land speeder in *Star Wars* was a recording of a Los Angeles freeway made through a vacuum cleaner tube.

Ben Burtt was tackling the job of recreating the take-off of the space shuttle for an IMAX film, and recounts:

"I was miking at various distances, but the sound still didn't sound full enough. I stuck a microphone out the window of a moving car and the wind totally distorted the recording. I took that sound, ran it through a subwoofer, took all the highs out of it, and when I added it to the production sound somehow it sounded more like the real thing than the real thing did. I can't explain that, but sometimes you have to experiment to get the best effect."

Sound shaping

The electronic revolution has supplied us with incredible tools like samplers, waveform modifiers, and a myriad of filters and editing techniques, in both analog and digital formats. We can manipulate the basic qualities of sound — such as rhythm, intensity, pitch, timbre, speed, shape, and organization (see Chapter 3, ***Sound qualities***) — as well as build relationships with the harmonics, and isolate different components to highlight, eliminate, or create Doppler effects. These are the perfect tools for experimenting with layering several sounds while still being able to manipulate each one individually in its relative attacks, decays, volumes, etc. When to do this shaping is discussed in Chapter 1, ***Experimentation and open options***.

TRY THIS

Find or record an isolated familiar sound that carries a distinct meaning or image for you. This could be an animal, a body sound, a machine, or something in nature. Look for five different yet still familiar sounds, each of which you will combine with the first sound in a pair. The idea is to create a third, new sound image for each pair, observing how much the original sound's meaning can be modified. Play with the levels, offset the attacks, try reversing a sound. Then give it a try with the original plus two added sounds.

Emotional impact

No matter how strange or out of context a sound may be, our minds tend to look for something to recognize. This happens when we are looking at a natural rock wall and end up finding the form of a face. These kinds of archetypal templates can work in our favor when we discover or create nonhuman sounds that appear to have vocal characteristics with an "emotional envelope." This occurs most often when there is some kind of air friction involved, as this is what creates the human vocal sounds like speech, laughter, crying, burping, hiccups, or groans. In recording we find squeals, squeaks, and hisses from compressed air hoses; groans from old wooden doors; and a laughter-like craziness from bending a saw. When we want to add something in post to give it an intelligence or emotional resonance, animal sounds can be layered to create strength (lion growl), wackiness (chimp yapping), or seductiveness (cat purr). Human vocal sounds can do this as well, but be sure to keep them at a level or with modifications so that their source isn't too obvious (unless you want exaggeration for comedy).

Another area to look out for is the potential for an out-of-context object or source to re-create a recognizable audio icon. One example you can perform by simply dialing 0005-8883 on any phone: Listen to the introductory tones of a very famous classical symphony.

CHAPTER 3

FROM VIBRATION TO SENSATION

How is sound created and how does it reach our ears? Using accessible notions of physics, anatomy, and neurophysiology, this chapter will explore sound from its various sources of energy, how it is transferred through different media, and how we can categorize different types of sounds by their basic characteristics of rhythm, intensity, pitch, timbre, speed, shape, and organization. The construction and function of the ear as receptor to these sounds is then introduced, so that we may understand what the effects of sound have on our physical body.

The source

Energy. Vibration. Our universe defines itself with the interaction of masses and forces, both visible and invisible, physical and emotional. The point of origin may be two galaxies colliding, a drop of rain in a bucket, or a child's wail of hunger. They all produce vibration, some reaching our auditory sensitivities, and some able to attract our attention more than others. They all contain motion, a dynamic seeking equilibrium, a goal. In the search for this equilibrium some will produce a wave of energy that sets into motion air molecules at certain frequencies and loudness, enabling us to perceive sound.

Friction between air molecules and solids can give rise to whistles, wind, and sounds from woodwind instruments. With liquid, the air creates gurgles, gargles, and busted bubbles. Water with water makes splashes and waves, and with solids makes cannonball dives, squirt guns, and garbage disposals. Solids against solids range from the lowest earthquake rumble of tectonic plates to the fizzy brush stroke on a cymbal.

Exploring the possible sources of sound-making is one of the most joyous processes for the sound designer. Tuning into what we already hear around us and separating the sources is the essential ability needed for creating new sounds and combinations. The **Sensitizing to sound quality** experimentation later in this chapter (see page 69, **TRY THIS**) will help you pay attention to the possibilities of the world of sound and to your talent to sense the vibrations.

The medium

Between the sound source and your ear is a space across which the vibrations must travel. This medium can be solid, liquid, or gaseous — usually our atmosphere transmits the sound at about 600 feet per second. (Did you ever notice the crack of the bat at a big ball game arriving a bit delayed from the hit, or the wait for thunder after lightning depending on how far away it is?) Due to the varying elastic, restorative properties of the different states, sound waves travel through water four times faster than through air, and even faster through solids. You can sense this phenomenon by tapping a 20-story metal stairwell with a friend on the other end who will feel the metal vibrate before the arrival of the air-transmitted sound.

While air molecules vibrate easily as sound waves pass through, water molecules are denser and slow down with friction between each other, allowing much less sound to be transmitted. An excellent example of this contrast between air and water occurs in the opening sequence of *Saving Private Ryan*. Sound designer Gary Rydstrom created the indelible sensation of a gun battle raging from the cliffs of Normandy down to where the soldiers in waist deep surf are being shot down. When the camera submerges, the sound environment transforms radically with the eerie isolation of underwater events, an illusory haven from the chaos above.

Why then would you hear a distant motorboat engine more loudly underwater than above? The surface is reflecting the sound energy from the propellers back into the water, with little escaping into the air, much as an optic fiber maintains the light beam intensity until it reaches the receptor.

Unlike light, sound can travel through solid materials like walls, although the high frequencies are usually filtered more than in the gaseous medium. Sound also bends around corners more easily than light, giving less privacy than our visual world. This property lends itself to telling much more of the film story than what is seen on the screen (see Chapter 7, **Sound and Image**).

Sound qualities

To identify, manipulate, and create audio in a system of **sound-plus-listener**, it is very useful to be able to label the types of sound by their qualities, which also facilitates communication between creative members on the film crew. The major attributes of sound fall into the categories of **rhythm**, **intensity**, **pitch**, **timbre**, **speed**, **shape**, and **organization**. Our ability to perceive these parameters and their extremes is governed by the physiologic limitations of the hearing apparatus, which we will discuss later.

TABLE 3-1
CATEGORIES OF SOUND QUALITIES

Quality	Extremes
rhythm	rhythmic-irregular
intensity	soft-loud
pitch	low-high
timbre	tonal-noisy
speed	slow-fast
shape	impulsive-reverberant
organization	ordered-chaotic

Rhythm

Rhythm, or the lack of it, characterizes sound through time, ranging from an absolutely regular clock tick or resting heartbeat to the spastic squeals of feeding pigs or the cacophony of a bicycle crash. Organic sounds can be either **rhythmic** (breathing, brushing teeth, woodpecker) or **irregular** (conversational speech, whale songs, volleyball game). Mechanical sound tends toward predictability, until it signals some kind of breakdown or outside intervention. The predictability of a sound can lend a certain tranquility and assuredness, or nagging oppression. An irregular sound can keep you alert, frightened, confused, or in fits of laughter.

Intensity

The **loud** to **soft** continuum is measured in energy increments called decibels, a logarithmic scale of sound energy with each ten points representing ten times the loudness. True silence is perhaps impossible to attain. At the extreme of zero dB (decibels), considered the bottom threshold of hearing, even the vibrations capable of moving the eardrum only a fraction of the diameter of one hydrogen atom can produce a measurable sensation. Our ear mechanism creates its own noise as well, so absolute silence is virtually impossible. Silence therefore must be tailored for dramatic needs, as will be discussed later. At the other extreme, sustained loud sounds can damage hearing, as may explosive attacks, and they cause fatigue in the listener if overused.

TABLE 3-2 INTENSITY OF SOUND

dB	Units of Energy	Examples of Sounds
0	1	threshold of hearing
10	10	rustling leaves
30	1,000	whisper
40	10,000	quiet home, city background
60	1,000,000	ordinary conversation
70	10,000,000	rush-hour traffic, average film dialogue level
80	100,000,000	loudest TV sounds
90	1,000,000,000	loudest peaks in analog theatrical films
100	10,000,000,000	shouting, jackhammers, motorcycles
110	100,000,000,000	loud rock music, loudest peaks in digital theatrical films
120	1,000,000,000,000	jet take-off
130	10,000,000,000,000	threshold of pain

Although our hearing extends over an enormous 1 to 10 trillion relative range, the actual energy of the human voice, for example, has only the power equivalent to one millionth of an ordinary light bulb.

According to "The Sonic Boom," an article published by *Playboy* in May, 1967, the loudest continuous sound ever heard on earth was a siren at

175dB, which could make pennies dance in a vertical position and burst a cotton wad into flames within six seconds! Of course film sound will never get near to this level, but the power of sound can be awesome indeed.

Pitch

The parameters of pitch follow the gradient of **low** to **high** frequencies, in normal hearing ranging from about 20–20,000Hz (Hertz, or cycles per second), although older people's upper range is often decreased. Very low pitches (known as infrasonic) are felt bodily as rumblings more than acoustic phenomena, since the frequency gets so slow that individual beats become distinguishable as rhythm rather than pitch. Frequencies above hearing range (known as ultrasonic) may not be audible but can cause uneasiness if emitted loudly.

TABLE 3-3 PITCHES OF SOUNDS

Hz	Examples of Sounds
10	earthquake
20	lowest range of hearing
27	lowest note on piano
50	low range of singing voice
80	low range of male speaking voice
263	middle note on piano
400	high range of child's or woman's speaking voice
1,000	high range of singing voice (fundamental tone)
4,186	highest note on piano
10,000	hiss of spoken consonants (s, ch, z, f, th)
20,000	highest range of hearing

Timbre

When sound waves pulse at regular intervals (also referred to as periodic), they create a pure or **tonal** sound, as opposed to a **noisy** sound made of overlapping and intermingling frequencies which produce highly complex waveforms (nonperiodic, irregular intervals). In the continuum between a pure tone and noise lie musical instruments that emit several frequencies known as **harmonics**. The harmonics for each instrument have regular waveform patterns, defined as timbre (pronounced *tam'-ber*), ranging from the simple harmonics of the flute or triangle to the complex pattern of the bassoon, violin, or timpani. The human voice has a tonal quality when it is singing, or more of a noisy quality when it is coughing or sneezing. At the noisy extreme we find explosions, wind, splashing, clapping, and what is referred to as "white noise," which is electronically generated with a completely mixed, noncharacteristic frequency range.

(Distinction should be made between this concept of a *noisy* sound with another definition of **noise** that refers to any undesired sound signal that impairs transmission of an intended message, be it musical, verbal, or otherwise.)

Speed

When acoustic impulses are repeated, they can fall between the extremes of **slow** and **fast**. When a sound slows down beyond our conscious ability to perceive it as continuous, with a pause longer than about a second, our attention becomes distracted. However, with additional acoustic cues such as a melody or verbal context, we can integrate information at a still lower rate. Resting cardiac pulse and the lethargic march of a funeral procession are examples of slow forms of soundmaking. At the upper extreme of 20 beats per second, the individual sounds begin to blur into a steady pitch (or low frequency). When speaking, the highest optimal speed for comprehension is about five syllables per second, with frequent interruptions to give the listener time to process the information.

Shape

Another technical term for this parameter is the **envelope** of sound, defined by its attack (onset, growth), body (steady-state, duration) and decay (fall-off, termination). The gradient of measurement of shape ranges from more **impulsive** to more **reverberant**. An explosive gunshot in an open area with no echoes would be termed as impulsive, beginning rapidly, peaking, and decaying rapidly. On the opposite extreme would be the reverberant sound of wind howling through a tunnel, gradually rising and falling. The listener's perception of the sound shape depends not only on the waveform created by the source, but also on the distance and reverberation properties of the surrounding space. Note that an echo differs from reverberation in that the former is a repetition or partial repetition of a sound, whereas the latter has no distinguishable repetitions.

Because every natural sound has a beginning, or attack, there will never be a mathematically pure tone or sine wave in a normal environment. The striking of a tuning fork, for example, sets up little imperfections called **onset transient distortions**, telling our ears that it is a tuning fork as opposed to an electronic oscillator.

TRY THIS

Sensitizing to sound quality

To fluently communicate with all these variables in sound, you should be very much in touch with the experience of hearing them. This is not a common form of observing. Set aside a moment and sit quietly in your home, a park, or a restaurant, and count how many different sounds make up the sonic environment. Look for sounds with particular qualities, for example, high-pitched, organized, or fast. What combinations do you hear? If there are sounds that are similar, which aspects are similar and which are different? Notice that the more the similarities, the harder it may be to distinguish between them. How does it feel to inspect every sound carefully during your search? This listening game hones the skills of a good sound designer, and you might find a simple joy in these activities — especially when they lead to creative discoveries for your film work.

At another moment after you have tape-recorded some conversation or group discussion, listen to the tape and concentrate on the sounds that were not intended to be recorded. What background noises, interruptions, or surprises appeared? How would you characterize them for their sound qualities, and what influence do these qualities have on the intelligibility of conversation or on the concentration of the participants? Later we will see how perception principles of the ear and brain relate to these questions of sound quality.

Organization

This quality pertains to how orderly the acoustic signals are to the human ear, ranging from **organized** to **chaotic**. Unlike rhythm, which derives from physical and biological parameters, organization depends greatly on the listener's social and educational background as well. A foreign language, for example, will seem utterly unintelligible and chaotic to the unacquainted until the meaning is learned, and then it translates into organized concepts. This can also apply to music, ambience, or effects, where organization delights in meaningful rhythm, tone, intensity, etc., while chaos reigns in cacophony, dissonance, and disarray.

Physical effects of sound

Sound energy can influence matter directly and be seen in physical forms and shapes of intricate geometric figures. Vibrations that pass through a drumhead with sand or through a basin of water can produce oscillating images of either beauty or chaos, depending on the organizational quality of the sound. A low *omm* chant, for example, produces perfect concentric circles that change to wobbly edges when a high *eee* is sounded.

The force of sound can be destructive as well as creative. Through the principles of resonance (see ***Entrainment***, Chapter 4) a strong soprano singer can shatter a glass with her voice and a lithotripter can break up kidney stones by using explosions of sound at the same frequency as the resonant frequency of the stone mass. These extremes are not often reached in film sound, but it is useful to know where your limits and potential lie, especially with respect to how you may be physically affecting the human body and mind.

As a general rule, the lower frequencies up to around 65Hz will resonate in the lower back region, pelvis, thighs, and legs. The timpani, or orchestral kettledrums, are a prime example of a sound that activates this region not through the ears, but directly — affecting sexual, digestive, and deep-seated emotional centers. As the frequencies increase, effects are felt more in the upper chest, neck, and head, influencing the higher biological functions of the nervous system and mind.

Sound can affect our body temperature, blood circulation, pulse rate, breathing, and sweating. Loud music with a strong beat can raise body heat, while soft, floating, or detached, abstract music can lower it. This phenomenon can be used in sound design to accentuate or counterpoint a scene with, for example, a cold winter day or a searing rocky desert.

Noises can energize, release pain, and dissipate tension, in particular those from our own voices. Helping break through to new levels of achievement, focused energy is emitted with the strong vocalization of a karate punch — *hai!* But a sound can also bring about negative changes, as with obnoxiously loud factories, jackhammers, or jet planes. A buzzing saw close to the ear can bring immediate headaches and extreme disequilibrium, and loud low frequencies can create stress and internal pains. Drones produced by air conditioners or the last days of a fluorescent light bulb that go on for hours can have an unbalancing effect, but the drone from a richly harmonic organ or your own voice can stir wonderful emotions and break down blockages in the body.

TRY THIS

Helen Keller, the college-educated blind and deaf woman, "heard" sound through touch and vibration. You can gain a valuable experience in replicating Helen's heightened sensitivity by temporarily removing your sight and hearing with a blindfold and earplugs. Select an environment that will not make you self-conscious. Begin projecting a tone with your own strongest voice, first in the lower registers, and place your hands on various parts of your body — abdomen, chest, throat, forehead. Notice where the sound vibrates on your hands. Raise the tone to normal speaking pitch, feel the vibrations throughout the body, then raise the pitch as high as you can, very loud. Does the sound move up your body as well? Try this now with a loud speaker that has a strong bass, playing a selection of music that isolates low and high frequencies at different moments. Move your body very close to the speaker and see which tones resonate with which areas of the body. By sensitizing to this, you will be conscious of an effect that for the most part will be unconsciously affecting the film audience.

The ear

"Our ears are open before we are born. Our consciousness begins with them. Is that the real reason why we can never, ever close our ears so long as we live?"
—Joachim-Ernst Berendt

Hearing development

Hearing is the first sense that develops in the womb. By the fifth month of pregnancy, the cochlea of the fetus's ear is fully developed and sounds from both inside and outside the mother's body are perceived. Someone asleep can accelerate their learning from instructional language tapes. When a patient is anesthetized or in a coma, the auditory fibers continue to transmit information to the brain that is later consciously recalled. It is said that hearing is the last sense to leave before death, and Tibetans believe that listening continues beyond this moment into the hereafter.

Nevertheless we often demote the ear's role to that of an auxiliary organ, almost a reflex in the same way that it maintains our physical equilibrium automatically. We become conscious of the ear's function only when the information provided by the eyes becomes totally inadequate. In a way, though, this gives the sound designer great power to work behind the scenes of the audience's attention, directly into their subconscious.

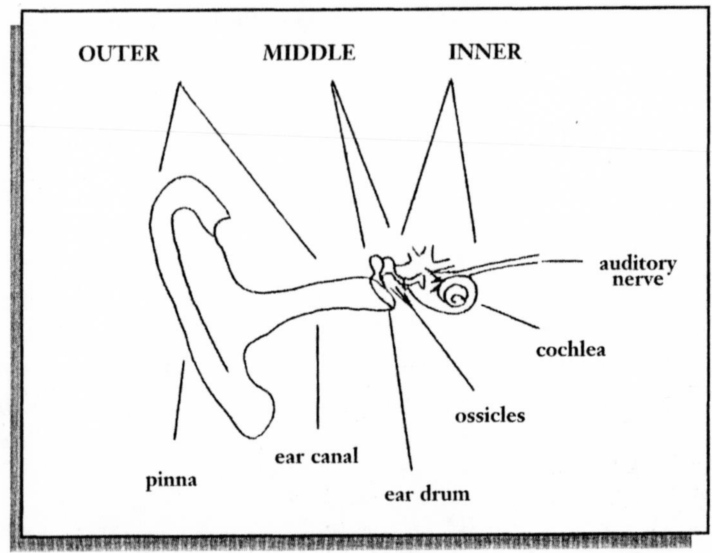

Figure 3-1 cross-section of ear (not to scale)

The function of the ear is intimately related to its structure, as are the sounds entering the ear related to the sensations we perceive. The three parts of the ear are outer (pinna/ear canal), middle (eardrum/ossicles), and inner (cochlea).

TRY THIS

Standing near a running shower, constant traffic, or radio static, gently place your fingers over both pinnae (plural of pinna) without blocking the entrance to the ear canals. As you alternate between covering and uncovering your pinnae, notice how the high frequency hissing sounds are influenced, but the bass tones remain constant. Notice also some loss of directionality when you turn your head with your pinnae still covered. Listening to the "ocean" in a conch shell is a related phenomenon in which the shell amplifies certain frequencies in the ambience to create the effect of a distant ocean roar.

Outer ear (pinna/ear canal)

The rubbery mass of folds and ridges we see on the side of our heads and what we generally call the "ear" is in fact just part of the outer ear. The pinna's main job is to amplify the ambient sounds and funnel them into the ear canal. It also accentuates middle-high frequencies between its folds, resonating in the range of the human voice, and helps us locate sound sources in space, giving minute clues through the varying resonance qualities from different sources. The sound then travels down the ear canal toward the middle ear.

Middle ear (ear drum/ossicles)

The sound energy next vibrates the eardrum, which is attached to three tiny hinged bones called the ossicles. Why the complexity? The ear is transforming sound energy from the medium of air to the medium of water in the inner ear, and requires an amplification of this energy to move the sluggish water molecules. Like the pinna, the ossicles boost the middle-upper frequencies of the voice over other sorts of sound. They also serve as a kind of pad or limiter for very loud sounds, with tiny muscles beginning to respond within 1/100th of a second of the onset of a dangerous sound. But these muscles can't react quickly enough to an explosive gunshot and will tire from constant assault, so they are not perfect in the protection against deafness. Our own voice sounds so different to us when we listen to it recorded, because we usually hear both by way of our ear canal and through direct vibration of the ossicles from the bones of our skull.

Inner ear (cochlea)

Finally, as the sound vibrations enter the wet inner ear, the energy is converted into information that the brain can use. Up until this moment the sound has been processed, transforming from the mechanical movement of air molecules to water molecules. Now the sound will be sensed and become information, with the mechanical energy being converted into neuronal energy in the **cochlea**, a kind of flesh-and-blood microphone. Inside the conch-shaped cochlea the vibrations agitate tiny hair cells like grass waving in the wind. Hair cells of different lengths correspond to different sound wavelengths, longer hairs for lower sounds, shorter for higher.

Curiously, there are a mere 14,000 sound receptor cells in an ear, compared to 1 million visual receptor cells in an eye. But if you play two pure pitches simultaneously you can distinguish them, while if you project or mix two pure colors together, they blend into one solid color.

Sensitivity

Pitch, intensity, and speed are sound qualities that the ear, because of its inherent physiology, will respond to differently than will an electronic measuring device. There is constant interaction between these parameters as far as our perception is concerned. For instance, intensity can influence speed perceptions (a loud tone will sound longer than a soft one), pitch will affect intensity perceptions (a high tone will sound louder than a low one of the same measured volume), and duration will affect intensity (a tone of the same loudness will appear to grow weaker over time).

Because of the physiology of the ear, the midrange frequencies are accentuated, helping us distinguish voice information in a mixed frequency environment. We can also sleep more soundly without the distraction of our internal bodily noises like heartbeat and breathing. So when you need more bass, you have to account for the extra energy to make it be heard, which may risk saturating the film's optical soundtrack. An example is the basso profundo voice of Jabba the Hut in *Return of the Jedi*, needing tremendous intensity to sound normal to our ears.

At lower volumes our ears are even less sensitive to low and high frequencies, so when music is played softly, the loudness button on the stereo will boost these frequencies to better match the apparent level of the middle range.

When two tones are heard within a frequency **critical band** of approximately one-third of an octave, the increase in perceived intensity is not so much as when the two tones fall outside this critical band. So a way to make a sound seem louder is to increase the spectrum of frequencies. If, for example, you want a rumble to be more present, then add middle and higher frequencies, not more lows.

The speed of the tone by itself or as a sequence can influence our perception. When it is singular, the loudness of the tone will take about a third of a second to register fully (called the **integration time**), so less than this will lower its perceived intensity. In a sequence of loud sounds, the later bursts will seem softer (termed **aural reflex**). This is fundamental to observe in big action movies: Avoid constant sound blasting, because the effect will be diminished with no aural relaxation for the audience. Contrast is essential for this and many other parameters to work on a dramatic level.

Masking

A specific phenomenon of diminished perception of sound is explained by masking. This can occur because of frequency or temporal causes. In general, our ears will not be able to hear softer sounds under a louder sound of the same pitch, which is called **frequency masking**. When editing production tracks this is extremely useful to solve the problem of background noises jumping from one cut to another. Placing over the entire scene another ambience track of the same frequency range as the production track, but a little bit louder, will smooth out all the cuts. For medium frequencies, the masking occurs when the signal is at least two and half times louder than the background noise (signal-to-noise ratio greater than 1:2.5 or at least 4dB).

In temporal masking, a loud sound will cover up a softer sound that follows a short time after. This happens because the auditory system has clamped down from the initial high volume and this is termed **forward masking.** But because the brain responds to loud sounds more quickly than to soft ones, **backward masking** can occur in the opposite direction. These physiological effects can help the sound editor cover up unwanted discontinuities, but also must be accounted for to avoid unwanted loss of auditory information.

Masking has a stronger effect when the two sounds come from the same direction. This can be taken care of in a pre-mix so that the sounds are on a single track, or the sounds can be kept separately and assigned to the same track in the final mix. In the latter case, remember to note future track assignments. Otherwise, the signals will need to have a greater ratio to affect the masking.

Phase shifting between two signals (when their sound waves do not strike the microphone at the same part of their cycle, therefore causing some cancellation or interference of the sonic energy) will emphasize their distinct sources. So if masking is desirable, the phases should be in sync. On the other hand, two similar sounds might be played with, to separate them intentionally using the phase-shifting technique. This is normally more detectable when listening with headphones to isolated sounds in each ear, so it would be more applicable to the new media on computers than to theatrical film exhibition.

CHAPTER 4

FROM SENSATION TO PERCEPTION

What is the difference between hearing and listening? Once sound has entered through our ears, we begin to perceive through various listening modes. As our sight is influenced by psychological principles (known as Gestalt) and forms of illusion, so is our hearing. The perception of space, time, and tone follows certain rules laid down by our sensory system and processed by our brain, while **entrainment** is a special case of our body and mind being able to syncronize with an external rhythm that can then induce a specific physical or psychological state. Understanding how the potential, limitations, and quirks of our physiological and mental capacities influence our perception of the world through sound will guide us towards concepts that can be applied in cinema.

Listening modes

"Listening begins with being silent."
—Joachim-Ernst Berendt

Hearing is passive and listening is active. While hearing involves receiving auditory information through the ears, listening relies on the capacity to filter, selectively focus, remember, and respond to sound. Our two ears together allow us stereophonic reception, helping us perceive distance, spatial relationships, and our place in the world.

Our ability to listen is multifocused, which means we can glean information through several different psychological and perceptual perspectives. Michel Chion, the French film theorist, distinguishes between three types of listening modes: **reduced**, **causal**, and **semantic**. A fourth type of listening is introduced here as **referential**.

Reduced

Reduced listening refers to the real-time awareness of all the sound quality parameters mentioned in the previous chapter. It is observation of the sound itself and not the source or its meaning — perhaps an unnatural mindset, but one that can disrupt lazy habits and open fruitful exploration to the sound universe. This might happen when you have your eyes closed, listening to a sound library of effects without needing to know what their sources are, while seeking only perhaps a low rumble or a high squeal.

Causal

Causal listening consists of listening to a sound to be able to gather information about its cause. This can assist in qualifying what type of space, object, or person is creating the sound. It can be accompanied by a synchronized visual or come from off screen, helping identify its source. This does not mean that the sound is literally coming from that source, but we can use its filmic logic to direct the audience's belief system in this mode. We usually treat a sound (other than speech) as causal, like answering the phone when it rings.

Semantic

Semantic listening pertains to the spoken language and other code systems that symbolize ideas, actions, and things. The study of linguistics delves deeply into this area and points out that the variation can be great in actual sound (gender, age, accent, grammar, even language) and still have the same meaning. But coupled with causal listening, we can understand so much more about a person and the message than simply linguistic meaning.

Referential

Referential listening consists of being aware of or affected by the context of the sound, linking not only to the source but principally to the emotional and dramatic meaning. This can be on an instinctual or universal level for all humans (e.g., a lion's roar), culturally specific to a certain society or period (e.g., a horse and buggy on cobblestones), or within the confines of the sound coding of a specific film (e.g., *Jaws*' famous *dah-Dah…dah Dah*). (For more, see ***Sound references*** in Chapter 8, **Sound and Narrative**.)

TRY THIS

Take a piece of paper and write down quickly all the sounds that you hear. Look at your list and see which sounds fall into which modes of listening, or into more than one mode. Now concentrate on all the sounds from a single mode for a couple minutes — first reduced, then causal, semantic, and referential — and note your different subjective experience of each mode. Adults sometimes don't notice the same things that children do (for example, their own body, breathing, heart-beat, voice, and clothing sounds). Open up to everything. This can help hone your skills in distinguishing the possible audience perception of the sounds you will choose in your design.

Less is more

With the expansion of awareness of so many possible sounds comes the opposing wisdom as to which — and how many — sounds will actually be most effective. Sometimes you can get the most impact with the least number of elements, allowing the audience to be more participatory by letting them fill in the gaps in their minds, as opposed to handing them a full plate.

Ben Burtt, sound designer for *Star Wars*, relates how the development of Darth Vader's sound began with many different elements of heartbeat, breathing, and machine to create his all-powerful, evil presence. But after testing all the combinations and manipulating many sonic elements, it was found that the most impactful sound was centered on a single breathing cycle with varying speed. The sinister simplicity helped generate a cultural icon.

Gestalt principles and illusion

Gestalt psychology (the theory that a pattern or unified whole has specific properties that cannot be derived from a summation of its component parts) uses terms in regard to visual perception, which can find equivalents in aural perception as well. These concepts help identify the mechanisms that our brain employs to analyze information, giving us further tools for creating an effective sound design.

Figure and ground

When a voice pops out of the restaurant murmur and you recognize an old friend or a hot tip on the stock market, this voice becomes a **figure** against the **ground** of the background ambience. Depending on your interest in the subject or person, you can "dial in" on any number of equally loud conversations. Your habits may also influence what you listen to (for example, the only voice in your native language among all foreign-speaking people).

Sound quality influences what might be noticed in a soundscape in the reverse sense of masking. When a frequency or timbre, for instance, pops out differently from the ground, it can become a figure. On the other hand, physical dimensions of the sound have much less influence on the figure-ground phenomenon than does the novelty or contrast of elements. A soft, quirky sound like a buzzing insect inside a sterile office will attract more attention than the loud grinding of the paper shredder.

Walter Murch, Oscar-winning sound designer of *The Godfather*, *Apocalypse Now*, and *The English Patient*, has pointed out that within one scene our attention can be focused only on a maximum of two sound elements simultaneously, because "three trees [figures] make a forest [ground]." As two sounds can be heard distinctly at full volume, the third can be rising or falling from our attention. This will strike a balance between a rich density and a simple clarity for our brains to absorb.

An aural illusion of figure and ground may be generated within white noises of constantly oscillating mixed frequencies, when in fact there may be no figure at all, like when imaginary voices are heard in wind or waves. Or the figure may be at such a low level as to become subliminal (below the conscious threshold). This is used in meditation and self-help tapes that play back almost inaudible voice information, which you may imagine as something else like a bell or machinery, but nonetheless it enters your mind as a complete message. Control of this phenomenon by the sound designer requires fine-tuning of these parameters and experimentation in the mix of the elements.

Completeness, good continuation, and closure

The mind likes to complete patterns, so if a melody, voice, or cyclic sound has paused before completing its intended trajectory, we will feel tension, conflict, and drama. This law of **completeness** can be expressed within a scene or across the entire film. It is what draws us toward a satisfying conclusion, whether it be a simple major scale or the archetypal story line of boy meets girl – loses girl – gets girl back.

Good continuation relates to the principle that changes in the frequency, intensity, location, or spectrum of a single sound source tend to be smooth and continuous rather than abrupt. If the change is smooth, then this indicates a single source; if abrupt, then a new source has been activated. Natural speech employs frequency glides that help hold together a single speaker's voice into a single perceptual stream. If a sentence is cut and edited from two takes, sometimes it doesn't sound right because there is too abrupt a change between the unnaturally stitched words. The solution is to find a cut point with as little change as possible between takes.

The law of **closure** states that the mind will tend to unite two disconnected lines lying along the same trajectory. This happens as well with melodic fragments, broken sentences, or any other interrupted sonic information. When a hole or defect occurs in a sound, say in some dialogue, a sound editor can hide it by placing another sound over this moment, e.g., a car horn. The result is that the audience will perceive that the dialogue continues non-stop, even filling in the actual words that may have been missing from the original track.

Proximity and similarity

The law of **proximity** explains how the brain tends to group nearby objects, like a bunch of grapes. When this rule is applied to audio, where proximity means nearness in time, adjacent sound elements tend to be grouped as a single sound object. If a squeak is followed by a bang and rattle, this could be a rusty screen door closing. A human wail mixed with a wolf howl becomes a single sound source. If an *uh-oh* is followed by a glass breaking, we can assume that someone is responsible for this catastrophe, or at least knew that it was coming. In music, this is illustrated when adjacent notes become a melody.

Another aspect of this concept regards the instance of large numbers of sounds grouped together, like crowd murmur, clapping, or cicadas. The aggregate sounds of these textures are not merely the sum of a lot of individual sounds, but something qualitatively different to our ears. If a ball bearing is bounced on the floor, it is totally distinct from a bucket of ball bearings dumped at once, or the single raindrop compared to a full downpour.

When listening to a group of musical instruments play a melody in unison, we are able to distinguish the separate instruments because they maintain enough separation of the onset (asynchrony) of their voices that the proximity effect does not apply, and they do not sound like one instrument.

The law of **similarity** states that similar sounds are grouped together even when separated by time. For instance, a telephone ringing once every five seconds, with all sorts of office sounds in between, remains a single sound object calling attention to the growing urge to answer the phone. A dog barking sporadically but with the same timbre in the distance will continue to represent that single dog, even if other dogs bark in between with other timbres.

In the specific case of musical scales or melodies, these patterns can be formed in our brain from two different instruments or ears (locations of source) sharing parts of the pattern. Composers have long known of this illusion, employing several instrumentalists to play two or more executable melodic passages that add up to a completion and seem to the listener to be a single melody that would have been excruciatingly difficult for a single performer.

Similarities have stronger bonds with the same timbre than with the same pitch. Two differently pitched bells struck simultaneously will sound more like one object than a bell with a whistle at the same pitch. If distinction is desired, it's better to avoid similar timbre.

Common fate and belongingness

Common fate refers to the phenomenon of two or more components in a complex sound undergoing the same kinds of changes at the same time, which then become grouped and perceived as part of the same source. This could be linked to the structure of the sound envelope (onset, decay, etc.), volume changes, pitch shift, or directionality, and can be applied to individual sound objects or entire environments. When a scene moves from exterior to a nearby interior, the exterior sounds may remain the same, but at a lower volume, with the high frequencies cut off.

Usually a single component of sound can only be assigned to one source at a time, which is known as **belongingness**. Once it has been used in the formation of one sound object or stream of acoustic information, it cannot be applied to another within that incident. For example, inside a bird shop next to a busy street, the sound of a traffic cop's whistle will most likely be assimilated into the twittering of the birds, unless a visual component pulls our attention away from the shop context. On the other hand, if the component has any level of ambiguity, the associated stream can shift depending on the context and focus for the listener. This can be utilized as a subtle dramatic shift of intention within a series of scenes, or played towards comedy, where intersecting realities can be full of double entendres.

Illusion

Have you always enjoyed magician's tricks and optical illusions? With the many principles outlined in this chapter, you too can produce some really fascinating acoustic illusions. While understanding how these function is essential to mastering them, they will remain cute, intellectual, or merely experimental if isolated from content. The challenge is to find how they can be integrated into filmic storytelling, using the lesson of perception to fit the human psyche as much as any technical requirements.

Space

Visual and auditory cues are what define our perception of space and its various aspects: size, distance, perspective, directionality, subjective/emotional space, and movement. The parameters of the space that convey these cues through sound include frequency range (pitch and timbre), intensity, and reflections (echo and reverberation, or reverb).

Size, distance, and perspective

The size or volume of a space can be sensed acoustically by the distance between its containing walls if they have a minimum amount of reflectivity. The longer the time required for the sound to leave its primary source and be reflected back to the listener, the farther away the reflective walls and the bigger the enclosed space. The duration of decay of the sound is not so much a function of the size of space, but of the degree of reflectivity of the walls. Usually reverb characterizes enclosed spaces, but echoes may also, in the case of a tunnel or rocky canyon.

To make a space feel larger, be cautious with the use of echo and reverb on all elements, which may just make it muddy. One sound alone with reverb, perhaps a distant voice or animal cry, might produce a vastly more effective expanse. Experimentation is the key.

If there is no reverb or echo, the sense can be of open space or an enclosed, very absorbent environment. The other sounds of the environment will give clues to where you are, as crickets will make you feel that you could be in an open meadow, while a ticking clock might hint that you are in a cozy bedroom.

Distance from a sound source is indicated by both its intensity and frequency spectrum relative to other sounds in the environment, and to our contextual expectations. The louder a sound, obviously the closer the source, but louder than what? When a dialogue scene transpires, the same dog bark will appear inconsequential if low in the background or intrusively close if louder than the voices. The contrast of volume is what determines the distance. However, there is also a loss of high frequencies when a sound is far away, so that this dog can seem very distant if the highs are chopped off, or very close if the highs are accentuated, especially relative to the other sounds in the scene and to what we have learned as being a normal timbre for a dog. Contrast will heighten many, many effects presented throughout this book.

To change the perspective, or relative distance between two objects in a single scene or between two scenes, other elements can be added as well. For example, a large crunching robot in the distance could have lots of booming truck door slams and heavy artillery, but when in a close shot it will be hyped with metallic clinks and clatters, chains, and knife sharpening.

Notice that when you change the timbre or intensity in the same direction at the same time with two or more sound elements, these sounds will appear to be joined in space and perspective, creating a uniform sense of depth. Conversely, if the changes made are not equal to the different sounds, these sound objects will not be bonded in the same space and can exist as independent elements. You must choose according to the storytelling necessity.

Echo and reverberation

There exist basic differences between an echo and a reverberation. An echo will occur when there is a discrete reflection of the sound from a specific direction and reflective surface, perceptibly repeating a single sound object. Reverberation is nondirectional with no singular repetition of a specific sound, but rather a longer decay rate that defines the overall volume and reflectivity of the space.

Directionality

We are able to locate sounds in the horizontal plane within three degrees by using the different signals that our two ears receive. There are two mechanisms that give clues, **temporal delay** and **sound shadow**. With the lower frequencies coming from one side of our head, they will take a fraction of a second longer to reach the ear on the opposite side of the source, which our brains will interpret as directionality. With the higher frequencies, the brain registers a similar directionality but using another factor, i.e., the shorter sound waves will be blocked by the head itself and therefore will have a different timbre for each ear. This will happen naturally when spreading sounds to a multispeaker projection system, but you might want to experiment with exaggerating this effect by intentionally using the delay or dampening the higher frequency between the right and left channels.

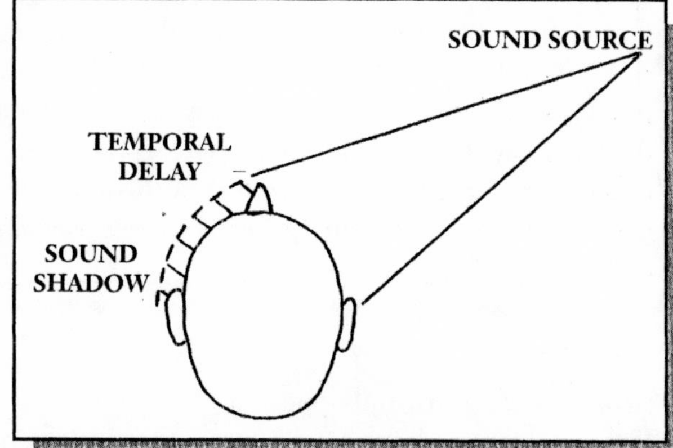

Figure 4-1 two ears help determine directionality (top view of head)

For the up/down and front/back vectors, our pinnae help clue us in to the finely detailed resonance that occurs differently from different directions. Because the folds are small, we can distinguish the direction of the high frequencies better than the low. Unfortunately, theater sound reproduction does not get the up/down vector, but with headphones some effects are incredibly authentic. If two microphones are placed in the well-formed ears of a sculpted life-size head and a recording is made in a concert hall, on playback you sense you are really there. A whisper behind your ear reproduces as if it is *just there* behind your ear because the sculpted pinnae recreate the actual listening experience.

Another unwanted effect called **precedence** may occur in theater reproduction because not all the audience will be able to sit in the ideal middle spot. If the same sound comes from two loudspeakers and the listener is much closer to one speaker, the sound may appear to come from only that one speaker. Not much can be done about theaters seating as many people as possible, but you might want to test your mix from the sides of the mixing room to see how badly this may distort the space you intend to create.

TRY THIS

Find a few sound-making objects like a rattle, a loud clock, a bell, a radio, etc. With a friend, record in an external, non-echoing space these sounds at different distances. Note the changes in intensity and timbre. Go to an enclosed space with hard walls and reverberation, and repeat the experience. Then do it in a room with soft walls and carpeted floor. Again note the cues for distance and size that each space provides. Play these sounds back for someone not involved in the recording and see how accurately they can describe the space where the sounds were made.

Subjective/emotional space

The space around the sound connotes a relationship that can be heard and felt on a narrative level. The conventional wisdom of recording is to get the very cleanest, most isolated sound elements possible, to be able to manipulate them in editing and mixing independently. But it is also worth it to grab the effect that a location space will produce as well, with two microphones in different placement (one close, one wide) onto two channels. Thus you will be able to choose in the mix which you prefer to use or manipulate electronically.

The space between the source and the listener can be likened to the acoustics of a concert hall, where we hear direct sound for localization, plus early reflections for intimacy, early sound for definition, strong reverberation for a big presence, and long reverberation for warmth. In this way, we can manipulate music and other ambiences to make the environment feel lighter and more spacious, or denser and more claustrophobic. These parameters can influence us to feel a space as orderly or chaotic, active or stagnant.

A room when it is being recorded may also influence the sounds that are being made, as when Paul Horn recorded his music in the Taj Mahal. Along with his flute, it was the *room* that was the instrument being played with its reverberations and resonance.

Consider also the very special position of where a character may be listening in a space. For example, the subjective experience of a child's hearing is quite different from an adult's, because the child is much closer to the floor; they will hear the ground reflection sooner than will an adult. Microphone placement can be crucial in capturing these subtleties.

Movement

The sensation of movement can be objective (observing objects in motion) or subjective (feeling like you're moving through space). The story and image will generally dictate which of these movements is occurring in any given scene or shot.

Objective movement is represented by the change of the spatial parameters, specifically distance and/or directionality. When the distance changes (intensity, timbre, or reverberation), a sound seems to move closer or farther away. This will usually occur only if there is a smooth change, because if the change jumps abruptly, the ear will probably register it as another sound object. The exception might be if visual cues indicate that it is the same object indeed, and a cut in the image transports the visual object as well. When the directionality (left-right balance) changes, the sound will seem to move from side to side, following the same rules as with distance changes.

An explosion effect in *Mission to Mars* uses all these cues for the movement from far away to engulfing the audience. The sound begins in the center speaker, low intensity, and both high and low frequency cut off. It quickly expands into the left-right speakers, then into the surround, increasing the volume and then adding high frequencies for proximity, with low frequencies for the physical shock to the whole body.

The **Doppler shift** is the effect of change of pitch when a wailing vehicle comes toward you, then drops in frequency as it passes. This is caused by the air being pushed forward to shorter wavelengths of sound, then being pulled apart to longer lengths with the change of pressure. In a film, this effect can be created artificially with a frequency shifter to give the impression of a noisy object moving by at great velocity (bullet, arrow, car, rocket, etc.). The real sound of the moving object may be too short or quiet or may have an inappropriate frequency for the scene, so electronic manipulation is commonly employed to create the Doppler shift.

When we are hurtling through space, the subjective sensation of motion uses all the objective cues above, plus the immediacy of friction between the moving elements. This is characterized by wind blasting through a crack in the car window, screeching tires, a rocket thrust accelerating in pitch, or a water ski slicing through a glassy lake.

Our ears also have the capacity to sense motion through balance. The inner ear fluids give us a sense of gravity and equilibrium (or lack thereof), which can be played with in hydraulic theme park rides, but traditional movie theaters keep you steady in your seat so that this effect will not contribute to movement in most motion pictures.

Time

Temporal resolution and integration

Our hearing carries constraints as to how well we can distinguish sounds in time and how they interact with each other in sequence. These limitations are an important dimension in hearing, since almost all sounds fluctuate over time, and information in speech and music is carried mostly in the changes rather than the stable portions of these sounds.

Temporal resolution or **acuity** refers to the ability to detect changes in sounds over time, like being able to detect a brief gap or change in a sound. The threshold for perceiving this gap increases at very low loudness levels (harder to detect), although it is fairly constant at medium to high levels.

When there are bursts of tones with repeated gaps just above the audible level, the sound becomes a continuous tone, based on the principle of **temporal integration** or **summation**. With increase in volume, the tones separate and a pulsation occurs.

The interval over which this kind of fusion takes place is not the same for all types of sounds. For single clicks, the upper limit is about .005 second, while for a more complex sound like speech or music this interval may be as long as .04 second.

The **integration time** for hearing refers to the finite amount of time for loudness to grow to its full value. If a loud sound has only one frame duration (about .04 second) then it will sound quieter than the same sound lasting .33 second or more, which is when the hearing mechanism will register the full volume.

Speed

Our neural circuitry has limits as to how quickly it can interpret acoustic information. When things get going too fast, we don't register individual sounds, so time can actually seem to go slower because we are overwhelmed and not involved. The challenge is to find those limits.

Ben Burtt comments about the challenge he had in developing the pod race in* Star Wars I*:

"We had a great difficulty with this sequence because the way the brain can process sound is slow. As the shots got shorter and shorter, the sound bites got shorter and shorter too, but became less distinctive even though they were different from one pod to another, just bursts of noise: *ing-onk-ook-eh*. There wasn't time for the pitch to be heard, sometimes only nine frames, so I really had to stretch things to develop distinctly different sounds."

We can first sense a sound when it lasts .001 second, and we can distinguish two sounds that are separated by .002 second. But to perceive the different sound qualities, we need .013 second for pitch, .05 second for loudness, and .1 second for timbre and speech consonants. This makes the speed of speech as much limited by our perceptive abilities as by our mouth and larynx. If you electronically (or with a speedy orator) accelerate dialogue beyond this point, there will be an effect of exhaustion for the listener, which should normally be avoided — or purposefully used to create a desired anxiety or comic moment.

The Gestalt principle of grouping by similarity comes into play when sounds are sequenced so rapidly that they lose detail and individuality, becoming texture, timbre, or pitch. With the blurring of speed, the detail may be reduced to superficiality, leaving no sense of deeper relations between elements. Although it is physically speeding up, it is perceptually slowing down. However, if the sequence is too slow, the brain will fail to observe any relationships between the sounds, as an extremely slow melody of music disintegrates into separate, independent long notes.

Subjective time

While objective time can be measured by the clock, dominated by the principle of similarity and the potential for intellectual discovery, subjective time is measured by the psychological disposition and attention

TRY THIS

Our perception of time may be changed by temporal illusions created by sound. To illustrate this, you need a partner. Ask the person to sit comfortably with eyes closed. Looking at your watch, hum a constant tone for five seconds, then a second and a third time, totaling exactly fifteen seconds. Let your partner open their eyes, stretch, then close their eyes again. Now whistle or sing some popular tune you like for exactly fifteen seconds' duration. Ask your partner to say whether the first or second fifteen-second block of music seemed longer. Either might, in fact, seem longer — since the first has more space and contemplation, maybe even boredom, while the other has more sonic information to process (pitch, rhythm, timbre, etc.).

of the listener. Whether listeners are bored, excited, amused, or in pain will influence their subjective sense of time.

Music can affect the apparent passage of time by slowing down or speeding up the scene. A brisk, repetitive march will quicken things, while romantic or New Age music tends to soften stress, relaxing the passage of time, even making it stand still.

Tone

Frequency perception

Upper frequencies in the range of speech consonants and higher musical melody lines are the first level of sound attention. A telephone emphasizes these frequencies over the lows, and we can clearly make out what the other person is saying, whereas a muffled voice behind a wall without the highs can be unintelligible. The high voice of a child or small animals makes us feel curious or perhaps tender, in contrast to adult or large animal noises. High frequencies can be soothing as well, as with the rustle of leaves or crackle of a campfire.

When a sound goes very high (above 5,000Hz) our perception of melody and pitch distinction breaks down, as well as our identification of a perfect octave. What is left has to do more with presence, rhythm, or a component of mixed-frequency sounds.

Next in importance to our attention are the bass notes, low frequencies that project strong extensive series of overtones that set a framework for the higher tones to be heard. The tremendous energy of the bass frames the entire experience, as our brains are mostly concerned with defining edges and contours. While the low frequencies carry more power, they are less influenced by diffraction and proceed around obstacles. Because they fill the space so uniformly, localization of the source is more difficult; this lack of direction can immerse the listener more inside the sound. Often the bass can represent a threat, like the lurking omnidirectional danger of the *Jaws* theme.

The middle voices in a musical score are the least important for commanding our attention, but these are the normal voice frequencies that are most notable at low volume. This is due to the fact that the ear is relatively less sensitive to very low and very high frequencies at low levels. The function of the "loudness" control on home amplifiers is to compensate for the loss of the highs and lows at low volume. Conversely, at high-level reproduction human voices often sound "boomy" because the bass is too accentuated.

Loudness

Normally, perceived loudness is independent of the duration of a sound (although it might seem to lessen somewhat after a long period because of habituation). But when a sound is shorter than a fifth of a second, the minimum loudness required for our ears to detect its presence increases as the duration of the sound decreases. If you are using very crisp, staccato sounds, they may need a boost in volume to have the same impact as the longer sounds (see page 89, ***Time***).

If two tones of equal amplitude and similar frequencies are played together, they will seem to have an increase in loudness. However, if those tones are separated in frequency beyond what is considered the **critical band**, then the perceived increase in loudness will be even greater, even though a volume meter will register them equally. This not only relates to the pitch of the sound, but to the timbre or frequency spectrum as well. So for a low frequency rumble to sound louder, it is effective to add some higher frequency elements as well.

How loud we judge a tone to be is also influenced by how far away we think it is (a low whisper in our ear may seem softer, but the objective measure of its volume is more than that of a scream next door) and how meaningful it may be to us (is it *my* baby that's crying?).

Recognition

When we identify a particular musical instrument, voice, or other source of sound, the attack or onset transients are essential for recognition. For example, if a piano is recorded and played back in reverse, the timbre will resemble an accordion. A flute needs the puff of air at the onset to make the sound realistic.

In speech we have a perceptual categorization that allows us to distinguish between consonants, for example "*b*" and "*v*." There is considerable latitude for each pronunciation based on intonation and expression, but there exists a quantum leap between the two when the "*b*"-ness is left behind and we begin hearing the "*v*." The experience of music and speech has less to do with the raw sensation of sounds than how our minds interpret these sounds.

Modifying sounds may influence our ability to recognize them, depending on what type of sounds are being treated. If a pitch shift is made to an explosion or a wind, we will not be able to tell that this is abnormal, it will simply be this new size or velocity that we perceive. However, a sound like a human voice or a telephone ring may lose its normal identification, seeming less recognizable and perhaps strange. Even stranger would be reversing the sound, losing the normal attack and decay expected.

We have a certain limitation on how many different inputs we can pay attention to simultaneously. If the sounds or voices are similar, only one can truly command our attention at one time, so with two going we usually flip back and forth, or perceive an overall pattern between the two without getting into details. When the two are distinct, like a low and high frequency, or speech and music, then we have more of a capacity to follow both at once.

One special case of tone recognition occurs pathologically, called **tinnitus,** which is the phenomenon of hearing sound in the absence of any external stimulation. This is a high-pitched ringing only heard by the affected person, but it may contribute to the sound design as a subjective experience of one of the characters in the film.

Habituation and hearing loss

Have you ever noticed that you are no longer noticing a rather loud sound in your environment, maybe a humming air conditioner, zooming traffic, or roaring ocean? This effect, **habituation**, is due to the tiring of the nerves, responding less as they are stimulated in a constant pattern. If this pattern changes in any of the sound qualities (speed, loudness, pitch, etc.) you will be much more aware of its presence. A real violin seems much richer than one synthesized, because the minute alterations of the bow, fingers, and strings give the brain more to respond to than a simple machine would.

The need for contrast pervades life, as well as drama and film that represent the human condition. Our physiology is wired to perceive contrast. We only notice our heartbeat, digestive system, or breathing when it is in contrast to the normal rhythm. In a soundtrack, contrast can be used in all sound qualities to keep the audience's attention, not bore or dull them. Thus the valleys and hills are what will keep interest.

Habituation can apply to various parameters of sound, including time as well as intensity. A case in point: With so many technological goodies in postproduction and such powerful theater sound systems, some movies are just too loud for too long. They lose their impact because the audience becomes numbed. This might happen because those responsible for the mix level spend hours on one scene, so maybe (ironically) are experiencing habituation and need to boost things constantly higher for their own deafened tastes.

There are two different processes coming into play with habituation, **adaptation** and **fatigue**. Adaptation occurs when a constant stimulus seems perceptually to diminish in volume until it reaches a steady low state, or perhaps no perception at all. Fatigue results when a constant stimulus "tires" the auditory nerves in a particular frequency range such that when the sound stops and then is introduced again, it must be at a higher volume to be noticeable than before the first stimulus.

Hearing loss in the higher frequencies is common as people grow older. Some specific problems may lie in the area of understanding sibilant characters like "*s*" sounds, making the listener request the speaker to repeat. When the speaker raises their voice, it is common to hear, "Don't shout, you're talking loud enough, but I can't understand what you are saying!" This is probably not a concern for which you will modify your film soundtrack, but it may be applicable to a special character's subjective experience.

Tonal center

In music the tonal center is the first note of the scale or lowest note of a chord (see also Chapter 5, ***Tonal center***). We sense a completion upon hitting this fundamental note. Dramatically, this represents the place of resolution after the conflict of so many chord changes and dissonance, resulting in a return to the safety of home.

The sound of a continuous fundamental tone can be compared to a **drone**, which in Indian music is considered to be a concentration point from which all other sounds are perceived tangentially. The relationship to the tonal center determines the meaning of any other sound.

When we hear the harmonics of this fundamental tone without the low tone itself, this lower tone can be subjectively perceived. Our ears produce this "virtual" pitch even though it is not physically present. The mid-frequencies of 1,800–2,000Hz must be contained within the harmonic series or we lose the virtual fundamental tone.

We can speak of a tonal center in our cultural environment as well. In countries operating on alternating current, the 60-cycle hum is present (or potentially so) wherever there is electricity (50Hz in Europe). It has been found with American students that the B natural corresponding to 60Hz is the easiest pitch to retain and to recall spontaneously, as well as the most common tone to be sung in a relaxed state. In Europe the tone most reproduced was G sharp. The use of the "electric" tonal center can contribute to the design of ambient sounds, allowing you to appeal to a sense of familiarity or strangeness.

Out-of-tune and beat phenomena

Our ears like to categorize musical notes into a twelve-tone equal-tempered scale (each note being proportionally higher than its neighbor). When the pitch strays from the perfect scale, wavering between one note and the next, our brains enter into a state of agony. We long to rectify this micro-imbalance, just as we seek the tonal center, a return to home, the tune-up to make everything run smoothly again.

When two notes played simultaneously are very close in frequency, a **beat** phenomenon occurs. For example, if an A 440 on a piano has one string out of tune at 436, at some point the sound waves will add up and at some point they will cancel in terms of air pressure. The beat will be at a frequency difference between 440 and 436, or 4Hz, and the audible effect will be a *wah-wah-wah-wah* pulsation at 4 beats per second. This can be used to create a powerful, low rhythm, as heard when the ominous ark was opened in *Raiders of the Lost Ark*.

The beats created from two strings on a piano are considered **monaural beats** because they travel through the air and reach both ears in equal pressure. In fact, these beats only occur if the tones have similar intensity. When headphones are used, however, the two slightly untuned pitches can enter separate ears (most effective between 300–600Hz), entirely isolated from one another to create **binaural beats**. The perceptual effect is similar to the monaural beat at first glance, but it is formed by a completely different mechanism of the brain, combining the sounds in the neural circuitry to make us "hear" a beat. With this neuronal pulsation, the binaural beat has the capacity to resonate and entrain the brainwaves, altering the listener's state of consciousness, discussed more in the section below.

Historical perspective

When making films of different periods, there should be a corresponding difference in the characteristic frequencies coming from the environment. For instance, in Paris of the 17th century, reports of noise included shouting, carts, horses, bells, artisans at work, etc. All these sounds came from specific directions and were very impulsive, rather than long constant tones, with few low frequencies.

In the mechanical age, big cities were introduced to the automobile and noise became more continuous with increased low heavy traffic. This sound is more omnidirectional and encompasses us, and we lose the sense of humanness.

In a postmodern environment, the sound may also be omnidirectional, but higher pitched, more electronic rather than mechanical. There is a certain sterility and predictability to the background hum of a computer, but humans have given character to their ever-shrinking, attention-demanding machines — like musically ringing cell phones, for example.

Entrainment

In the 17th century a Dutch scientist, Christian Huygens, discovered that two pendulum clocks swinging side by side would enter into a remarkably synchronous rhythm, way beyond their mechanical accuracy. This phenomenon, known as **entrainment**, has been found so ubiquitous that we hardly notice it. Everything that vibrates in the universe seems to lock in and swing together, like the vertical setting on an old TV matching the station oscillator, women's menstrual cycles in a college dorm, and two individual muscle cells from the heart when they approximate one another. Even two people in an involved conversation will have a synchrony in their brain waves, as does the enthralled audience with a charismatic preacher.

So as we react in resonance with the vibrations and fluctuations in our surroundings, it follows that our physiological functioning may be altered by the impact of sound waves, from the digesting activity of our intestines, lungs breathing, heart beating, to the rapid firing of neurons in the brain.

Music has long been used to induce specific states of consciousness through entrainment. Shamanic drumming in the frequency of 4–8Hz induces the **theta** brain wave, which is characteristic of a deep sleep pattern and trance states. A powerful example of this was used in the magic mushroom sequence of *Altered States*, which synchronized this intense pulsation with rapid image cuts (3–6 frames each).

The Balinese gamelan orchestra is made of many xylophone-like instruments that are purposefully tuned at slightly different pitches so that they create a beat phenomenon. Not coincidentally, the beats have been found to be in the 4–8Hz range as well, inducing a theta state in the dancers as well as in the audience watching the choreographed drama unfold.

Entrainment can be reflected in the global environment, architecture, and even in our physiology. An electromagnetic field vibrates between the ionosphere and the Earth's surface at 4-8Hz (called the Schumann resonance), which synchronizes not only with that theta consciousness state of "oneness" and harmony with the universe, but is also said to be mathematically related to many sacred sites such as Stonehenge and the Pyramids.

But we can just as likely be invaded by destructive sounds, such as a chalk screech, that can vibrate in our brains like fragile glass on the verge of shattering. This is an international sound phobia, excruciating even at low volume, and the only conjecture of its cause is some form of neurological entrainment.

Loud, low frequencies at around 12Hz that are below hearing level (called infrasonic or subsonic) can cause nausea, very likely due to the resonance in different organs of our digestive system. An entrainment can be very unhealthy for long periods in heavy industrial settings, and a bad mood or illness can result without knowing what the source is. An example has been cited in the literature of police crowd control utilizing a loud 77Hz siren that would resonate with the human anal sphincter, less harmless than tear gas, but certainly something to avoid.

At the other extreme of repetitiveness of rhythm, if entrainment goes on too long we become bored or habituated, which will ultimately inhibit the resonance. In music therapy, which depends upon the vital link of a patient to musical rhythm, the **iso principle** has been developed to counteract this negative effect. Through a gradual change of pace in rhythm, speech, or emotional content, a steady entrainment is achieved that can bring the patient/audience from one physical or emotional state into another. In fact, this is a basic rule of good drama, that things must grow and transform, moving from one level of intensity to another. A classic example in orchestral music is Ravel's "Bolero," which builds ever-so-slowly in speed, loudness, timbre, and general emotional expressiveness. Note that this must be a gradual transition to maintain the entrainment, for any abrupt change will induce surprise and a "jump cut" into another reality. If you bring your audience members into an altered state, you as the sound designer must be aware of where you have taken them, and when and how (and if — there is some responsibility here) you are going to bring them back.

We seem to be wired for imposing order on our perceptions, as the brain will pull out patterns from chaos even if none objectively exist. Watching a person walk on screen and putting music to that image, it will seem that their steps are in sync with the music, just because we tend toward entraining sound and image. This natural tendency can be manipulated consciously, working in conjunction or in counterpoint — by pulling our organic system to its limits and then breaking into new realities, like with the intentionally out-of-sync footsteps in *Yellow Submarine*.

CHAPTER 5

MUSIC TO OUR EARS

"Music creates order out of chaos, for rhythm imposes unanimity upon the divergent, melody imposes continuity upon the disjointed, and harmony imposes compatibility upon the incongruous."

— Yehudi Menuhin, master violinist

How can music contribute to our appreciation of a good story? Music not only plays the obvious role of scoring for film soundtracks, but also is a nonverbal language that can reveal many insights to the sound designer. By tracing the development of music we can observe the distinction between its ability to elicit emotions and to order our universe. Various genres provoke different responses, and structure can help define the actual purpose of the composition. The building blocks of music — rhythm, melody, harmony, tonal center, silence, and contrast — can be applied to other elements of sound design as well.

The essence of all music is communication, whether it is personal expression, spiritual messages, political persuasion, or commercial appeal. The genres can be identified with local radio station themes: classical, rock, jazz, rap, country, world, fusion, etc. And of course, incidental music for film scores is written specifically to help tell the story.

To fully access the potential of music within sound design, and to apply music history and theory to the other elements of the soundtrack, it will be useful to take a glance at the origins and structure of music. Basic music composition concepts such as synchronization and counterpoint can provide clear analogies as to how to manipulate the interface between audio and visual elements, producing specific emotional and mental states in the audience. When you work with the film composer, this will help you understand each other's terminology.

Origins of music

An infant will express itself with song (crying, gurgling, laughter — see ***The vocal instrument*** in Chapter 6) long before speaking, and these same sounds can be heard in every culture of the world. Every baby gropes for the same sounds towards words, the *mmmm* often being the first to convert to some form of *mama*.

Throughout the world, song marks the major events of our life cycle of birth, rites of passage, and death. Finnish women sing to the "pain spirit" to lessen the pain while in labor; Apaches mark the transition of girls to women with song; and in New Guinea, songs of grief by the tribes mourn the passing of their loved ones.

Music serves as a communal memory bank for the Australian aboriginals, who use songs inherited from their ancestors in the same way as birds affirm their territorial boundaries. The contour of the melody describes the contour of the land with which it is associated, to help them find their way about the world. In their Dreamtime, when they sing out the name of all things that cross their path — animals, plants, rocks, and water holes — they also sing their world into existence.

From ancient times, Hindu holy men and Vedic philosophers have used chants and simple, single-syllable sounds called *mantras* to attain a state of consciousness that will bring them into communion with "the divine essence of the universe." The school of Mantra Yoga is founded on the idea that sound exists at several levels of awareness, ranging from our ordinary, daily existence to the auditory sensation that manifests itself only when we enter into a state of deep meditation.

To the Sufis, sound is nothing less than *Ghiza-I-ruh*, or "food for the soul." They were among the first to explore the physical basis of the mind-body connection through music and sound, finding that both physical and emotional healing can take place by transporting us beyond our immediate pain and suffering to put us in touch with a spiritual reality greater than ourselves. The use of horns, flutes, bells, and gongs generates the sacred sounds, reflecting this potential to transcend the physical realities.

Tibetan overtone singing emphasizes the higher harmonics in the monks' chanting, so that one person is able to sing a chord by himself. This very other-worldly sound not only touches us with its unique audio quality, but symbolizes, as good sound design should, a greater relationship between our ordinary lives and the universal truths. The vocal capacity to elevate overtones from the normally subliminal to a focal awareness helps point to a greater spiritual quest of experiencing life. The overtones tell of a reality that can be sensed but not seen, heard but not explicit. (You can hear these incredible sounds on *Freedom Chants from the Roof of the World, The Gyuto Monks,* recorded by Mickey Hart, released by Rykodisc.)

Igor Stravinsky, one of the 20th century's musical geniuses, affirmed as well that "the profound meaning of music and its essential aim is to promote a communion, a union of man with his fellow man and with the Supreme Being."

The Greek philosopher and mathematician Pythagoras could be considered the godfather of sound medicine, composing specific melodies to cure problems of the psyche, ranging from despondency and mental anguish to anger and aggression. His famous phrase, "the music of the spheres," has alerted the world to the vibration of each atom and celestial body existing in "a universal harmony in which each element, while having its own function and character, contributes to the whole."

At the other extreme of human nature, music has been functional in stimulating aggression in warfare to frighten the enemy — with horns, trumpets, and percussion in remote primitive regions of the world, as well as in European battles and the American Civil War. Music can also accompany rebellion and anti-government sentiments, with chanting and song protests to generate a feeling of solidarity against oppressors.

Feelings vs. order

"Ravel's 'Bolero' is a myth coded in sounds instead of words; the musical work furnishes a grid of signification, a matrix of relationships, which filters and organizes lived experience; it substitutes for experience and produces the pleasurable illusion that contradictions can be overcome, and difficulties resolved."

— Claude Lévi-Strauss, cultural anthropologist

Good music, that which works on the many levels of our being, allows us a greater grasp of the world and who we really are. We respond not just to the beauty of the sustained deep relationships that are revealed, but also to the self-reflexive fact of our perceiving them. This is the same wonderful satisfaction that comes when we see a good film, one that resonates for hours or a lifetime after watching it. It encompasses both the emotional and the intellectual — feelings and order.

These two poles can be epitomized by two Greek legends of the origins of music, Apollo and Dionysus. Apollo is the god of order, measure, number, control, serenity, and the subjugation of unruly instinct. The harmony of the universe is contemplated as Apollo plays upon the strings of a turtle-shell lyre, an external gesture. Structure is strongly defined in Apollonian music, such as J. S. Bach and Haydn.

Dionysus, in contrast, is the god of liberation, intoxication, and orgiastic celebration, inspired by human emotion or animal cries. His instrument is a flute or reed oboe, both instruments of exaltation or tragedy that conceive sound internally to break forth from the human breast. Irrational and subjective, as in Romantic music, Dionysian expression employs tempo fluctuations, dynamic shadings, and tonal colorings.

The physicality of music makes it immediately relevant to the ebb and flow of our subjective, sentient life, while its mathematical order can provide the aesthetic revelation to organizing our universe. Great art cannot exist without human feelings, nor without means of ordering and expressing those feelings, and in this way great music restores a link between mind and body.

Emotional signifier

Openness

According to the psychoanalytic theory of development, our auditory sense as infants is really a sonorous envelope without distinction between the self and the world. This inside-outside fusion with the mother never ceases in our psyches; thus we continue throughout our lives with a longing to return to this melodic bath of the maternal voice.

Music helps us return to this oceanic feeling and at the same time diminishes our critical faculties, allowing us to be more susceptible to suggestion. In a kind of trance with music, our lowered threshold of belief is essential to watching films and being immersed inside the story. As in nonverbal therapy, music provides a suspension of judgment and a lack of intellectual resistance that gives power to the emotions over rational words. When scoring the emotional wave, the music can conduct the relaxation-tension cycle, taking us on the ride.

Music can initiate us into a fantasy world, effectively hypnotizing the spectator and bringing down defenses that might be erected against the realm of monsters, spaceships, cyberspace, ghosts, and the irrational in general that predominate in horror and science fiction. In the dream world where there is a loss of control and logic, music plays an important factor in drawing us into the illusion-reality.

Insights

When music allows the listener to relinquish control, peak experiences are invited — moments of great insight, surrender, wisdom, or awareness of profound human relationships. Guided Imagery and Music (GIM) is a technique originated by music therapist Helen Bonny, acting much like a personal movie for each person's transformational needs of the moment. It serves as a field of safe combat and a comfortable container for the patient's various subpersonalities to interact, much as the characters of any film live out the drama of their fictitious lives.

Within these therapeutic settings, different kinds of music have been used to stimulate different kinds of experiences. Mozart's accessible melody and harmony have been found to stimulate learning, clarity, and creativity. Haydn's orderliness can dispel irritation and depression. Wagner's Dionysian style can either reveal transcendent mysteries and emotional truths, or overwhelm and repel an audience that may be fearful of letting go into such an intense experience.

In the entertainment arena, sometimes we want to seek the negative emotions of melancholy, bitterness, rage, and tragedy. Oscar Wilde wrote in *The Critic as Artist*, "After playing Chopin, I felt as if I had been weeping over sins that I had never committed, and mourning over tragedies that were not my own.... Without being conscious of it, [the soul] had passed through terrible experiences, and known fearful joys, or wild romantic loves, or great renunciations." Surely one of our goals with sound design is to bring the film audience as well to such intensities.

However, there exists another extreme in **serial** music, which has imposed intellectual, mathematical parameters that prevent any identifiable rhythm, melody, harmony, or even a tonal center. With no reference for our natural senses and no short-term memory functioning, we lose any anchor or location sense. The music of Schoenberg and Hindemith has been likened to a nauseating amusement park ride in which one is tossed in every conceivable, unpredictable direction for too long. It is not enjoyable, makes the ears hurt and the body want to escape. Indeed this may be a desired effect at a particular moment in a film.

Then there is the kind of music that is challenging and might require that the listener get to know it over a period of time, like characters who do not immediately reveal themselves or who may appear to erect barriers against intimacy. Stravinsky's "Rite of Spring" created such a critical uproar in its 1907 premiere that it is hard to imagine how so many millions have watched the dinosaur sequence in *Fantasia* and were utterly enthralled.

Groups

Music can intensify an emotion which issues from a particular event by simultaneously coordinating the emotions of a group of people. In a wide variety of human activities like marching, worship, marriages, and funerals, music imposes an order so that the emotions aroused in the group peak at the same moment, even if they are not identical in quality. What matters is the general heightened sense of the importance of the moment.

The highly suggestible crowd can experience with powerful music a loss of critical judgment, which can become a dangerous element of mass behavior. The gigantic bands that played before Hitler entered at the Nuremburg rally of 1936 prepared the huge gathering to believe thoroughly in the self-made Messiah. Hitler's speech itself was not intended to convey information so much as raise the emotions through a kind of incantation. Not incidentally, Wagner was Hitler's favorite composer, one who also overwhelmed people emotionally.

In *Air Force One* the two ideologies in conflict are the American and the Communist; at the peak confrontation of the President with his hijacker, their two "anthems" play in strident confrontation. As described earlier, the scene is masterfully mixed with gunfire, shouting, and body thuds, but the genius comes in the cultural entanglement of the two opposing musical themes, each being cheered by their respective armies and able to clarify the passions so necessary to political revolutions or defenses.

Social stability or instability can be reflected in the type of music heard within the culture. In a well-ordered age, both the music and the government are calm and pleasant. A people who are anxious for change will listen to and play excited or wild music. When the state of things is in decay, the rulers are imperiled and the music is sad.

The emotion signified by classical film music can raise the literal to the symbolic, the ordinary to the poetic, and the particular to the universal. We feel the sense of belonging to all of mankind as we live the lives of those individuals on the screen.

Emotional inventory

An early attempt was made to categorize definable mood states and emotions according to specific musical rhythms, tonal progressions, and harmonies by Friederich Marpurg, one of the foremost students of sound in the 18th century. His ideas have transcended into today's literature on singing, public speaking, and other forms of soundmaking, and can be related to much of what we experience in the soundtracks of films. Some of his terms might be considered more personality attributes than emotional characteristics, indicating a bias of social rules and perhaps even cliché, but a certain universality can be gleaned from his observations. And knowing when something is a cliché allows you to play with it, build expectations, satirize, create irony, or surprise with something unexpected.

TABLE 5-1
ACOUSTIC EXPRESSION OF EMOTIONAL STATES

According to Friederich Marpurg (1718–1795)	
Emotion	**Expression**
sorrow	slow, languid melody; sighing; caressing of single words with exquisite tonal material; prevailing dissonant harmony
happiness	fast movement; animated and triumphant melody; warm tone color; more consonant harmony
contentment	a more steady and tranquil melody than with happiness
repentance	the elements of sorrow, except that a turbulent, lamenting melody is used
hopefulness	a proud and exultant melody
fear	tumbling downward progressions, mainly in the lower register
laughter	drawn out, languid tones
fickleness	alternating expressions of fear and hope
timidity	similar to fear, but often intensified by an expression of impatience
love	consonant harmony; soft, flattering melody in broad movements
hate	rough harmony and melody
envy	growling and annoying tones
compassion	soft, smooth, lamenting melody; slow movement; repeated figures in the bass
jealousy	introduced by a soft, wavering tone; then an intense, scolding tone; finally a moving and sighing tone; alternating slow and quick movement
wrath	expression of hate combined with running notes; frequent sudden changes in the bass; sharp violent movements; shrieking dissonances
modesty	wavering, hesitating melody; short, quick stops
daring	defiant, rushing melody
innocence	a pastoral style
impatience	rapidly changing, annoying modulations

Genres

Music therapy has opened up the use of various genres of music for changing the energy of the listener. The physical, mental, and emotional changes that occur can well be applied to the dramatic elements of films as well. The comments in the table below are general, and within each genre are certainly variety and exceptions. For example, hot jazz will get your adrenalin pumping, while cool jazz can put you in a relaxed mood.

TABLE 5-2
PHYSICAL, MENTAL, AND EMOTIONAL IMPACT OF MUSICAL GENRES

Genre	Impact
sacred, hymns, gospel, shamanic drumming	grounding, deep peace, spiritual awareness, transcend and release pain
Gregorian chants	regular breathing, openness, lowered stress, contemplation
New Age	expansion of space and time, calm wakefulness, gentle detachment from the body
slower Baroque (Bach, Vivaldi)	security, precision, orderliness
Classical (Mozart, Haydn)	lightness, visionary, regal, three-dimensional perception
Romantic (Tchaikovsky, Chopin)	emotion, warmth, pride, romance, patriotism
Impressionist (Debussy, Ravel)	feelings, dream images, day dreaming
African American — jazz, blues, Dixieland, reggae	joyous, heartfelt feelings, sly, playful, ironic
Latin — salsa, rhumba, samba	sexy, heartpounding, body stimulating
big band, pop, country/western	centered, feeling of goodness, contained movement
rock	aggressive movement, building or releasing tension
heavy metal, punk, rap, hip hop, grunge	animating the nervous system, rebellious behavior

By utilizing the contrast between genres, we can help lead the audience from one state or level of involvement to the other. For example, the normal waking beta brain waves can be slowed to the meditational state of alpha with Baroque or New Age music. If shamanic drumming enters with a 4–8Hz frequency, entrainment will cause the listener to go into a more dreamlike theta state where perception of altered realities or dimensions is opened.

Mozart will increase alertness and mental organization, while jazz or Romantic music will do the opposite by loosening up mental processes. Jazz in particular moves away from linear order to help find nonlinear solutions to problems or conflicts, presenting chaos and then a way to find order from chaos. Wynton Marsalis, the virtuoso trumpet player says, "Playing jazz means learning how to reconcile differences, even when they're opposites." That holds for dramatic conflict and resolution in film as well.

Fast, loud rock'n'roll can produce shallow, fast breathing, superficial and scattered thinking, mistakes and accidents. The opposite effect will occur by slowing the tempo of music with a calming Gregorian chant. But if there is an emergency, a need for action and quick thinking in a perilous situation, New Age and ambient music might be deadly, and jazz could even save your life (or at least that of the character on screen). Once again entrainment functions here, with the heartbeat following the music's rhythm.

Robert Jourdain has made a different analogy referring to how people use music, like drugs, for mood enhancement. "We 'take' a certain kind of music to steer our central nervous systems toward a particular condition: hard rock as the frenzied rush of cocaine; easy-listening genres as a martini; cheery supermarket Muzak as a pick-me-up cup of coffee; cool jazz as a laid-back marijuana high; the far-flung landscapes of classical music as the fantasy realm of psychedelics."

Structure and function

Musical patterns are reflected in the physical and mental makeup and behavior of human beings, and vice versa. The cycles of motion and rest, excitation and release, preparation and fulfillment, are just a few of the structures that provide an organic, sensory basis for corresponding musical designs.

The bond that an audience has with a symphony, a sports event, or a feature film can have a lot to do with the approximately 90- to 120-minute length, for it has been discovered that we have what is known as **ultradian** biorhythms. (The more commonly known **circadian** rhythm is a 24-hour cycle; ultradian is several cycles per day.) Our muscles, hormones, neural activity and awareness levels fluctuate at night with the rapid eye movement (REM) 90-minute sleep cycle, and this continues throughout the day as well. So this can be a reason why we bond with this duration, being a kind of entrainment for our attention span.

Within this macrostructure are the interweaving tensions from dissonance, melodic contour, and changing rhythms, the building blocks of emotional life. There exist specific recipes for certain musical forms like the blues, which has three groups of four bars each following a prescribed harmonic progression. The sonata form also reflects a very specific dramatic structure and will be discussed later in this chapter. These give the composer parameters within which to create, and the audience a container to experience a complete musical "story line."

While the repetition, interaction, and variation of musical themes can contribute to the clarity of the dramatic story line of a film, note that when the music remains absent in a film for more than approximately fifteen seconds, the link is severed for any given **tonal center** that was established (see this topic later in the chapter). In other words, within this period of time our brains will retain the musical reference of the tone and chords, lending a unifying effect to the film. The sound designer and music composer should be aware of this constraint or maybe intentionally break it for a jarring effect.

World music

Examining music from non-Western cultures, we can see how universal human drama has been portrayed through sound. Although the styles can seem at first unfamiliar to the ears of Westerners, with a little study and immersion, the listener can enjoy many levels. The audience's experience of each film can be oriented by several reference points as well (see Chapter 8 on ***Sound references***).

The **ragas** of India are musical modes that correspond to times of the day, seasons, and moods, and are named after gods and goddesses with a corresponding array of personalities and colors. The emotional expression of human laughter or a sobbing trill is duplicated by both instruments and voice. Each raga is based on one of nine sentiments: pathetic, angry, heroic, frightening, romantic, comic, disguising, peaceful, and wonderment. It is a musical archetype and, as Ravi Shankar has said, "is discovered as a zoologist may discover a new animal species or as a geographer may discover a new island." The intervals are related to animals (e.g., octave = peacock, major second = bull, third = sheep, etc.) and the individual tones to parts of human beings (e.g., soul = tonic, head = second, arms = third, etc.) Similarly, Chinese five-note scales represent the basic elements of their spiritual tradition: earth, water, fire, metal, and wood.

Another Indian form, the **tala**, is a rhythmic sequence that can be as long as 108 beats (as opposed to our Western norm of 4/4 or 6/8 measures). However far apart the musicians wander during the tala, they always return in sync at the "one" beat, which can elicit loud cheers from the audience. The tension builds and builds, with the looming question, "Are they going to find each other again and resolve the drama?" Even the concept of tala signifies a cosmic as well as erotic musical union, generating multiple storytelling levels.

Both Indian and African music work with the principle of call and response, like conversations between musical parts. Modern music with its roots in Africa exhibits this as well — big band, jazz, Dixieland, etc. Musical "battles" and "chases" have been made famous between Alla Rakha's tabla and Ravi Shankar's sitar, as well as between tenor sax players Gene Ammons and Wardell Gray. In films we find a guitar showdown in *Crossroads* and dueling banjos in *Deliverance*.

The descending scales of Native American music begin with the calling down of the sky spirit to meet the spirit of the Earth. The immaterial entering into the material world is a theme opposing most Western belief systems, which strive to rise from the material into the spiritual, and therefore we have developed ascending musical scales to symbolize this movement.

Feminine form

A very simple cyclic pattern appears in the seasons, the lunar rhythm, the menstrual cycle, and a woman's form of orgasm. In music, this feminine form has a similar structure to a **rondo**, which states a main theme, then contrasting theme(s), then returns to the main theme. One example is the folksong "Oh, Susannah," which has its middle portion rise in pitch, then fall to the original level, conducive for singing repetitively and in rounds.

The feminine form has the uniqueness of a contrasting middle section that is shorter than the beginning and end sections, with a different, intensely emotional, or transformational theme. These orgasmic moments of personal revelation at the center, being bounded by a gradual buildup and relaxation, put the point of tension in the middle rather than at the end. This contrasts with the more traditional film story arc that reaches a climax at the end with a quick resolution, mirroring the male orgasm cycle.

Violating form

There exist opportunities to explicitly go against the expectation of a musical form, and in so doing make a dramatic statement. This happened at various moments in the evolution of classical music. For example, Stravinski's symphony "Rite of Spring" provoked a famous riot in the concert hall when first performed in 1907 because of his audacious breaking of the rules.

In film this can be applied to the drama. The opera montage in *Citizen Kane* shows Kane creating a singing career for his girlfriend, using a montage of music as well. In a most unorthodox way, the music is layered upon itself so that it turns into total cacophony, indicating that this manufactured career is doomed. This manipulation of the movie music is contrary to the customary respect we give composers and musicians, but is exactly what has been done within the story by Kane — disrespecting the artistic standards of the opera for the sake of his personal interest.

TRY THIS

Usually we try to find music that reflects the visuals and story when we are designing the soundtrack. We can invert this process by letting the music mold the space through our body. Imagine that you are a conductor of a symphony orchestra and listen to one of your favorite pieces by a classical composer. Close your eyes. As each section plays — the strings, woodwinds, brass, percussion — let your body move, sculpting the air to guide each sound into its evolving shape. Unlike dancing, you should feel like controlling where the sound goes, caressing, luring it to its full potential. It is important to conduct a piece you really enjoy, so that you can repeat this over a several-day period. Notice how your familiarity allows you to discover new layers, relationships, and ways to interact with your body. This session can also help get your heart and lungs working, oxygenating your brain, which in turn will stimulate healthy brain wave patterns and your creative mind.

The case of the sonata

During the Classical (Haydn, Mozart, etc.) and Romantic (Beethoven, Brahms, etc.) periods of music, the **sonata** form was developed with a distinctive architecture relating to a beginning, middle, and end typical of dramatic storytelling. Two thematic ideas are presented in the opening section (exposition), then these are brought into tension in the middle section (development) through key changes with transforming or opposing themes. In the final section (recapitulation), we are brought back to the opening themes and the "home" key, bringing the whole piece to closure.

In emphasizing tension and release, change and resolution, the sonata form mirrors the emotional lives of the listeners. They are able to take the non-verbal expedition that is reflected archetypally in the "hero's journey" myth so well described by Joseph Campbell (and referred to in Chris Vogler's *The Writer's Journey*). In this myth the protagonist begins with a set of known themes/virtues/goals, confronts opposition to reaching these goals with both inner and outer conflict along the way, and finally finds a resolution and returns home with the hard-won treasure and personal transformation. The contradictory pressures and relief of tension are experienced the same way in life and society, and in all great storytelling.

Dane Davis comments on how musical structure is mirrored in sound design:

"I'm consciously aware all the time of the developmental possibilities of sound effects. I think that audiences are aware of that in an even more subconscious way than they are of music. With the sonata, the audience may not know exactly when the second theme comes, for example, but you feel that it is evolving in some way. I think that the audience is affected by sound effects in this way too, but I also know the limits of it and I don't pretend that it is more than it is. With the exception of mundane sound effects (which are more than 90%), I try to have all the sounds be associative in some way. I'm doing a Pirelli tire commercial now and my approach is to do all the sounds from tires, really make everything integrated in that way. It's a creative limit like any artist sets. If you're going to write a fugue or a crime novel, you've got a set of rules. So this keeps me from thinking of the millions of possibilities. I could have done the whole thing with animal sounds, but because everyone else would have cut in these lion roars and such, I chose to do it with tire sounds. I think it really worked and that everything you're hearing could have happened. So in movies it's often the same thing. If a particular character has cat sounds integrated, I try to make sure that character always has those cat sounds, because there is an associated quality and people will remember the previous time you saw that character. I don't think they remember consciously; I hope not, because then it's a cartoon."

Rhythm and anticipation

Rhythm of the body

Rhythm is rooted in the body with our breathing, walking, heartbeat, brainwaves, and sexual ecstasy. Through entrainment it can be relaxing, help learning, induce altered mental states, and in rare cases even provoke an epileptic seizure.

When rhythm confuses the natural resonance of the body, for example with the heavy rock *chic-boom* opposing the heartbeat, our muscles lose control and go weak. Or if a sound engineer deletes all the tiny moments of breathing from the recording of a flautist, listeners may be left literally gasping for air because their own breathing rhythm cannot synchronize with the music. These may indeed be desired effects in a film scene, so be alert to use them intentionally.

Meter and phrasing

Mapping the flow of time in music, there are two distinct concepts to consider: **meter** and **phrasing**. A balance of both is necessary to captivate the audience.

Meter is the pattern of accentuated beats, instrumental in the sense that it is created by hands, as in a drumbeat. It is repetitive, predictable, and gives order to time. Without meter, music sounds like a Gregorian chant.

Phrasing is the rhythm of organic movement, considered vocal because it naturally arises from the throat in song and speech. It works through the inherent meaning of the sound it contains, the flow of ideas in groups or musical objects. Without phrasing, music would become mechanical and boring.

Repetitiveness

Through the repetitiveness of a phrase (for example Pachelbel's "Canon in D," Ravel's "Bolero," or Philip Glass' works), listeners can become familiar with it and comfortable. In so doing, they will become more receptive to other inputs on an emotional level. However, if the phrase repeats identically like a mantra, this can either draw the listeners totally inward and away from the external storytelling (even into sleep if they are not accustomed to meditational states) or drive them away from the music or film because of boredom and distraction. So it is essential for dramatic storytelling that there be sufficient direction and evolution to keep the audience alert. This may also be accomplished with interactivity between the sound and the visuals (see Chapter 7, **Sound and Image**).

Perception of rhythm

Some interesting phenomena happen in our hearing system with respect to rhythm. The **pulsation threshold** refers to a repeated beating sound that appears as a series of tone bursts when it is loud enough, but when the sound drops in volume the same series of bursts is perceived as a continuous tone. This could be used to blend or distinguish certain sound elements, depending on the dramatic moment and context.

The subjective sense of rhythm is more influenced by the timing of the elements and the pauses between them than by the patterning of the elements themselves. In other words, a group of notes regardless of their pitch will be clustered together if they are separated from other groups by a beat of silence. So sound design will be influenced more by the placement and temporal relationship of similar sounds than by the variety of sounds within the cluster. The controlled use of silence can help deliver a stronger rhythmic and temporal message.

Holding information into a rhythmic pattern, this message has been found to increase memory and learning as well. For instance, school children are helped in their spelling when they associate sounds with their body parts and movements. With the addition of violins pulsating at 64 beats per minute (a slow heartbeat) with rich harmonic overtones, learning of complex tasks such as designing dresses or machine tools has been found to increase dramatically.

Anticipation

The foundation of listening is anticipation, seeking patterns and variations within expectation. As Robert Jourdain so aptly puts it, “A musical object is not so much something that strikes our brains as something that our brains reach out and grab by anticipating it.” This principle of music theory coincides with the dramatic storytelling structure, whether it be a comedy, thriller, or action-adventure film. We try to figure out what will happen next and revel in the surprising twists and turns of the plot that ultimately bring us to some kind of climax we are all expecting, even if we don’t know the exact outcome.

When we anticipate an event, be it musical or dramatic, we test our hypothesis to see if it is confirmed or not, allowing for adjustments in our next anticipations because of any mismatches. These are the deep relationships that create not only the structure, but the emotion as well. Imagine that you need to pay for a movie ticket and you think you have a ten-dollar bill in your wallet. If that is correct, there is no emotion in the act. But if you only have $5, that could make you pretty upset; or if you find $50, you would be pleasantly surprised. Emotion bursts out in music and storytelling when anticipation is not met.

The distance from the anticipated outcome can affect the audience as well. If the deviations are too big, the structure becomes incoherent and senseless. If the anticipation is always met or there is too little change, then the result is boring or mechanical. However, the violation of anticipation can have a rhythm in itself, ideally with a balance between deviations of rhythm, melody, and harmony in music, or possibly between dialogue, music, and sound effects in film.

By violating one moment, the next anticipated moment that is fulfilled can be intensified. A classic example is in the horror film with the fake scare of a bat screech being followed by the real threat of the monster howl. This same mechanism of pleasure derived from the unexpected has its basis in our neuronal makeup, and is seen by Jourdain in the excellent sport of good lovemaking, "taking its good time satisfying anticipations. It teases, repeatedly instigating an anticipation and hinting at its satisfaction, sometimes swooping toward a resolution only to hold back with a false cadence. When it finally delivers, all resources... are brought to bear at once."

Dane Davis refers to the difference of anticipation in drama and comedy:

"By introducing a sound a few times during a scene, it can grow and become functional on a score level dramatically and emotionally, like the train in *The Godfather* or the boat in *On the Waterfront*. The audience allows it, as it sneaks up on you. The opposite happens in a comedy, like when someone is cursing in a movie where they're not supposed to be cursing, and you'll have a really loud car horn right on the spot. It's funny because you know why it's there. It doesn't matter that it's coming out of nowhere because it is a comedy, but if it was a drama, you'd have to have it get louder and louder and louder. It's either a developmental curve or a trick, or ruse."

Melody

Out of the chaos of all the noises and pitches in the world, our ears can distinguish over 1,300 possible tones, but our Western-cultured hearing has conditioned us to recognize only 88 tones in the musical scale. The perceptual mechanism quantizes the tones, allowing them to leap from one level or tone to the next. Notice that when the tone is sliding between pitches it tends to lose its sense of melody, with no beginning or end, rather like swirling water. With a fixed pitch and duration to the tones, our brain can use these anchor points to discover relationships.

As with rhythm, melody can stretch the experience, challenging the brain to find the relationships. We tend to be more attracted to music that has very little melodic information (lullabies), than too much, although as we grow older the preference goes towards the more complex (jazz, symphonic orchestra). When children sing a melody, they generally can hold the overall contour, but the intervals between the tones might be distorted and the effect may be like a vocal roller coaster. Applying these age-related concepts to melody can help define film characters as well as the appropriate music for a given target audience.

A specific effect can be drawn from melody, as in the case of the singing of "Farinelli" for King Philip of Spain, alleviating his chronic pain, depression, and mental illness, as portrayed in the film of the same name. Well-known melodies can also stir the audience to associated memories, especially for period pieces that link with a certain cultural identity from the past.

The two phenomena of **fusion** (sequence perceived as a whole) and **fission** (split into separate patterns) can affect our perception of melody. In fusion, several instruments may play interleaved notes, creating the illusion of a single melody. Fission occurs when a single instrument plays alternate notes from very distinct frequency ranges, appearing to be playing two themes at once. This is often heard in Bach's flute concertos and guitar pieces. These concepts can be applied to dialogue and sound effects as well, offering profound, funny, or provocative sound design. In *Close Encounters of the Third Kind*, there is a wonderful moment when Richard Dreyfuss is pleading on the phone with his wife to believe him, and simultaneously the TV newscaster is claiming a false disaster has occurred to help evacuate the region. The sum of the two bits of dialogue create a fusion and a foreshadowing of the unfolding drama.

Harmony and dissonance

Harmony in music refers to the balanced proportions between the frequency of tones, for example, the 1:2 ratio of the octave or 2:3 ratio of a perfect fifth. But we can also find harmony in many other aspects of the universe: planetary orbits, DNA, leaves, snowflakes, crystals, the atomic nucleus, the Chinese I Ching, and the shape of our bodies.

A curious journey into discovering the harmonies of the heavens was undertaken by Willie Ruff and John Rodgers of Yale University, who programmed a synthesizer with the angular velocities of the planets. They found the song of the six visible planets to cover the eight octaves of the human hearing range and blended in remarkable ways, corresponding with the conceptions traditionally attributed to the different gods: Mercury as fast chirping; Mars as aggressive; Jupiter as majestic and organ-like; Saturn as low mysterious droning.

Within the microcosm of an oxygen atom there exist twelve steps in the nucleus and protons, the same as in a Western musical scale. In the normal state of the nucleus, seven of these intervals are filled and five are empty, exactly the same situation as in a major musical scale. Modulations or filling the empty intervals occur in both the oxygen atom and the musical scale, signaling a transition period or dissonance to be resolved.

This language of subatomic particles is mirrored on the human scale as well. When there is an affinity recognized between people with harmonic vibrations, we sense collaboration, love, and compassion; harmony is expressed both figuratively and literally. The soothing effect of harmony can also help people transcend physical pain, moving their consciousness away from identification with the body sensation and attachment to the pain, and into a focus upon a positive energetic state.

Certain harmonics can also generate transformation in our consciousness and even in our physical body. A specific interval called the augmented fourth or diminished fifth lies between being harmonic (or consonant) and dissonant. Considered by the German musicologist Wilfried Kruger as having a "touch of freedom," like in bebop or swing, this corresponds to the "jumping" function of the incoming photons that instigate cell division in living tissues, paths into new life.

The harmonic intervals have been described by various musicologists and sound therapists to have the following characteristics:

TABLE 5-3 HARMONIC INTERVALS

Interval	Ratio	Emotional Characteristic
Unison	1:1	Strength, solidity, security, calmness
Octave	1:2	Completeness, openness, togetherness, circularity
Perfect fifth	2:3	Power, centering, comfortable, completeness, feeling of home
Perfect fourth	3:4	Serenity, clarity, openness, light, angelic
Major third	4:5	Hopeful, friendly, resolved, comfortable, square, characterless
Minor sixth	5:8	Soothing, but delicate and sad
Minor third	5:6	Elated, uplifting
Major second	8:9	Happiness, openness, lightness, though irritating
Minor seventh	4:7	Suspenseful, expectant, rich but unbalanced
Major seventh	5:9	Strange, discordant, eerie
Major second	9:10	Anticipatory, unsettled
Minor second	15:16	Tense, uneasy, mysterious
Diminished fifth	5:7	Malevolent, demonic, horror

At the time of publication, a Web site has available the sounds of these intervals at *www.fortunecity.com/tinpan/lennon/23/sec2.html.*

The lack of harmony, i.e., dissonance, that we hear in certain musical relationships or chords is reflected on a physical and physiological level. In the study of **cymatics** and **Chladni** forms, patterns are created when sounds vibrate on drumheads or cymbals that have a layer of sand on the surface. When the sounds are harmonious, the patterns are balanced, mandala-like, and steady. But when they are dissonant, the forms are in constant flux, turbulent and eruptive, like waves crashing or the Earth coming into existence.

This is what happens at the neurological and cellular level as well. Our bodies are perturbed, especially when the dissonance is emphasized by rhythmic accentuation (for example, on the down beat, when we expect a musical resolution). The equivalent moment in drama and film occurs when a plot twist takes us by surprise, evoking an unexpected emotion through conflict and increasing our engagement in the drama. The delicate balance between harmony and dissonance creates a sensation of real life, of human imperfection, with the deviations from precise proportions necessary for true beauty.

Joaquim-Ernst Berendt finds parallels in the difference between the proportions found in male and female bodies, and the corresponding difference of the harmonics created by these proportions. For example, the triangle formed between a woman's breasts and thighs generates minor sixths, or "soothing, gentle, sad," while a man's proportions form major intervals, or "power, centering, square." These certainly are stereotypes, but knowing that there is this relationship between the sound and the sexes can help steer the sound design toward clarity.

And just as opposite sexes attract (and repel and attract, etc.), so do both music and storytelling rely on the balance between harmony and dissonance. Without conflict, there is no climax and resolution, no growth, nothing to be learned or surmounted. Too much dissonance leaves us with a lack of order, no relationship, a barrage of static and unpleasant noise. Too much harmony leaves us lulled into complacency, boredom, a pleasant death. Harmony requires dissonance just like a good story needs suspense.

The acceptance of what is harmony or dissonance depends on our environmental conditioning, as well as on the human ear and brain, since different cultures use different languages (ordering words), religions (ordering spiritual beliefs), political systems (ordering society), and musical scales (ordering sounds). All cultures tend to create order out of chaos, and this happens in our soundtracks as well, depending on the conditioning of the audience members through their culture and the film's specific audio language.

Tonal center

In drama the resonating theme or question sought to be answered by the protagonist's journey always drives the audience back to homeplate. It wanders off into the woods, sneaks behind the house, and comes up with a million variations, but always (in good drama) returns to an established reference point. Each time we return, there is new light thrown on the situation, so this reference becomes more profound and multilayered.

In music, this reference point is called the tonal center (see also Chapter 4, ***Tone***), which establishes the root of melodic and harmonic movement. When the structure moves away, the listener maintains anticipation as to how and when we return to the tonal center. The stronger this center, as with the use of a drone, the farther the music can wander, leaving the composer freer for harmonic adventure. In more complex music, there can exist a hierarchy of tonal centers, shifting the expectations as the piece moves along. One classic example is the blues progression, a 1-1-1-1-4-4-1-1-5-4-1-4 sequence of tonal centers on the keyboard. Each bar moves its center between the 1, 4, and 5 notes on the scale, but the overall progression uses the 1 as its master tonal center.

The underlying emotional principle in utilizing the tonal center concerns our need to return home harmonically, allegorically, or literally. As in real life, we can be reminded about this return by melodies that hint at this without actually making the full return. Men may be attracted to a woman's voice that has some aspect of their mother (or vice versa), an ice cream truck jingle can remind you of your pleasant childhood summers, or a popular song may throw you back to a very comfortable sensation.

But we need new stimulation, new desires; it is this seesaw of voyaging and returning to the tonal center that alleviates boredom and drives us onward, yet implies that there exists a place for us to return. Heightening expectation and postponing resolution, like in the blues which uses the dominant seventh, offers us this excruciating pleasure, the sexual tease, the wafting smell of freshly baked bread to the beggar on the street.

Musical or dramatic meaning arises when these expectations are contradicted. If there is a conflict between the "background" (conventional genre, expected structure) and the "foreground" (specific harmonic structure, story), then the tension becomes the clearest, most pungent to the audience when there is a maximum of contradiction and maximum of unity between the elements. A filmic example would be the spoof *Airplane*, which uses the tonal center and convention of the disaster movie as its home base. The comedy arises from the conflict between the convention and the specific treatment, creating an absurd juxtaposition of background and foreground.

A tonal center may also be implied, as with the missing fundamental in an overtone series, which you might hear when a guitar is strummed with stops to produce only these shimmering overtones. This "undertone" is a kind of acoustic illusion, an "unstruck" note that we feel must be there to produce the upper harmonics that are sounding together. This phantom or virtual tone may be utilized in parallel with a dramatic element that is implied as well, for example a character or event in someone's memory, or an emotion below the surface.

The high art of working with the tonal center requires a fine balance between reinforcing and violating it, to allow us the sense of adventure and journey before finally making the return home.

Silence

John Cage says, "There is no such thing as silence." Put yourself in an anechoic chamber with absolutely no external sounds and you will still hear your own blood pumping and the high pitch of your nervous system. So silence is always relative to some sound that is louder than the "silence" of which we are aware. In a movie theater, silence on the soundtrack will have some electronic background of the projection system (much greater on 16mm optical tracks than on 35mm Dolby or the equivalent) and audience noises.

So some sound is usually designated on the track as the baseline "silence" for any given scene. This can have the color of room tone, silence in the country, or a nighttime quietness, each with actual sound registering on the track. Walter Murch used the tone of the vast Exploratorium museum in San Francisco for the huge emptiness of the white void in *THX 1138*.

A synonym for silence may be used, such as faraway animal calls, clocks in the next room or leaves rustling. If reverberation is present with an isolated sound like a drip in a well, this helps indicate a surrounding silence, because we would normally not be able to perceive this low-level reverberation if there were any other masking sounds present (e.g., the hum of daytime traffic, TV background). More subjective uses of created sounds to represent silence include those in *Marooned*, a space sci-fi film that utilized the stroking of piano strings, looping and reversing the recording, then adding echoes and filtering.

Silence can also be present inside the scene with no ambience, effects, or dialogue, but still with an off-screen, nondiegetic (i.e., from outside the world of the film story) music track, for example. This silence differs from nondiegetic silence, when the film is completely without sound. Working with this fact that a certain sound was present in a given scene, or associated with a certain character, the lack of this same sound in a similar scene later in the film will create an expectation and make the audience aware of the previous sound's absence. This can create a striking shift in the emotional language. An example would be if the earlier scene(s) had music bouncing in the background lending a happy feeling, then the withdrawal of this music could lend a loss of frivolity and a sense of more reality to the new scene, or even emotional disinterest between the characters.

Psychologically, humans like to make sounds and surround themselves with them to nourish the concept of perpetual life, so that silence can represent aspects of negative attitudes such as oppression or solemnity. Silence can remind people that they are alone, that they have been rejected, or that there is no hope. The absence of sound can evoke the fear of the absence of life.

But silence can also take on different meanings, depending upon the context. In *Alien*, silence is portrayed with a tiny clock-like sound fading into the oblivion of the space void, a sinister external menace. In Bergman's *Face to Face*, a profoundly depressed woman lies down next to her ticking clock, which becomes the only sound heard, growing so loud that we are left with a horrible anxiety of being alone — exuding from the silence around this indifferent mechanical beating.

Other examples of the diversity of film silence are:

The Blair Witch Project — The night silence, elimination of all natural sounds of the woods, creates the forum for strange, indistinguishable sounds to attack the sanity of the lost kids.

The Conversation — While looking towards the insignificant wall of a hotel room, trying to understand muted scuffling and voices in the next-door apartment, the protagonist is suddenly confronted with the silence of only distant traffic. The double indirection forces him and the audience to create an imagined scene in their own minds.

All That Jazz — As the protagonist is having a heart attack while reading a script, all the sounds subjectively drop away, leaving only the tapping of a pencil on the table as an extraordinary exaggeration of what would be normally a minor element, suddenly breaking the pencil against a blanket of silence.

Gary Rydstrom used different styles as he moved from sound to silence in two very different films. In *A River Runs Through It* he drops out the constant burbling water sounds very gradually, so that the audience does not notice the change as the whip of the flycasting sings clearly over the softened background. But in *Backdraft*, the jumpcut from the hectic roar of a fierce fire to silence creates a shock and imbalance that contributes to the dramatic impact. The timing of when to go loud or soft, and how fast the change should be, is dictated by the storytelling and genre.

Robert Redford loves to have family dinner scenes that are all about communication and noncommunication. Often there are awkward silences that occur; as a sound designer, Rydstrom had to be careful not to fill them up with too much sound, so as to let them play with their intended pregnant emptiness.

The selective elimination of sound, called **suspension**, occurs when the sounds that we would naturally expect in a situation disappear. Kurasawa's *Dreams* has a howling snowstorm sequence in which the wind sound slowly dies away, even though the long hair of the woman continues to whirl in the gusts. Several films of the great French comedian Jacques Tati take this creative courage to remove all sound in certain scenes, emphasizing the comedic or absurd aspect of the situation. In *Aladdin*, the evil Jafar slides across the floor without any footstep sounds, a lurking menace. With this technique, the spectators feel the effect but usually are not consciously aware of what is causing this sensation. Conversely, they are drawn into examining the image more carefully and actively, seeking something to explain the strangeness of the silence.

Silence may or may not work for a film. *Armageddon* uses enormous sounds to portray the power of the spaceship, even though reality would dictate that nothing is audible in space without air to transmit the sound waves. It plays for the drama, and the audience would feel something were wrong if there were no sound. In contrast, *Apollo 13* is more reality-based and takes this interpretation of space literally by having the ship move silently. This also contributes to the drama of these astronauts who in fact were in a very fragile position so far away from home. The choice in both cases is dictated by the story, whether it is "authentic" or not.

TRY THIS

Silence is a pocket of possibility, which can be broken by anything imaginable. It is like the blank piece of paper waiting for the first word, the white canvas open to the first brush stroke. As a sound designer, your own mind and awareness must be able to reach that state of nothingness, so that you can allow the most perfect sound to begin to color that emptiness. There are all sorts of Zen meditation techniques that can be practiced to acquire this internal silence, but one of the simplest is just to stop speaking and focus on listening. Declare a moratorium on speech for a full day. See what fills up the aural space in the environment, as well as in your inner thoughts. What sounds are you suddenly aware of for the first time? What might you want to hear that you don't? Can you find a pocket of absolute silence? Relative silence? Do these silences have any significance? How do these silences make you feel?

Contrast

All of our senses work on the concept of contrast: sight (light-dark), touch (hot-cold), taste (sweet-sour), smell (fresh-musty), and sound (loud-soft). If we stay in any one position or mode, after a certain period we become habituated and the environmental effect becomes neutral or has no effect. At the other extreme, if changes occur rapidly, repeatedly, and at the same intensities, we can either become insensitive or hypersensitive and exhausted, even to the point of that particular sense failing to function.

Every dissonance demands its resolution in a consonance. Every consonance demands a dissonance to disturb its boring life. The two are like intimate enemies, ying-yang, night and day. Changes occur over longer periods as well, so that we can evolve with the seasons (spring, summer, fall, winter), life (birth, adventure, marriage, death), and story (beginning, middle, end).

All these principles hold within the realm of sound design: adaptation, habituation, and contrast. Combining the neurological factors with the storytelling necessities, contrast becomes an indispensable item in the strategy of capturing the audience's attention. High frequencies lead to low, loud volume to soft — increasing the impact of, for example, an explosion which could be preceeded by a moment of silence or soft sucking-in of air, then *BOOM*! *Terminator 2* is full of such scenes, rising to the challenge of making everything seem loud when there are so many impacts one after the other. Contrast in pitch, loudness, timbre, rhythm — anything that can avoid numbing repetition — will accentuate the impression of aural force.

Gary Rydstrom applies contrast to much of his work:

"You might have a *rat-a-tat-tat* kind of dialogue, and want to orchestrate it like a piece of music, using it as one element on top of another kind of element to help it stand out. I'm always looking at how a sound might stand out not just with level, but frequency range. I think of it as arranging your knickknacks in your cabinet so things look good, the short next to the tall, using contrast most of the time to make things stand out."

An interesting phenomenon in sound can occur because of habituation, rather like what happens when you stare at a green circle on a white wall, then move your eyes away to see a phantom red, or complementary circle, floating on the white. If a white noise is heard in isolation, it is normally considered a colorless, neutral timbre. However, if a tone is played previous to the white noise that has a notch, or dropout, in a certain frequency range, then when the white noise is played it will sound as if it is centering on exactly the frequency that is absent in the previous tone, that is, the inverse sound spectrum. This phenomenon can happen with speech as well by creating a harmonic complex that is the inverse of speech sound, e.g., a vowel, then playing white noise which will accentuate the inverse of the previous tone, making the white noise sound like a voice. This illusion of voice harmonics will last for a short while, then disappear as the habituation effect wears off. Normally a change in these elements helps us distinguish a new source or sonic environment, but it can also be a manipulation to emphasize dramatic movement in the film.

Clapping represents a very specific breaking of concert music that can destroy the solemn, joyous, or exciting mood with a tidal wave of noise. Or it can signify an entry into an altered state of meditation, dispelling illusions and purifying the atmosphere. This is a very old shamanistic technique used to set boundaries between two states of mind, shifting the focus radically and instantly. Like a doorway into another world, the contrast of sound serves as the key for transformation.

CHAPTER 6

THE HUMAN VOICE

Besides vocalizing the dialogue in a film, how can the voice contribute to affecting an audience? We have been making sounds and expressing ourselves since the time we were born. The ability to do this is based on the anatomy of our vocal instrument. As speech develops, along with verbal understanding, we continue to receive nonverbal messages through voice inflection. Personality is often communicated by types of voice patterns, while alien languages that we might want to create for films can be formulated based on elements of speech, nonverbal expressions, and animal sounds.

The vocal instrument

The human voice is like a little orchestra of wind instruments: The vocal cords are like the reeds of an oboe, and the vocal cavities in the throat, mouth, and sinuses are like the muted whistles of an ocarina. When the vocal cords do not vibrate but air passes through the vocal cavities, we hear a whisper and can distinguish the resonance of an individual's voice pattern.

Vowels were probably the first sounds to be developed by humans, as they resemble animal calls in a mid-frequency range that carry enough energy to carry a good distance for communication in the wilderness. By themselves, however, they make indistinct language, needing the consonants for separation of the sounds.

We create and perceive harmonics through the vowels. The vibration of the vocal chords resonates in the vocal cavities to create specific frequency spectrums or **formants**. As the vowels represent the harmonics, we are speaking or singing the mathematics of the physical world. A trained listener can perceive this as numbers made audible and can actually focus on this for a patient's benefit in various therapeutic situations.

These formants not only allow us to hear vowel sounds, but also to interpret emotional states (e.g., calm, happy, angry; see ***Voice personalities*** later in this chapter) and identify who the speakers are or their type. For example, a young boy and a woman might have the same fundamental frequency voice range, but because the woman's skull is usually larger, her formants will register in lower frequency ranges, giving a more "mellow" tone.

In the highest formants, the upper frequencies are heard as consonants. The position and movement of the tongue generates the consonants by narrowing or constricting the vocal tract, creating **fricatives** (*f*, *z*, *j*), **stops** (*t*, *d*, *k*), **nasals** (*m*, *n*, *ng*), and **approximants** (*l*, *r*, *wh*). Some frequencies go above the highest notes of a piano (like the *sss* sound). One of the main functions of these high frequencies is to separate the vowels from each other, producing intelligible words.

From the 6,500 modern languages, UCLA linguist Peter Ladefoged has distinguished 200 possible vowel sounds and 600 possible consonants. Commenting on this diversity, he points out that according to Genesis, God created Earth's many languages to confound those who had grown too powerful by speaking a single tongue. And in a contrasting legend, Iatiku, the mother goddess of the Acoma tribe of New Mexico, caused people to speak different languages so that it would not be so easy for them to quarrel.

Beyond the language distinctions, we are endowed with the ability to recognize individual voice patterns from not only a word or two, but a cough or even a characteristic intake of breath. This imprinting comes as part of our natural makeup, the fine-tuning of the ear to the utterances of significant others in our lives.

Development of speech

With hisses, whistles, barks, squawks, and roars, communication by sound is a basic trait of most animals, alerting for an approaching enemy, attracting a mate or locating food. Some animal sounds can resemble the abnormalities of human speech, like the cricket's chirping similar to stuttering or **echolalia** (the uncontrollable and immediate repetition of words spoken by another person). They can transmit emotion as well, clearly expressed in an angry growl versus a happy purr of a cat.

TRY THIS

To perceive how your own mouth and tongue create different overtone series for the different vowels, speak the word "why" very, very slowly, exaggerating the changes. Try holding your nostrils shut and hear what happens when that cavity is closed. Say the word in a very low tone, then in a very high tone. Each time listen (and feel) where the resonance is occurring. What happens to your mouth and the vowel overtones if you try imitating someone else's voice (John Wayne, Donald Duck, Mae West, Homer Simpson, or someone you know personally)?

What distinguishes most animal sounds from human vocal expression is not the air coming from the lungs or the vibration of the vocal cords, but the changes in the mouth that transmute the sounds into words, music into meaning.

However, before we are capable of the creation of words, we are infants with a tremendous range of communication, able to cry, scream, burp, vomit, gulp, sneeze, cough, hiccup, gargle, whine, mutter, squeak, whimper, and, considering no barriers to social decorum, fart. After the first year, we can add to that laughter, humming, and babbling, on the way to recognizable speech.

Adults are capable of making all the above sounds, but a social regulation comes into play telling us what is appropriate for "grown-up" behavior — no farting around, please. There are certain conditions when this is appropriate, like applause, laughter, or whistling in the theater, or in response to a speaker. But for the most part, these behaviors are literally outlawed as a disturbance of the peace. So these sounds occur usually in the following circumstances:

a) When the person is mentally ill or emotionally disturbed. A brain lesion can impair inhibition against the creation of any imaginable inappropriate sound (sucking, babbling, humming, chewing, biting, licking, spitting, swallowing, breathing, laughing, crying, etc.).

b) When people are physically ill they may be unable to control their soundmaking (burping, vomiting, hiccups, sneezing, or some other protective process against intoxication or infection).
c) When the intent is to provoke anxiety or humor with out-of-context human noises. (This can be a very effective tool in film sound design.)

The development of verbal speech patterns is gradual, as a child moves through adolescence to adulthood. A compromise usually takes place between reflexive, more infantile sounds and coherent, meaningful sentence structure. The typical teen-speak mixes all levels of soundmaking, and some people never do become fully "adult" in their vocal behavior. Recognizing these characteristics in the voices of the actors in the film for which you are creating the sound design will enrich your possibilities of supporting or counterpointing the emotions and relationships of the personalities on screen (see ***Performance analysis*** in Chapter 8).

Speech recognition and verbal understanding

For a film audience, speech recognition is even more important than speech reproduction. What we pull out of our aural environment as symbolic meaning ties us into powerful possibilities. "In the beginning, there was the word."

Within our mother's uterus, we heard her internal rumblings of digestion, heart, and breathing, while her voice vibrated through these embryonic sounds. If a child has difficulties in either listening or speaking, the French physician Alfred Tomatis discovered that these sounds can reproduce an emotional nourishment and unconscious primal return to a sonic birth. After hearing accompanying recordings of their mothers' voices with a low pass filter to recreate a fetus' hearing, the children had incredible breakthroughs in their communication development.

Speech stimulates different areas of the brain distinctive from other sounds. When measuring the capacity of the brain to recognize **phonemes**, the smallest building blocks in speech, a maximum of 30 phonemes per second can be distinguished, but only 10 musical notes per second can be recognized. This brain specialty allows us to separate sound objects that have no meaning by themselves but which can combine into a subjective, abstract entity with meaning.

Take for example the phonemes of *s* and *t* and insert different vowel sounds between them: site, sat, set, sit, seat, sought, soot. Another example of changing a single phoneme in three different places is with the word "bit": pit, bet, bid. A slight change of the harmonics in the vowels, or timbre, changes dramatically the perceived meaning of the sound.

However, these changes are not gradual, but categorical. They make quantum leaps in meaning when they change enough, or no leap at all if the change is too small. Our brains require the words to fit into our known vocabularies, so no ambiguity exists. If the sound lies in the middle of two meanings, people may disagree over each other's interpretations, which can then create interesting material for subtle drama.

Phonemes join into bigger blocks as syllables, which build into words, then phrases. Another cue for meaning can be the pauses or silence, or the accents, between the syllables or words, as in the distinction between "lighthouse keeper" and "light housekeeper." When an electronic voice recognition machine receives these acoustically similar sounds, it usually cannot compete with the human brain for understanding the correct meaning. This can also be related to the context of the conversation, which the machine may not be programmed to perceive, as in comparing "recognize speech" and "wreck a nice beach."

A very creative application of this emphasis on changing meaning with a tiny shift occurs in *The Conversation*, for which Walter Murch designed the sound. Throughout the film an audio tape plays the line, "He'd kill us if he got the chance," implying the couple is in danger. Finally at the end, the reading shifts from an emphasis on the word "kill" to the word "us," inverting the whole context of who is truly in danger, and revealing that they are really the killers, not the victims. The filter of the mind of the protagonist who has recorded and listened over and over to this line is finally revealed as well. This sound design was not in the original script, but a found element in postproduction that illuminated a crucial plot point.

To be able to distinguish between speakers, several qualities may come into play, including the fundamental frequency, timbre, rhythm, and variation of tones. Following the Gestalt concept of **good continuation** (see

Chapter 4, ***Gestalt principles and illusion***), if there is a smooth continuum between the speech styles, rather than a sharp or abrupt contrast, this will more likely appear to be a change from a single source indicating that one individual is talking with some variation. A ventriloquist takes advantage of this phenomenon by creating the illusion of a dialogue between two "people" with drastically different voices and sudden changes.

Another application of this principle occurs if there is a break in speech. It may be covered with a cough, for example, making the separation in the dialogue unnoticed, with the illusion of continuity. This can be a tool in sound editing to cover up a hole in the production track, or the joining of two different takes.

The intelligibility of words in popular song lyrics (rock'n'roll, country, folk) depends greatly on the consonants to distinguish and infuse the sound with meaning, as opposed to more classically oriented song (opera, kabuki theater, Gregorian chanting) that relies on vowels, subordinating the symbology to the overall harmonic good. Audiences for music as art will listen more to songs in languages they cannot understand, appreciating the pure sounds beyond meaning.

Retention of meaning in speech can be greatly influenced by having more than one voice present, or by having interactivity with other kinds of sounds or images. A saturation point may be reached where the information overload prevents any understanding. The variables and outcomes of this kind of interaction are sometimes unpredictable and need experimentation.

Notice in an airport at what distance you must be from the entrance gate to be able to understand the amplified voice announcing which rows are to be seated. As you get further away, the voice is heard but no longer comprehensible, being masked by the other sounds and distorted by reverberation, so that another sound may take your attention, or you may be able to take a snooze without the interruption of a verbal message demanding your attention. (See also Chapter 7, ***Dialogue in film,* Emanation speech.**)

TRY THIS

Record your voice for about two minutes on one track reading an exciting story that relates to a video tape you can show, and on another track an instruction booklet for some electronic appliance. Play this back in stereo headphones to your friend and see what your friend remembers hearing. Could your friend focus on anything? Is it dependent on content?

Do this again while your friend watches the video image. Is it easier for your friend to follow the voice track that relates to the image?

Select one dialogue sequence and experiment with various kinds of music or environmental sounds as a second track to see which distract from focus and retention of the verbal meaning.

Meaning vs. feeling

JABBERWOCKY
"'Twas brillig, and the slithy toves
Did gyre and gimble in the wabe:
All mimsy were the borogroves,
And the mome raths outgrabe."

— *Through the Looking Glass*
Lewis Carroll

It is practically impossible to listen to someone speak in your native tongue, even with the most esoteric or nonsensical of words, and be able to hear only the pure acoustical characteristics of their voice, the hisses, whistles, and buzzes. This involuntary urge for understanding is triggered when we think we should be understanding. In contrast, if a foreigner speaks or if a computer is producing a poor voice synthesis, we tune out significance. But if instructed to listen to the computer's speech, then we suddenly are able to recognize the meaning.

Meaning versus feeling is paralleled in language versus music. Words divide up our reality into things, whereas tone unites the things into a continuum. Language can translate from one idiom to another (e.g., English to Spanish), but music is usually untranslatable (e.g., Mozart to Indian raga). Overlapping tones create harmony, but overlapping voices create confusion. Words represent the contents of the world beyond our skin, while music represents the experience within our body.

Disconnecting words from semantic meaning (as in the poem "Jabberwocky") creates a code switching and the possibility of increased emotional communication. Archaic words, nonsense sounds, technical jargon, baby talk, or foreign accents are a few of the speech tricks to release the analytic mindset into a more feeling mode.

Prosody — vocal melody and emotion

When a mother calls out to the playground for her child with "A-lex-ANNNN-der," this sing-song of her voice is reminiscent of a bird call. The tonal inflections are as important to transmit the message as the symbolic meaning of the words. This vocal melody is known as **prosody**. Expressing shades of emotion and intention, another example of prosody is found in comparing the following sentences:

"I always wanted to *do* it." The martial, staccato insistent rhythm shows determination in the sound. The consonants are decisive and attention-getting. With the accent on the word "do," it is likely that a major key is struck with the tonal intervals between words, eliciting the sense of triumph.

"I don' wanna." This slow, lazy phrase reflects the feeling of procrastination. The whiny, slurred manner of speech lacks a tonal center and definition of purpose. There is likely to be a minor key created between the syllables in the "wanna," which contributes to the pessimistic attitude.

As speech carries two meanings, one verbal that describes the speaker's experience, the other intonational that reflects the speaker's feelings, our brain hemispheres have developed to specialize in these distinctions. Much study has been done on how the left hemisphere (in the majority of the population) performs verbal tasks, while the right hemisphere performs spatial and nonverbal tasks; but the essence for our purposes as sound designers is to distinguish the type of communication available with the voice.

As mentioned earlier in this chapter, a nonverbal expression is the only type available to infants, but we continue to communicate — with cackling laughter, shouts of anger, and the sexy breathiness of a lover's whisper. By manipulating the rhythm, intensity, pitch, speed, shape, or orderliness of our voices, we can increase or decrease the emotional range of speech.

Tension can be released through the voice, as when a weight lifter grunts under the irons or a karate cry sounds before a strike. With this escape valve for pent-up energy or pain, new life is brought forth through a type of inner sonic stimulation.

Grief and sorrow are released through wailing, combining a moan and cry in unison with others who share a similar emotional state. By focusing with this sound, hysteria is avoided and true social bonding accomplished, as in political protests against the war policies of the Pentagon in 1982, as described by Garfield in *Sound Medicine*. The end of suffering or release of pain can be accelerated by the sounds we make — and these sounds, in turn, can bring pain to empathic listeners.

A baby's cry demands attention, evoking a variety of reactions, from "Oh, what's wrong with that poor child" to "That damn brat won't ever shut up." In fact, this sound is usually 20 decibels louder than normal speech, assuring priority to the situation, and is mimicked in the siren of an ambulance and its tonal glides, or the insistent ringing of a telephone cutting through any other interaction.

Peter Oswald describes an experiment with the sound of babies crying that could have interesting applications in film sound design. When listeners are presented with this sound under a masking white noise, they perceive a variety of sources: cry of an animal (bird, hawk, coyote), dog barking, people shouting to each other, a trumpet, somebody hammering. For a short film I directed called *Electric Night*, I was recording a washing machine in a laundromat when fortuitously a baby began crying in the background. This generated one of the most powerful audio images I have encountered: a helpless growing wail inside of a rumbling, relentless ocean, mixed with a cold voice track spoken through a clarinet that develops into hysteria — all describing a terrifying sleep laboratory experiment. A different application of baby sounds occurs when the recording is slowed down by an octave or so; the modified voice resembles that of a woman in sexual ecstasy. In contrast, an adult's voice that is pitch-raised becomes more childish, to the extreme of the animated chipmunk characters' squeaky voices.

The speech pattern of an autistic child holds little if any verbal meaning, appearing as an acoustic game. Sounds are produced because they rhyme or are **onomatopoeic** (sounding like the thing it means, e.g., *hiccup, oink, splash, crunch*), and perhaps just because they are fun to mouth. This can create a double bind situation for the listener, who is invited to pay attention, then frustrated by meaningless utterances, leading to conflict and tension while trying to understand and ignore simultaneously. A conscious use of this language absurdity has been employed by comedians like Danny Kaye by mimicking foreigners with intonations characteristic of those idioms without actually using words of that language. Ben Burtt created fantastic new languages for *Star Wars* and *E.T.* based on these concepts of prosody (see page 146, ***Alien language***).

Elements of music (rhythm, pitch, volume, timbre, etc.) can be applied to emotional expression in the human voice. When we are in a heightened emotional state, the range of intonation increases, giving our declarations an arresting, spectacular quality. Even animals like chicks express distress or sadness with descending frequencies and pleasure with ascending tones.

In her analysis of *Zéro de Conduite*, Claudia Gorbman points out a dialogue that happens between the characters and the steam locomotive. Purely through the rhythm of human speech and that of the machine, an acoustic exchange occurs and there is a bonding between the boys and their environment.

Mirroring this interplay of human dialogue, Beethoven sets up a musical inquiry with an unresolved melody and harmony, like "Please, please... I implore you...," stretching out the urge through his composition until an answer is finally offered, which often returns with another question.

Similarly, the talking drums of East Africa imitate the human voice and its emotional communication using a recognizable phrasing.

Peter Ostwald in *Soundmaking: The Acoustic Communication of Emotion* cites a curious 18th-century article that relates each orchestral instrument to a personality type:

TABLE 6-1
MUSICAL INSTRUMENT VS. PERSONALITY TYPE

Instrument	Personality Type
Drums	Blusterers, loud laughter and a torrent of noise to domineer in public assemblies and stun their companions.
Lute	Exquisitely sweet and very low, easily drowned in the multitude, men of fine genius, uncommon reflection, good taste.
Trumpet	Capable of exquisite turns and modulations, fashionable education and refined breeding, but have shallow parts, weak judgments.
Violin	Lively, flourishes of imagination, sharpness of repartee, glances of satire.
Bass	Grumbles, tempers the sweetness, rough and unpolished, do not love to hear themselves talk, but with agreeable bluntness.
Bagpipe	Repetition of a few notes, perpetual humming of a drone, tedious storytellers.

Engaging musical improvisation has similarities to the prosody (as well as the meaning) of stimulating conversation. The quality of both depends on the depth and flexibility in the hierarchy of tonal, rhythmic, and contrapuntal ideas. Both run in real time, with spontaneous exchange and acute listening.

In more formal storytelling, the prosody (and plot line) can follow a more structured pattern, with a formula for repeating and developing themes (see examples in Chapter 5, ***Structure and function***). Folk tales have very marked melodies (characters), themes (subplots), and harmonic progressions (mood and transformation).

Poetry works with meter, rhyme, and tone as powerfully as with the meaning of the words, giving the speaking of a poem an entirely different experience than that of reading only. One example that goes to an extreme is Gertrude Stein's "A rose is a rose is a rose is a rose is a rose..." By pronouncing this for a few minutes, the words begin to lose their meaning, becoming only sound with no external reference, intensifying the structural elements and possibly eliciting unexpected emotional properties.

Mantras, nonsense, and beyond

Untranslatable sounds called **vocables** are used by Native Americans to evoke the sounds of nature and call upon spiritual guides and powers. The Tibetans call this the language of the *dakini*, which cannot be interpreted by the rational left hemisphere of the brain. Like a short musical phrase being repeated over and over, these sounds have an intoxicating effect (narcotic or stimulant) and an affinity for magic and trance. (Philip Glass and Steve Reich have composed music with similar structure and effect.)

Mantras from India and Tibet are repeated sequences of sounds that transcend their verbal meaning, kneading the flesh of the body and emptying the mind to nurture feelings rather than thoughts. In America we have the equivalent in the world of sports with the energizing mantras of "Hold that Line!" and "Go team, go!" This primordial, prelinguistic chanting transcends ordinary reality yet binds people into a shared experience.

The effects of mantras and ragas (see Chapter 5, ***Structure and function, World music***) sung by advanced yogis with complete control of their minds and bodies, have been said to light fires, bring rain, cause flowers to bloom, and attract wild animals, as well as heal. According to legend, some of the world's great stone monuments were constructed by the use of sound. These powers certainly go beyond our normal use of the human voice, bordering on the supernatural, but are worthy of our study to maximize the potential of sound in our films.

Glossolalia, speaking in tongues, i.e., in a language usually not understood by the listeners or by the speaker (who is often in some kind of trance state in a religious ceremony), creates an extraordinary acoustic space that transcends verbal expression. Between singing and speaking, the intent can be powerful and held within the emotional impact of the voice.

TRY THIS

To discover the power of such nonverbal, but vocally significant soundmaking, get together with a partner. The listener gives the speaker three (and only three) distinct nonverbal sounds which the speaker is allowed to utter, as they describe a particularly stressful incident or situation in life. The listener simply listens, while the speaker invokes a kind of secular glossolalia of nonsense sounds that tap into the nonverbal right brain hemisphere and the emotional midbrain. With access to this style of communication, as a sound designer you will be able to play more with the prosody of the voice and the voice-like elements that contribute to the emotional message underlying the sound.

As mentioned above, **onomatopoeia** describes the category of words that actually sound like what they mean: *bang*, *hiss*, *clap*, *swish*, *bark*, *thump*, etc. This kind of soundmaking is like pointing, a direct way to indicate the meaning, with listening to the sound more important than thinking about a symbol. The possibilities of fun acoustical games and playful mimicking invite children to participate and can be greatly helpful elements for comedy films. Dane Davis, Oscar-winning sound designer for *The Matrix*, describes how during the dailies the directors accompanied the images with a full-out onomatopoeic vocal rendition of the kind of sound effects they imagined. This gave Davis a tangible handle to be able to provide a totally integrated soundtrack with the image.

Reversal of speech will reduce it to a meaningless noise, but there are certain fascinating things that can be done with this technique. In *Twin Peaks*, the actors in a dream sequence performed their motions and spoke their lines backwards, then the film was shown in reverse so that the actors were moving and speaking in a "normal" direction. This effect is often used for certain visual effects, but coupling with sound creates a truly bizarre experience.

Voice personalities

Stereotypes are rampant in the media, so we can certainly find many historical examples of voices that transmit a peculiar character type: John Wayne's cowboy, James Cagney's gangster, Mae West's seductress, Cary Grant's gentleman. More contemporary types include the surfer dude, valley girl, and ghetto rapper. These voices are identified through their rhythm, melody, timbre, and vocabulary, usually appearing in a specific social context, but they can create wonderful comedy when taken out of the normal context.

When analyzing the voice as a form of noise (ignoring the phonemic variability and construction of syllables, words, and meaning), different frequency bands, or formants (discussed earlier in this chapter), can help define several aspects of the speaker's identity and personality. Peter Ostwald's studies suggest that by running recorded voices in reverse, the energy peaks of the formants can be analyzed without the distraction of the verbal context. In analyzing the dialogue on production tracks, these concepts can be applied to sound design as well (see Chapter 8, ***Performance analysis***).

The fundamental **Formant 1** allows us to judge whether the person is speaking (or singing) as a bass, baritone, tenor, alto, or soprano. **Formant 2**, made of middle-range frequencies, produces the resonant energy of the voice, exhibiting the level of power or enthusiasm present. Located between 1,000–2,000Hz, **Formant 3** peaks give a kind of whiney or infantile sound to the voice. **Formant 4** is composed of the sibilance and friction sound at the front of the mouth, and is very weak with poorly articulated speech, but very strong with giggling, whispers, or other displays of emotion.

Ostwald identifies four voice acoustic stereotypes: **sharp**, **flat**, **hollow**, and **robust**. The **sharp voice** has a "twin peaks" effect in the formants, meaning that Formants 1 and 2 are strong and exactly one octave apart. This creates a strengthening of the sound, a technique often used by singers to enrich a musical structure; for sharp-voiced speakers, this helps them to be heard better. On the psychological level, this stereotype defines a kind of sound which nonverbally carries the message "help me," an underlying distress call no matter how calming the words may appear to indicate.

With a **flat voice**, Formant 2 is literally flattened on the spectral graph. The sound is weak, without energy, and is heard from people who are listless, tentative, resigned, or depressed, regardless of what they say they are feeling. Often accompanying this stereotype are speech errors, mispronunciations, sighs, pauses, "uhs" and other nonverbal sounds, with the voice trailing off before the end of phrases.

The **hollow voice** carries almost no energy in any frequency band but Formant 1. This precipitous drop-off creates an empty sound and is found in people with severe chronic illness, and accompanies the states of general debility, depression, or profound fatigue related to brain damage. The physical appearance of someone in this state is that of a person with ashen skin, eyes fixed and sunken, like someone who has recently witnessed a catastrophe.

The **robust voice** is characterized by symmetric formants with evenly spread out energy. The acoustic stereotype is of a booming, successful-sounding voice, emitted by people who are extroverted, aggressive, and confident. Public speakers will use this voice to influence others in sales, lectures, or dramatization.

Alternating these voice stereotypes is typical of someone with insecurities and overcompensation. For example, a shift from a high-pitched loud voice projecting resentment, rage, or provocation to a low soft voice of defeat, hypochondria, and helplessness can exhibit a kind of schizophrenic personality.

Repetition of words or phrases can indicate insecurities as well, or may be used as emphasis and showing confidence, depending on the acoustic energy delivered.

In a psychologically healthy individual who is integrated with their thoughts, emotions, and relationships to others, there is less need for an unconscious acoustic expression. Only one mode of communication is needed, as the words and subtext of feelings are unified. This, however, is not the case with most interesting characters in film and television; and it is exactly the subtleties and conflicts between the obvious and hidden agendas that make for good drama.

Another approach to the link of voice with personality derives from the use and study of the vowel sounds and how they differ both physically and psychologically. Joscelyn Godwin identifies the vowels to resonate in different parts of the body, each inducing a characteristic state of mind in the speaker. (This is perhaps less so in the listener, but may be useful in designing sounds to support a certain atmosphere.)

TABLE 6-2
THE EFFECT OF VOWELS ON THE BODY AND MIND

Vowel	Body Region	Effect
A	Top of thorax, esophagus	Calm, peace, serenity
E	Neck, incisors, thyroid glands	Self-confidence
I	Bridge of nose, crown of head	Laughter, humor, gaiety
O	Lower thorax, upper abdomen	Seriousness, completion, perfection
U	Lower abdomen	Gravity, sweetness

Alien language

In the specific case of creating a new language for nonhumans, the search consists of a mix between intelligible and unrecognizable sounds.

Three sound designers have done extraordinary work in this area: Mark Mangini, Gary Rydstrom, and Ben Burtt.

Adding nonhuman sounds to dialogue can give specific characterization to a voice. In Disney's *Beauty and the Beast*, Mangini took the lead voice of Robby Benson and augmented it with growls from tigers, bears and camels, both before and after the dialogue, giving the Beast a ferocious animal-human quality. (Conversely, in *The Bear*, with all real animal characters, a human voice was added to the baby bear's to help emotionalize its utterances.)

Rydstrom designed the sounds of the beautiful aliens in *Cocoon*, giving them a friendly, smooth feeling. He combined cymbals, hisses, ringing champagne glasses, and a wispy flute with a human quality. An emotional envelope was created with real-life sounds that held some organic characteristics so that the audience could more easily empathize. Experimenting in several films with squeals, squeaks, and air hisses, he has found and isolated those that gave a hint of human communication.

In* Star Wars *and* E.T., *Burtt broke new ground for creating alien languages, as he describes here:

(Wookie, *Star Wars*) "We needed a voice for the Wookie Chewbakka before we started filming so we'd know how he would sound and relate to other characters, very important for the director and actors. George Lucas said, 'I think it should be some animal sound, like a dog or bear.' I initially went to the zoo, but all I got were animals sleeping and flies buzzing around. So I found an animal trainer with a bear who was docile enough to work and loved bread soaked with milk. I could take little snippets of sound, like little word bits, that sounded angry, or cute, or like a question. Then I processed and edited, changed the pitch and slowed it down, and out of all these I built a whole library of sounds, then taped them together into phrases which ultimately became the voice. There were some other things added, parts of a walrus, some lions, and dogs to balance it out.

(R2D2, *Star Wars*) "Probably the most difficult assignment in all the *Star Wars* movies was to create the voice of R2D2. The script just said R2 whistles or beeps, but didn't say what he sounded like. We were trying to create a voice that didn't use words but had a personality, acting with Alec Guinness. George figured it would be some kind of electronic language, which was a challenge to give personality, and we did a lot of trial and error. Synthesizers and electronic circuits were very cold, and playing around with voice speeds and processing was always recognizable as a person. So one day I was talking to George and asked him what did he really think it sounded like and he said something like, 'Maybe it's a kind of *beep-beep-beep-beep*.' I go, '*whoop-whoop-whoop-whoop*.' And we started making sound effects and we realized that's what we want — baby talk, with the intonation but not the words. So I start making baby talk, then copying it with a circuit on a primitive synthesizer. I recorded my own voice at a lower pitch, then speeded it up when I was done. I made a few hundred different components of sound, which I put together different ways to build up sentences, a very slow process working part of every day over a six-month period. I actually wrote out R2D2's dialogue in English, like 'C'mon, let's go this way!' just to give me a guide. I did this for about half the movie, reading the lines, then cutting them in, and I tried to build something that rhythmically related to the literal lines. This got me comfortable with R2, what elements gave an emotional and informational impression, and from that point I stopped with the literal lines and proceeded from what I understood of R2's character, more intuitive like a puppeteer.

(Hutese, *Star Wars*) "There was a bounty hunter's dialogue that became Hutese, kind of based on Zulu. My approach is to find samples of real languages that are exotic and interesting, because a real language has all the cultural evolution attached to it. By extracting interesting parts you can basically create a kind of double talk. [Another example was Danny Kaye speaking fake Italian.]

(*E.T.*) "There were about eighteen different animal and human sound sources for E.T.'s voice, as E.T. evolved from a kind of animalistic-sounding alien to an English-speaking alien. I heard a woman speaking in a store and asked her if she'd like to be an alien. Her voice was very neutral in gender and age. Spielberg would send some cut scenes and I would put a voice in without telling him how it was done or who it was, whether it was a person or a sea otter, so he would have an unbiased judgment. It made a big difference if it was heard out of context."

TRY THIS

This area of sound design is one of the most fun to play with. Here are two simple techniques that can open a whole dimension of interactivity between sounds.

1) Record three different nonverbal voice sounds (e.g., blow, snort, burp, tongue click, hum, laugh, cry, sigh, groan, whistle, etc.). Record or select one short, expressive nonhuman sound effect (e.g., gun shot, animal sound, water, kitchen appliance, etc.). Make three different mixes, each with one of the three nonverbal voice sounds together with the single sound effect you selected. Notice how the combined effect creates a synergy beyond the individual sounds.
2) Record one nonverbal effect and mix it three times with three different nonhuman effects. Again note the third sound event you have formed from the two original sounds.

CHAPTER 7

SOUND AND IMAGE

How does the interaction between our eyes and ears produce a whole that is greater than the sum of its parts? When we dive into the storytelling of the film, the sound tells us what is happening within or outside the character's world, using music, effects, and dialogue coupled (or not) with image. Space and time are determined by the audiovisual combination, as are the bridging and breaking of scenes. We usually expect the sound and image to be synchronized, but this too can be manipulated in service of the story, while there may be more than one meaning to a scene when these audiovisual elements are juxtaposed in purposeful ways.

Eyes and ears

As we work in the audiovisual media, this implies the use of both our sight and hearing for receiving and processing information. Comparing these two senses clarifies the capacities and limitations of each.

TABLE 7-1 EYES VS. EARS

Quality/Ability	Eyes	Ears
frequency sensitivity	(4 to 7.2) x 10^{14}Hz	20 to 20,000Hz
wavelength sensitivity	(4 to 7.6) x 10^{-7} meters	16.5 mm to 16.5 meters
speed of light/sound	300,000,000 meters/sec	331 meters/sec
can distinguish ratios	no	yes
primary brain processing	intellectual/reason	emotional/intuition
focus	narrow/pointed	broad/omnidirectional
open or closed	either	only open
habitat	space	time
transmission	time	space

A very broad electromagnetic spectrum certainly exists in nature (x-rays, radio waves, etc.), but for whatever reason our eyes have narrowed down what is functional light for our visual perception. In comparison, the ears have an enormous range of perception with regard to frequency sensitivity.

The eye does not abstract numbers from light as the ear does from sound, nor does it perceive mixtures of light in separate tones as the ear hears separate notes creating a chord together. The ability to distinguish ratios allows the ear to hear whether two notes are exactly an octave apart or not (a 1:2 ratio; see Chapter 5, ***Harmony and dissonance***). We sense the mathematical nature of the universe through the ears, music being the beauty of numbers manifested in energy.

The intuitive nature of sound, unlike the obvious, categorical presence of sight, allows our minds to create more internal images and relationships. When we are at the height of lovemaking, our eyes will often be closed, but our ears will be wide open, gulping in the volumes of sensory excitement as we bridge to another person.

While the eye trains itself on an object, a word, or a face, then scans to another point to focus on a different aspect of the visual field, the ear is sensitive to all sounds from all directions at the same time (although spatially distinguished; see Chapter 4, ***Space***). We can shut our eyes or turn our head to avoid a sight, but our ears will not close on their own, but only with a forceful hand or earplug to artificially stop the vibrations from entering.

Our ears and eyes inhabit different, complementary regions. In the arts, drawings and sculptures inhabit space in a gallery, but are transmitted through time as they remain in one spot for us to observe them. Music, on the other hand, inhabits time as it begins, continues, and ends, while being transmitted through space, moving the air molecules along the way.

On screen, off screen, and outside the story world

As I've mentioned, the word **diegesis** refers to the world of the characters and story within the film. Everything that happens to those people and in the environment portrayed on screen is considered diegetic. The opposite is **nondiegetic**, or elements that are not of the characters' story world, for example in the film image this would be titles, dissolves, scratches, out of focus, etc.

The origin of sound that is heard in a film can be from an object, person, or event that is either diegetic (on screen or off screen) or nondiegetic.

On screen
The sound comes from a source we can see on the screen. Typical types of sounds are dialogue with lip sync, door slams, footsteps, cars, ocean waves, children playing, etc. These may occur without the visual accompaniment as well, but to be defined in this category a synchronization of image and sound is needed.

Off screen
We hear the sound without seeing the source, although this source is implied by a reference to what we do see or know about the film scene. If the characters are reacting to a sound of an unknown origin, then this too is a diegetic off-screen sound. Examples are ambient backgrounds (traffic outside a room, birds in a meadow, wind), thunder, an off-screen character calling to an on-screen character, music from an unseen radio, etc.

Another distinction in the off-screen sounds is whether they are **active** or **passive**. Active sounds raise questions and curiosity to see what is making the noise: What is it? What's happening? What does the monster look like? Passive sounds create atmosphere and environment, enveloping and stabilizing the image across edit cuts to make them seamless.

Michel Chion has coined the term **acousmatic** to mean listening for the sounds one hears without seeing their originating cause. In the specific case where the source of the unseen sound is revealed, this effect is known as **de-acousmatizing**. The classic example occurs when Dorothy pulls back the curtain to reveal the little man making the big voice in the smoke in *The Wizard of Oz*. The dramatic impact of this is to disempower the previously unidentified sound, taming and draining it of its mystery.

Nondiegetic

Any sound that would not be heard by a character or is not emitted from a sound event in the story is considered nondiegetic. Typical examples include a voiceover narration and incidental music. More recent creative sound design has incorporated stylized ambiences and unexpected sound effects that are charged with emotional content. A wolf howl might pierce the downtown redlight district or an exaggerated clock ticking can loom over an office worker under a heavy deadline. In general, the nondiegetic sound functions as an interpretive element, guiding the listener towards a certain feeling, subjectively beyond the visual elements.

***Sometimes what happens inside the film story contrasts with how the audience perceives the filmmaking process itself, and may provoke a question of acceptability. Dane Davis speaks of this challenge in* The Matrix:**

"I wanted the sound to help define the limits of the system (of the Matrix) itself. When things happened quickly, I wanted the resolution to drop down as if the system wasn't quite up to it, which you see whenever you work with any computer or video. The more automation, the less dependable it is, so I assumed that the processors that the Matrix used were also limited. I wanted certain rules to be broken, to seem like hack sound-effects editors were using the same car horn every time. The footsteps would all sound exactly the same, sounds looping in the background or going out of sync. You could notice if you were paying attention, giving subtle clues to the character, *if* he was conscious enough, and [to] the audience too, that this wasn't really real. But we ran into this dangerous line about what would be perceived as limitations of the Matrix and what would be perceived as limitations of the filmmakers — like bad filmmaking. In the end, we did almost none of that, just in the Construct, which was like their little laptop model of reality."

The three types of sound discussed above are all **on track**, meaning that we actually hear them on the soundtrack. There can be **off-track** sounds as well, which the diegesis leads us to believe exist but are not audible. When someone speaks into a telephone and the audience hears only one side of the conversation, the unheard other telephone speaker is implied to exist, and perhaps we can even imagine what that person is saying. Another case occurs when a masking sound obliterates a certain assumed sound; for example, when a character is seen shouting something we may or may not understand from watching the lip movements, but a roaring jet overwhelms the soundtrack.

Music in film

Classical film scores or incidental music serve specific functions in the technical, aesthetic, and emotional aspects of the film: emotional signifier, continuity, narrative cueing, and unity.

Emotional signifier

Music helps to hypnotize us into the make-believe world of the film, making plausible all that constitutes such genres as fantasy, horror, and science fiction. In all types of films, rather than supporting the realistic image on screen, the music allows us to sense the invisible and inaudible, the spiritual and emotional processes of the characters portrayed.

Continuity

When a gap occurs in either the image or sound, music serves to fill in this hole. By smoothing over these rough areas, music hides the technological basis of the medium and prevents this from being a distraction for the audience. A sense of continuity is maintained when music is played over spatially discontinuous shots.

Narrative cueing

Music helps the audience orient to the setting, characters, and narrative events, providing a particular point of view. By giving an emotional interpretation to the image it can cue the narrative to give, for example, advance knowledge of a threat or a setup for a joke.

Narrative unity

Just as music composition has its own structure (see Chapter 5, ***Structure and function***), it can aid in the formal unity of the film by employing repetition, variation, and counterpoint, thus supporting the narrative as well.

The irony of a good musical score is that it is not meant to be heard, at least not consciously, normally remaining subordinate to the dialogue and the visuals as the primary narrative vehicles. If the music is so bad or so incredible as to attract our attention, then it most likely is distracting from the narrative action. If it is too complex or decorative, it may lose its emotional appeal rather than intensifying the psychological aspects of the story. The intent is to guide the audience towards an unambiguous identification with the feeling of the scene.

Programmatic music

This particular style represents some action or event in the world, and when coupled with exactly the same visual is nicknamed "mickey-mousing." An example explored in great detail by Robert Jourdain is the "Pink Panther" theme, as the cat stealthily climbs, then falls down, and climbs back up again. The rhythm replicates the animal motion, modulating the harmony for bodily stresses and releases, as the melody follows the physical action. In general, this style is considered old-fashioned for dramatic films, but can be very effective in comedy.

Anempathetic music

While most film music rides with the emotions of the on-screen characters, anempathetic music deliberately takes an indifferent stand to the drama and feelings taking place. When the music does not care what is happening, irony can build a strong counterpoint for the spectator to seek more actively what is really happening. This involvement can be heightened when there is a great tragedy or catastrophe depicted, using the juxtaposition of happy music that simply challenges us to identify more closely with the victims, as in *A Clockwork Orange*.

Dialogue in film

Theorist Michel Chion has made useful distinctions on how dialogue can function, contribute, and be modified in film. The three types of speech possible are theatrical, textual, and emanation.

Theatrical speech

Characters in the scene are generating the voices, serving to inform and affect one another on dramatic and psychological levels. Their words have no specific power on the structure and form of the film image itself beyond what they can create within the story. The action contributes to focusing on the content of the dialogue, generally in a unified direction to create an audiovisual integration. Watching the lip movements can influence the actual understanding of some words. (E.g., if someone utters "tata" which is synced with the sound "mama," the perception may be that the person is saying "nana.") When there is an impasse in the theatrical speech of a romantic scene, a kiss can release the pent-up, unspoken energy.

Textual speech

This is generally produced as voiceover commentary to change a setting or call upon a memory, characters, or place, at any moment. The diegetic sound and images are at its mercy, as this voiceover status is reserved for certain privileged characters for a specific moment of entry. One film that has taken this to comedic extremes is *Annie Hall*, which accentuates the difference between theatrical and textual speech, creating contradictions, conflicts, and gags that make fun of the rules.

Emanation speech

When speech is not heard or understood completely, or not tied directly to the narrative line, then it can be termed emanation. It is verbally unintelligible, avoiding emphasis on the meaning of the text, yet serves as a kind of silhouette or emanation of the characters.

Manipulating the dialogue beyond the conventional use of communicating information between the characters can be a very powerful, yet subtle, storytelling device. Techniques of elimination, ad lib, and foreign idiom are a few that can aid in the construction of the sound design.

Elimination

Certain moments can be striking if the characters are speaking on screen, but the audience cannot hear what they are saying. This is similar to emanation speech, except that there is no sound at all relating to their mouth movement. This could happen if the characters are seen behind a window, in a distance, or in a noisy crowd. It demands participation by the audience to imagine what is being said, and can serve to build mystery or anxiety in the plot.

Ad libs and proliferation

Words can cancel out one another if they are accumulated through proliferation or overlapping, either in the production track or when superimposing several tracks in the editing. As several characters talk at the same time, overlapping or speaking "superfluous" lines like in large meal scenes, they have the effect of becoming an ambient background. **ADR** (automated dialogue replacement) groups specialize in creating these atmospheres, ad libbing dialogue that may never be listened to but contributes to the feeling of the scene.

Multilingualism and foreign language

With an English-speaking audience, for example, the use of any other language in a scene can create specific responses. The intention may be to conceal or reveal information, either to other characters or to the audience, or to create an ambience of a foreign locale. There are several variations on the use of a foreign language by the on-screen characters:

a) None of the characters, other than the speaker, understands. This would be setting the foreigner isolated from others, most likely "a stranger in a strange land," as in *Dances with Wolves*. If there are subtitles, the audience would tend to identify with the plight and point of view of this foreigner more so than without subtitles, which would generate the point of view of the other non-understanding characters in the scene.

b) Some of the characters understand, but not others. This can lead to intrigue, comedy, or multiple meanings, as when the Africans fail to communicate to the Americans in *Amistad* and also leave the audience perplexed when there is no translation. If some of the characters are translating for others, this sets up a certain complexity of interaction. If there are subtitles as well, there can even be clever play with incorrect translations, lending rich subtext to the characters' intentions, as is seen in the barracks scene in *Life is Beautiful*.

c) All the characters understand each other, as in any foreign language subtitled film seen in the U.S. A film like *Schindler's List* has German characters speaking English as if it is their native tongue, but there are some scenes where minor characters are speaking German with no subtitles. This gives an added sense of the ambience of being in Germany, but used more as emanation speech rather than theatrical speech.

Dialogue recording and postproduction

Some interesting techniques of recording dialogue can be applied to develop the theoretical concepts mentioned above. If there is a desire to use only emanation speech in the scene (the director "barely wants to hear it"), it is a good idea to get that quality with a boom mike at a distance from the actor, but also to mike another channel close up for protection so that the final choice can be made in the mix.

Distortions of dialogue can be accomplished in the recording, or in rerecording a reproduction of the original track through speakers that might even be in movement or in unusual acoustic environments (known as **worldizing**) or through a ham radio signal that lends delightful perturbations.

The delivery style of dialogue and the manner in which it is recorded can also create different acoustic effects. In *Apocalypse Now* the narration was recorded in a whisper with the microphone very close, then spread to all three speakers behind the screen, creating a massive, unfocused presence. This contrasts with the normal dialogue in the film, which only emits from the central speaker.

The energy and realism of ADR work can be judged in the final film by the performance, pitch, tempo, and emotional intensity synchrony with the image and original track. What can help recreate this dynamic is to keep the looping actors in movement, perhaps even getting a boom operator on the sound stage to follow them around.

Serendipity can play a role in designing the dialogue track, so listen to all your material to see where it might go into something unexpected. Skip Lievsay discovered, in the many minutes of wild track recordings of babies in a nursery he had made for *Raising Arizona*, a tiny voice snippet sounding like "I'm Larry." He synced it up with a baby that Nicolas Cage picks up who has a name tag of Larry, creating a hilariously realistic scene.

Spatial dimensions

Sound can help induce the sensation of space, volume, and texture in a film. The dimensionality and distance is coded by our own body's ability to process the acoustic information (see Chapter 4, ***Space***), so that with the addition of visual information we can be immersed in a more complete virtual reality.

3-D space

When sight and sound combine to define space and movement, sight generally has an overwhelming priority in our orientation. For example, when the jet fighters zoom off screen in *Top Gun*, we hear the sound follow them over the exit signs at the side of the theater, when in fact the sound may not have literally flown in that direction.

With the use of surround channels (see Chapter 1, ***Pre-mix decisions***), a tremendous variety of aural movement can accompany images that come and go on the screen. Any such occupation of the real 3-D space of the theater helps break through the 2-D film image to create a 3-D visual space as well.

The representation of rooms, walls, caves, cathedrals, or any other space that has the possibility of reflecting sound can be extremely enhanced by treating the sound elements with appropriate reverb, echo, or filtering. A pitch black space can be made to feel like a giant hall, a sewer, or an interstellar space void depending on the ambience and reverb used.

Layers of the space can be distinguished by their respective sound qualities and the proportion of direct to indirect signals. If characters are close, their voice will have more high frequencies and less reverb from the ground and walls; as they retreat these qualities invert. In this manner, the space and distance can actually be implied by the sound, even if we don't see the character or source of the sound event.

If different sounds have the same reverb or filtering, then their associated sources are all perceived to be at the same distance or in the same space. If they have different reverb settings, then they will appear to be in different visual planes, helping to design the audio space.

A curious experiment cited by Brian Moore was performed to illustrate how visual and auditory inputs can influence our perception of space. The subjects' heads were fixed inside of a rotating cylindrical screen which was covered with vertical stripes. After watching the movement for a few moments, the subjects would perceive themselves in rotation and the screen at rest. Then a stationary sound source was placed directly in front of their heads — but the perception was that the source lay either directly *above* or *below* their heads. So this shows how the integration of image and sound can create a new perception of space, something to experiment with in sound design.

The acoustic size and shape of a space represented by the reverb level and echo can also contribute to a more narrative aspect of the scene. For example, the sound of a very large single room with hard walls will evoke the spiritual sense of being in a cathedral. Or a multirhythmic echo will denote a labyrinth-like space, confusing and complex. Conversely, the type of space that generates these sound reflections will also induce a certain tempo of activity. Church music is slow, chamber music faster, and the high-speed conversations and electronic beeps of a contemporary office building with small dry cubicles is even faster still. As mentioned before, when Paul Horn played in the Taj Mahal, he was in a dialogue, playing the room more than the flute.

Hi-fi vs. low-fi perspective

In the countryside, in the wee hours of the morning, or in times long past, the sparseness of the sounds allows us to sense from where they are coming and how far away their source is. The relationship between the silence and recorded sound levels is distinct (a high signal-to-noise ratio) and is labeled in this context as **hi-fi** (high fidelity). When we are surrounded by the unrelenting noise of the city, there is no sense of distance, only presence. The ambience lacks perspective and seems like an acoustic wall, and is considered **low-fi**. This relationship between fidelity and space helps define how we perceive the image and ambience of the scene.

Landscape design focuses on sound as well. An important analysis of the natural environment comes before the creation of the manmade space, including what sounds will be disguised or enhanced. A film sound designer can listen for what is on the synchronized production track and the ambience tracks taken in that location, then build upon those to see what may be eliminated or increased. Keeping the fidelity in mind helps portray the space more appropriately for the narrative.

Once a space is defined acoustically, the change of space from one scene to the next can be more clearly announced with the change of ambient sound. In *Raiders of the Lost Ark*, the shift of the very present rumbling ambience in the collapsing cave to a more distant rumble looking from outside the cave, marks a dramatic cut when Indy must escape disaster. It is not a realistic sound change, but helps the audience perceive the potential safety outside.

Gary Rydstrom discusses how he shifts the point of focus with sound:

"Like with the camera going in for close-up shots sometimes, the sound can be decided like all the visual elements. What do you hear? You don't just follow along blindly with what's going on screen. You might be on two people in a room, starting with sounds of traffic from outside, then focusing closer and closer with your sound, choosing your sound 'angles,' so to speak. In *Saving Private Ryan*, there is a scene where the two snipers are facing off in this courtyard in the rain. You hear people in the town, artillery in the distance, sound of war going on all around us. At the climax when the two snipers see each other in their scopes, we focused on the water drips only. The German's drip was a drum-like rhythm on the window where he's hiding, and then the metallic drip where the American is hiding. We cut to that drip, then that drip, in this case following the visuals. You don't always have to, because you can choose what you hear. Think like a director or a DP, staging a scene with equivalent techniques like depth of field, and choose what the audience's ears are focused on."

Size

The **degree of expansiveness** of a scene can be suggested by sounds, ranging from the extremes of **null** (e.g., a single character with an internal voice) to **vast** (e.g., from a full range of close-ups of popping a beer bottle, through nearby layers of urban sounds, to the siren in the great distance). This can be regulated by the number of spatial layers present, whether the sounds are off screen or not. A film can use the degree of expansiveness to contrast between scenes (e.g., *All That Jazz*, *2001: A Space Odyssey*), or it can adopt a specific degree for the whole film as a style (e.g., *Blade Runner*, *My Dinner With Andre*).

The apparent size of a sound-making source can be manipulated by changing the speed of the original recording. In *Terminator 2* the bubbling mud sounds recorded in post were slowed down to create the sense of a much larger tank than was on the screen. In order not to lose sync with the speed of liquid movement, the original sounds were mixed together with the decelerated recording.

Other techniques for inducing a sense of size include the setting of the volume level in the mix compared to other surrounding sounds and the placement in the center speaker (far, small) vs. the side or surround speakers (close, large). Contrasting with other sounds spatially and temporally is always a factor in making the size apparent.

Point of audition

In the same way that a camera can have a point of view, the perspective of sound can have a point of audition. This can be purely spatial; for example, listening to an orchestra from far in the balcony with the reverberation of the hall, versus from the intimacy of the conductor's podium. Or this can be a more subjective sense, relating to which character in a certain scene or place in the story is associated with what the audience is hearing. An example is the audible sound of a filtered telephone voice; this would be the subjective point of audition of the telephone listener, not the realistic sound heard in the space where the camera sees the listener with the phone to the ear.

Another distinction of this perspective is between the type of sound made when a person is facing towards or away from a microphone (which may or may not coincide with the image on screen). The voice will have tone color fluctuations, diminishing the higher frequencies when the person's back is towards the mike. This can help create a sense of reality in the space, but it must be balanced with the momentary loss of intelligibility. On the contrary, a lapel mike will pick up everything clearly and consistently, but will not offer a feeling of perspective.

Sensation and texture

The feeling of what an object sounds like can give it elements of weight, speed, resistance, solidity, and texture. Types of matter are characterized by their acoustic qualities: glass, fire, metal, water, wood, tar, mud, plastic, compressed air, rubber, stone, or flesh. These different materials can interact as well: rubber against glass, metal into flesh, compressed air in mud. They can move and transform with resistance, explosion, scraping, puncture, brushing, popping, or hissing.

In special cases, objects are created for a new reality that does not exist outside the film world. Animation employs the ultimate invention of sound for the make-believe world. In *Who Framed Roger Rabbit?* the cartoon bodies make noises of friction and contact that give an impression of being a balloon-like material — thin, hollow, and elastic. In the Brazilian fantasy film *Super Xuxa*, I created the sound for a caterpillar puppet, but the very deflated balloon I used in foley work was filled with water and a little bit of air, giving a much more squishy feeling rather than hollowness.

Temporal dimensions

Rhythm of life

The sound of a 19th-century scene will be different from a 21st-century scene because our environments have changed, and we have changed in the rhythm of our lives. In the past, the sounds were based more on the movement of our human bodies doing manual labor such as pumping water, sawing, knitting, etc. Our conversations and thought patterns are now interrupted by phone calls, TV sound bites, and electronic beeps as we dodge the acoustic shrapnel of modern life. The pace has changed and should be reflected in the story setting, with both the types of sounds and their rhythm or lack of such (see Chapter 8, ***Sound references***).

Linearity

An image, particularly a still image that does not give reference to passage of time, can be coupled with sounds that imbue the scene with temporality. The use of diegetic sound (as opposed to nonstory audio like a music track) will create a sense of duration. For example, a quiet neighborhood with no movement will sit like a historical record in silence, but if a dog barks off screen we know there is life there, and that soon someone will wake up, feed the dog, open the garage, and get on with daily life. The routine of living is implied through the sound.

Narrative cueing
To help set up expectations for narrative events to unfold throughout the film, an acoustic theme may be stated that will be heard repeatedly. An example might be the beating of a heart, which could identify the subjective sensations or emotions of a character throughout the story.

Another possibility for sound to define time would be in the slowing or acceleration of a rhythm that produces the effect of a change of motion on the screen. An example might be in a train sequence that does not necessarily show the change of motion with the image of the train, but through slowing down the beat of the tracks or the accompanying music, the illusion of deceleration will hold.

Dane Davis discovered the power of sound to transform the rhythm of a scene:

"Very early on in post with *The Matrix*, the picture editor had gotten feedback from the producers and studio people on the first cut of the fight scene in the subway, that it was long. Then I put in some of the sound effects with the hits and the *wooshes*. They cut it into the Avid and presented it again, and everybody said it worked so much better and told the picture editor that it was great the way he had tightened it up, cutting out all the dead time. And he hadn't done anything, just added the sound effects. This made us decide that we had to put sound to any picture before we present it to anybody else, so that it will look better. If you have time, it really pays off."

Bridging and breaks

An ambience track can provide a unified space for the action to play in that may not have been there at all during the shooting. When there is a continuation of the sound across a picture cut, we sense the illusion of continuity in the image as well. With ambience or a background music track it can be useful to have available fairly neutral sounds that can be stretched or trimmed since the final cut of the image may be lengthened or shortened. In music, pauses and sustained notes can provide this as well.

On the other hand, sound can introduce or terminate a scene with an abrupt shift in such parameters as rhythm, volume, or timbre. We know we have shifted to another moment in the story world when, although the same character may be on screen, the ambient sounds are no longer the same, helping create an ellipsis in time that may be essential to moving the story along.

Sudden cessation of sound can also give rise to a feeling of aesthetic perplexity or emotional anxiety. The power of silence at an unexpected moment can be deafening (see Chapter 5, ***Silence***).

An entry or exit by an actor or object, or a specific sound event like a doorbell or phone, can trigger a shift in the ambience or music, lending a greater emotional significance to the event. This newly introduced, more subjective sound goes less noticed because our attention is on the more commanding element.

To aid transitions, sound can overlap from one scene to the next, either lingering or anticipating. This can occur in dialogue, effects, or ambience, and may create some intriguing tension between the dual temporal realities of sound and image.

Synchronization

To fortify the illusion of the diegesis, sound is most often synchronized with its normal visual partner to create the virtual reality. The dictum "See a dog, hear a dog" refers to hearing exactly what we are seeing, forming a redundancy that is normally part of our daily lives.

Releasing from this image-sound constraint allows the dog to bark off screen to create an atmospheric mood, say a neighborhood under siege. This flexibility permits the sound designer a freedom to interpret the scene and offer the audience more insight than would be possible with only the pure synchronization.

A more radical step would be to synchronize the dog's bark with an unexpected image. If a character is complaining with exaggerated mouth movements but we hear the barking instead of any words synchronized with his lips, this will produce a very strange, perhaps funny, perhaps threatening effect. Jacques Tati uses this freedom in *Mon Oncle*, replacing the sound of ping-pong balls with footsteps.

Point of synchronization

The specific point of synchronization can be made in several ways:

a) An unexpected double break in both the audio and visual tracks may occur, jolting the audience with the shock of transition into an entirely new scene.
b) Separate tracks can converge after being on their own course, then gradually or suddenly fall into sync, at which moment a greater relatedness occurs between the two sound sources. This can happen within certain audio elements, as well as between effects, music, dialogue, or ambience.
c) When the image cuts to a close-up and the sound grows louder, or when the grand orchestra theme accompanies the epic landscape wide shot, the physical punctuation creates an emphasis.
d) The meaning of a word, a particularly emotional musical chord, or a sound effect imbued with storytelling meaning all can lend strength to the meaning of an image that synchronizes with a particular sound.

There may also be a **false sync point**, where the anticipation of image and sound match is not fulfilled. This can happen when, for example, a gun is pointed at someone's head and there is a cut to another image with the sound of the shot. We fill in with our minds this synchronism that doesn't exist on the screen, which can make our involvement even more intimate because we are participating internally in the action.

Consider that the speed of sound is much slower than that of light, so thunder reaches us much later than lightning or a crack of a baseball bat will sound in the outfield bleachers a while after the ball is hit. Convention tells us to put all sounds in exact sync with image, but filmic reality can sometimes be better served by recognizing the physics of light and sound. The decision to follow convention or physics depends mostly on what the story calls for or what effect has more emotional impact in the scene.

The lack of a normally expected synchronization, either in terms of physical events on screen or emotional shifts in the story line, can create a sense of irony. This indifference to the human condition and events can actually provoke an emotional response in the audience that might normally not be elicited with the realistic treatment. Perhaps having become jaded by the media's saturation of sound-synced video coverage, the intense events on the evening news do not affect us so personally. Using the disassociation of sound and image at the right moment can stun the audience into an internal realization.

TRY THIS

With some mixing and matching, you can discover how synchronization of sound and image can manipulate the meaning of the scene. Select a single recorded visual event with some explicit moment that may or may not normally generate a sound (e.g., a punch, fall, explosion, contact, body movement, facial gesture, etc.).

a) Sync up with three different sound effects.
b) Sync with a verbal text, a sound effect, and a clip of music.
c) Experiment with different mix selection and levels of all three of the sounds used in b.

What different emotional, storytelling, or character shading can be felt through the various sounds you synced to image? How realistic, subjective, or absurd are they?

Added value and multiple meanings

When sound works well with image, the impression is that the sound is already contained in the image itself. This can derive from the interaction between the natural world and our physiological responses (see Chapter 3, **From Vibration to Sensation**), and how our muscles and nerves tell us what's happening "out there." If there is a lot of energy and motion, the sound is usually loud; if relaxed, usually soft. If there is tension building, whether it be a teapot whistling or a violin string tightening, the sound rises in pitch.

But in fact, the combining of sound with image in the filmmaking process has nothing to do with our physiological mechanisms, unless we choose to imitate them consciously. The sound designer has freedom to create **added value** to the scene through the unlimited possibilities of juxtaposition of image and sound — whether it be text, music, or effects.

Inserting text (narration, off-screen dialogue, etc.) over an image will direct the viewer to interpret the scene through the symbolic construct of the words. "In the beginning, there was the word," and we continue to give it priority, as the mind will seek a meaning based more on the text before it begins to interpret any other kind of sound. Of course, the aesthetics must be considered as to how much a voice over should be used to manipulate the scene. It may alleviate confusion, help the story line, and allow us into the mind of one of the characters, but it may also be intrusive and at worst redundant, preventing the audience members from participating fully and coming to their own conclusions.

The addition of music to a scene can add **empathetic** value, reinforcing the filmmaker's intended emotion for either the character or spectator (see Chapter 5, ***Emotional signifier***). The shifts of intention can be extreme, depending on the type of music used (see Chapter 5, ***Genres***) and the relation it has to the other sounds in the mix. If the music does not relate to the action or the character's emotion, it is considered **anempathetic**, producing an irony or distance to the event, which may serve the story line just as well.

Sound effects will give added value to a scene any time they venture from the "see dog, hear dog" realism. An example in *Star Wars* shows how sound can create the illusion of movement, when a *psssht* accompanies a straight cut from a closed door to an open door.

A single sound can have different meanings, depending on the visual context in which it is placed. A sigh might be someone's last breath on

Gary Rydstrom talks about the synergy between sound and image:

"Some of the most horrific images in *Saving Private Ryan* are in the hearing loss scene, but they have this tableau feeling to them, like we're not experiencing them in reality anymore, more like a slide show. We take them in a different way, focusing on them more with the sound so simplified. We see the guy carrying his severed arm, not knowing what to do with his own arm, people going up in flames. The thing to think about is this interplay between sound and picture. In unimaginative filmmaking we use the sound and picture to tell the same part of the story, and we don't make use of these two major halves to do two different things to add up to something even better. The good filmmakers like Cameron and Spielberg are going to use the camera and visual to tell you one thing and the sound to tell you something maybe completely different, like the off-screen world."

their deathbed or a pleasant recognition of a cute little baby. A car horn can indicate imminent danger or celebration of a hometown victory. A hiss might be that of a rattlesnake or a kettle boiling. This ambiguity is not only a function of added value, but also extremely fertile ground for creating sound effects from sources other than what would be the norm.

Another level of sophistication in storytelling can be aimed for by developing a "sound arc" with a single type of sound as it progresses through the entire film. Each time it occurs, the context may shift according to the emotional or character development, such that the added value actually represents a flow in the drama. The intention of the sound of a clock ticking, for example, might range from control, to anxiety, to danger, to horror.

A shift may also take place over the course of the film with the amount of added value that the sound contributes. In *The Blair Witch Project*, the sounds are quite realistic and linked to the characters' identifiable physical environment, until the evening brings in unknown noises from the dark woods. Furthermore, at the end when they reach the house, the ambience tracks go completely wild and subjectively overwhelming, adding to the full-blown fear of the experience.

TRY THIS

Michel Chion's educational experiments with sound and image, called **forced marriage**, are wonderful illustrations that you can experience in a group. Someone selects a film scene that is unfamiliar to the others, and shows this without any sound. Then replay the scene three to five times, each time with a different piece of music, as varied as possible. Look for moments of synchronism, and whether they create drama, comedy, or surprise. What music is awkward or fits like a glove? Finally, show the scene with the original sound and look for a sound element that may not have occurred in any previous sound/image combination. Observe the fundamental artificiality of this relationship.

Another variation in this experiment of observation is to take a single scene and show it five times. The first two times show sound and image together, getting familiar with the event and the details of audiovisual interactivity. Then show the image with no sound, followed by the sound with no image, and finally sound and image together again. Based on observations made during each of the five replays, look for the added values, where illusions of time and space may be occurring, and how memory may be playing tricks from the interplay of sound and image. Focus on the descriptive factual elements that compose the scene, as opposed to the psychoanalytic interpretation which may result from this interaction.

CHAPTER 8

SOUND AND NARRATIVE

What story is being told? And how can sound help convey the narrative? Through analysis of the script and characters, the primary (characters') and secondary (audience's) emotions can be identified. Environments and sound objects can be created that enhance the dramatic evolution, paralleling the production design in support of the story. Performance by the actors is also analyzed to complement their talent. References on the soundtrack can be formulated within the archetypal human psyche, a specific culture, a historical period, or a specific film, which is examined in the case study of *Pleasantville* at the end of this chapter.

Narrative analysis

The first audiovisual presentations were around the campfire, with long shadows cast upon cave walls, throbbing drumbeats, and shivering rattles, while the primitive storyteller's reverberating voice recounted tales of the hunt, their ancestors, their gods, providing sense and wonder to the listeners' existence. Joseph Campbell's in-depth study of world mythology, in particular *Hero with a Thousand Faces*, identified common dramatic elements and story structures of the Hero's Journey that appear from the dawn of man to the modern saga of *Star Wars*. Lajos Egri's *The Art of Dramatic Writing* develops a fine analysis of character; the books by screenwriting teachers Syd Field, Bob McKee, Chris Vogler, and Richard Walter, among others, offer rich analyses of story structure and show how to weave the various elements into an effective script. See the **Bibliography** for more ideas.

To discover the full potential of sound, an understanding of the dramatic principles behind storytelling and script analysis must also take place. In its most noble and satisfying execution, sound will reveal something that the image does not or cannot, be it the unconscious intent of a character, a hidden emotion, or a sudden surprise. But to know that this is indeed serving the whole film, rather than simply calling attention to itself, the sound designer must have a thorough understanding of the story, theme, and subtext.

Whether beginning your sound design work with a script or an edited image, the process of narrative analysis requires the identification of the goals, conflicts, confrontations, and resolutions. Over the course of a two-hour feature, these dramatic ingredients (if the script is well written) will vary, repeat, mutate, and rise to higher orders and bigger risks for the characters and the audience. Your task is to identify these movements, separate the distinct elements, and begin associating the obvious and not-so-obvious sounds with the image.

What makes a great story? Plot, character, and emotional bonding for the audience must be present with a strong sense of beginning, middle, and end. Although most obvious in plot, this structure is just as essential in the transformational arcs of the character growth and empathetic reaction of the viewer. In the Hero's Journey model, for example, the main character is dissatisfied with something in everyday life and ventures outside the known world (sometimes involuntarily) on a quest for a treasure. Along the way there are all sorts of guardians, mentors, rascals, and dragons, and finally after winning the treasure, the hero brings it back to the home community. More importantly, the hero has also vanquished certain inner demons along with the outer ones; it is this story structure that must be clearly perceived so that the sound design will support all the twists and turns, ups and downs.

When reading or viewing the film for the first time, take it in like any moviegoer, letting yourself merge with the experience, enjoying the drama, comedy, or surprises (see Chapter 1, ***The first script reading***). After you have had that unique first-time opportunity, you will automatically slide into an analytic viewpoint and begin to perceive this structure. It will consist of specific turning points in the drama that will shift from one scene, emotion, or act to the next. As the structure begins to unfold, use the techniques in Chapter 1 to develop the sound design to support this narrative.

Music and story

Some excellent examples of how classical and pop works have conveyed story through music are: Vivaldi's "Four Seasons" tracing the universal cycle of birth-life-death; Prokofiev's "Peter and the Wolf" illustrating characters with specific instrumentation and melodies; Wagner's many operas (including "Tristan and Isolde" and "Parsifal") created not for the sake of the music but as an emotional expression of naked human instincts suppressed by civilization. In Chapter 5, **Music to Our Ears**, the relationship of music to structure is developed in detail.

By comparing the elements of music theory, composition, and performance with those of filmmaking, we may find inspiration to extend the possibilities of storytelling in the audiovisual medium.

TABLE 8-1 MUSIC-STORY RELATIONSHIP

Music	**Story**
melody	character
harmony	setting/production design
dissonance	conflict
rhythm	pace
phrase	beat/scene/sequence
score/composer	script/screenwriter
performers	actors
conductor	director

The melody forms a trajectory of dramatic intent, exploring different regions of the scale of a particular instrument, with specific definitions of tonal center, range, and timbre. Character is defined by type (instrument), goals (tonal center), abilities (range), and emotional latitude (timbre).

Harmonic structure provides an emotional and spatial context for the music to be expressed. The location setting and production design provide a visual context for the story to be enacted, supporting the drama through the visuals.

When dissonance occurs, two sounds clash to our ears, the opposite of harmony. In the story, this happens when two characters or ideologies conflict. In both cases, these elements are necessary to build tension and drama, which create a yearning in the audience for resolution.

Both music and film are art forms that work with time (as opposed to painting or sculpture), and the passage of time can be both objective and subjective for the audience. Rhythm or pace is perceived by the literal frequency of events occurring, how much information is transmitted within a period of time, and how involved we are viscerally, intellectually, or emotionally (see Chapter 4, ***Time***).

A musical phrase consists of a complete idea made of melody, harmony, rhythm, and intention, serving as a building block for the entire composition. Similarly, a script or film will have building blocks of a beat within a scene that focuses on a single idea, a complete scene within one setting with the purpose of joining individual ideas into a physical flow, and a sequence of scenes whose joint purpose is to move the story into a new dramatic direction.

The blueprint of both music and film is in the written form, not discounting improvisation that can provide essential creative juice to the process. The musical composer uses nomenclature that translates through the score; the screenwriter uses the word to communicate through the script. Then the score or script is performed by musicians or actors, guided by the overview of the conductor or director.

The obvious and major difference between music and film is that the latter works with image and in fact incorporates the former into its expression. Chapter 7, **Sound and Image**, delineates some of these differences.

Character identification

What does the character sound like to the audience? What does the character hear? How does a nonliteral sound affect the way we perceive the character? These questions raise the distinctions between objective and subjective points of view that sound can have in the film.

Objective audience perspective

When actors perform with complete visceral involvement, their sounds extend beyond the dialogue to the musicality of the voice (see Chapter 6, ***Prosody — vocal melody and emotion***) and other nonverbal body sounds. The natural communication of the voice range — coughs and sighs, finger tapping and punches, tiptoeing and stomping — all convey something about who that character is at that moment in the scene. Some of these may be recorded during production, others added in postproduction, but the common factor is that they create an identity for us to listen to from an outside viewpoint.

A character may also be an object or an ambience. George Watters discusses how a submarine can take on different characteristics in the hands of two different directors:

"*Hunt for Red October* and *Crimson Tide* both featured submarines, which were treated quite differently. The directors, John McTiernan and Tony Scott, had different concepts of what they wanted. The sound in *Red October* contained many sonar pings and a large variety of torpedo sounds. John always used musical terms to describe what he wanted. It was evident to me that real sonar pings and torpedo sounds was not what John was going for. Subsequently we ended up making new pings with partial musical tones and torpedoes with strong piston motors. Whereas, in *Crimson Tide*, Tony did not care so much where the origin of the sound pings and torpedoes were derived from, but wanted them strong sounding and loud enough to cut through the musical score. Tony wanted to surround the audience with the feeling of being in a metal structure, to increase the feeling of claustrophobia and what it was like to be on a submarine. He likes sounds to be big and aggressive. A director's feel for both the sound and the film is individual and key to the process."

Subjective character experience

By getting inside a character's head, hearing what he or she is hearing, the audience can have a strong bond with that experience, especially if it is shown to be distinct from other sections of the film in which the viewpoint is contrastingly objective. Focusing on something away from the obvious allows distinction of the character's point of view from what everyone else might notice. Having the character in the scene, intercutting the image with what the character is seeing, strengthens this association. This also provides the possibility, in a later scene without the character's presence, for the sound to continue in order to evoke this subjectivity.

In *A Civil Action*, a man must decide whether he is going to give information to the lawyers about the toxic water quality, and he is watching his own children drinking water. We hear the isolated sounds of the kids drinking to realize what he is focusing on, rather than seeing a visual close-up on the lips of the kids, making for a psychologically powerful scene.

***Gary Rydstrom relates how he accomplished subjective character experience in* Saving Private Ryan:**

"When Tom Hanks is suffering a momentary hearing loss from shell shock, the visuals don't change much, but we did a radical thing with the sound by shutting down the outside world. You get distorted bits and pieces of the outside, but mostly just this seashell roar as if you're inside his head. There is a wonderful shock coming out of the hearing loss when one of his men is screaming at him and he can't hear a thing, then we use another explosion for him to snap to, and now we can hear the guy. There's also a rising tone, like a teakettle boiling up to that point, then it snaps back to reality. When you are in intense experiences, you have this sense of closing down, almost more aware of your own sounds than the sounds around you. The blood in your ears is going so fast, you're more self-aware than outside aware. Those moments are simple, but work remarkably well to help the audience identify with the character even more, because they feel like they've been in his head for a short period of time."

Nonliteral sound

The most common nonliteral sound to accentuate character personality or emotion is music, while more and more use is being made of sound effects and ambience to support this area as well. The "right" or literal sound

Dane Davis also speaks about the objective vs. subjective experience in films:

"With the director we define: whose movie is it, whose scene is it, and where is the audience — and this is usually defined by the script. What does the audience know that the main character knows, and what does it not know that the character knows, which defines the subjectivity. When the movie is about drug experiences or hallucinations, it can go really far by taking the audience all the way inside the character's head. *Matrix* played with all these rules and we had to structure very carefully about what was real and what wasn't. In *Drugstore Cowboy*, the characters were breaking into hospitals to steal pharmaceuticals and their world was completely defined by how high they were or how much they were integrated into their reality. You hear more and more of the real world, trucks, trains, a trumpet playing, all the parts of a scene independent of the characters. Then they would do the drugs, all that stuff would disappear and you would hear specific sounds they would focus on, like the spoon bubbling or hypodermic going in, all exaggerated sounds. This was about the degree of focus, the space collapsing."

may actually not be the best sound for the expression of the character, and in fact if this is avoided, the richness of the film and storytelling is multiplied with infinite possibilities. The task of the sound designer is to find the best of such myriad possibilities and build a consistency with the genre, plot, and character's transformational arc. It must be the right sound for the script and for what the director is trying to say on the screen.

Emotional associations

Characters will also be defined by the things and environment in which they act. The associated sounds of the wildest, most dramatic scenes may be very familiar things from everyday life (e.g., a cat purring with a vivid sexual fantasy sequence), or just the opposite, with a mundane scene using extraordinary audio references (e.g., knotting a dress tie to the sound of a strangling shriek). In *Star Wars*, Darth Vader's laser sword electronic drone is pitched to a foreboding minor key, while Obiwan Kenobi's is pitched to valiant C major. When they are in battle, the two sounds waver dissonantly in conflict.

The character of a whole society can be colored by sound, as in *Witness*, which contrasts the rural Amish using old-fashioned, hand-worked devices against the city police scenes of hyper-violence and jarring telephone rings. In *The Hunt for Red October* three submarine sonic ambiences (American, good Russian, bad Russian) each exhibit their peculiarities with familiar vs. unfamiliar effects and languages to emphasize the dramatic distinctions.

The personality of a crowd can be sculpted by the kinds of sounds accompanying the image. If there is a whispering quiet or low murmur, this produces a totally different sense than a hooting, whistling, catcalling crowd. A feeling of bigness can be accentuated by mixing in foreground voices, either verbally identifiable or with nondistinguishable vocal sounds, applying a dynamic to the presence and depth of the crowd.

Footsteps can lend an identity to the walker, even if they do not appear on camera. Literature has described many: felt boots screeching angrily in the snow (*Doctor Zhivago*); the slap, slap of Gran's carpet slippers (Emily Carr); the impish echoes of footsteps in the cloisters of Oxford (Thomas Hardy); booming floor timbers under strong rough feet (*Beowulf*).

Even dead bodies can have a sonic character, not simply silence. In Remarque's classic war novel *All Quiet on the Western Front*, he describes the unburied corpses lying in the heat with "their bellies swollen up like balloons. They hiss, belch, and make movements. The gases in them make noises." William Faulkner also writes of the noise of the dead as "little trickling bursts of secret and murmurous bubbling."

Animal sounds produce a particularly rich territory to explore for enhancing audio character traits. We respond so primally to a snake hiss or gorilla roar, that these sonic events can symbolically infuse an associated character with a sense of deadliness or ferociousness. In *Jungle Fever* the world of the drug addicts careens into a zoo of wild sounds with walrus grunting, lion growls, and bats flying (see also comments on *Beauty and the Beast*, *Star Wars*, and *E.T.* in Chapter 6, ***Alien language***).

In* House on Haunted Hill *Dane Davis created a character personality and growth for an object, which was essentially a principal of the film:

"The house had to go from just a building to a monster. I wanted it to have life, like a heart beating and respiratory level, but also on a mechanical level with all these machines and torture chambers. At the beginning it's quite subtle. We could have started full-on horror movie sounds at the beginning, but the director and I wanted it to grow. It started with the slow pulse, very low, and grows during the movie with these contrapuntal rhythms of these machines, as the house comes into its own and becomes alive. The respiratory level goes from almost static air to roaring wind sounds. Everything had to keep growing without ever becoming obvious to the audience. As things got more noticeable, it was still in the arc that the audience would buy. If I ever did anything too extreme, people would look at it and think, 'Where are all those noises coming from?' But it kept you engaged with the life of the house without making you forget what the actors were saying."

TRY THIS

Find an animal that represents the emotions of the main character. Imagine the sounds. What would the other characters be as animals? How would these animals interact? What kind of jungle chorus would result?

Primary and secondary emotions

When Laurel "accidentally" bangs Hardy on the head with a ladder, we may have a laughter reaction, but certainly Hardy isn't laughing. This distinction is made between the **primary** (character's) emotions, and the **secondary** (audience) reactions. Sound can induce either primary or secondary emotions, so it is useful to analyze the intention of each scene from both of these perspectives. Ask, "Which character are we identifying with and what is the character feeling?" and "What should the spectator be feeling?"

An example of this distinction in sound would be in a suspense film where a woman is walking by herself in the woods. Suddenly we hear the cracking of twigs. If the woman turns in curiosity to see what it is, this is a primary emotion sound. But if she doesn't hear it (and perhaps it is reinforced with a visual close-up of a boot) and it is for the ears of the audience only, to heighten their anxiety in contrast to the woman's ignorance, then it would be a secondary emotion sound.

Music can serve for either primary or secondary emotions as well. Claudia Gorbman refers to these styles as **identification** or **spectacle** bonding traits for music. Identification music acts as a psychological container for a melodramatic dialogue scene, for example by underscoring, delaying, amplifying, or otherwise nudging the audience to feel empathy for the character's emotional state. It provides a depth above and beyond the literal spatial depth into a nonverbal psychological human depth. Spectacle music lends a sense of epic scale to a scene, like the theme from *Star Wars* or *Platoon*. Rather than involving the audience inside the narrative, the larger-than-life spectacle dimension places us in contemplation of the moment in order to externalize and make commentary.

Environments and the "soundscape"

Stories happen in a time and place, and these parameters are characterized by their acoustic environments or **soundscapes**, a term coined by the Canadian composer R. Murray Schafer. His work has traced the historical development of soundscapes from primordial nature to the ever more complex and mechanized world of modern man, helping us to listen, analyze, and make distinctions. As sound designers, we can take this information and creatively apply it to the film narrative.

The soundscape is composed of several types of sounds: **keynote sounds**, **signals**, **soundmarks**, and **archetypal sounds**. The keynote is equivalent to the tonal center in music (see Chapter 5, ***Tonal center***) in that it represents the anchor and reference point to all other sounds. As a constant, it may be listened to unconsciously, but its omnipresence suggests the deep influence it may have on the characters' behavior and moods. Indispensable to the environment, it serves as the ground for the figure (see Chapter 4, ***Gestalt principles and illusion***).

The signal is considered the figure or foreground sound to be consciously heard. These include sounds that demand attention, like sirens, whistles, and horns, which can also transmit more complex messages like the number of bell chimes of a clock tower.

A soundmark establishes a particular place, as does a landmark, possessing some unique quality for only that location. It might be a foghorn, an unusual birdcall, or a consistently irritating water pipe screech.

***George Watters comments on being able to experience the reality of Alcatraz in* The Rock *and being on a real World War II airplane in* Pearl Harbor:**

"Authentic location recording is invaluable. It provides the opportunity to do as much field recording as possible, while you experience firsthand what you are trying to convey to the audience when you are putting the soundtrack together. Spending two days on Alcatraz Island for *The Rock* brought home the eerie, lonely feel to the sound. Anyone who spent any time there and heard the soundtrack would be instantly transported to this place, which has its own unique sound signature. It is very windy, so you have lots of wind whistles setting the mood, combined with seagulls and a lighthouse electric horn, interior jail cell ambiences, and the jail door sounds. These individually common elements, when combined, became quite distinctive in this particular location.

"Riding on a B25 and a P40 during recording sessions on *Pearl Harbor* gave me the chance to hear not only the sound, but also experience what a pilot feels. This direct experience made it possible to recreate an authentic and accurate soundmark for this film. Sometimes in life, there's no substitute for the real thing. Direct experience is best if you're striving for authenticity or nostalgia."

Archetypal sounds stir our ancestral memories, bringing us into an environment through a universal emotional reaction. Light wind blowing through the grass, birds twittering, and a babbling brook elicit a sense of peace in the world. Thunder, cracking branches, and pelting rain tell us that we had better look for shelter.

The natural soundscape can create not only a wide range of emotional spaces, it can also link with our human environments through analogy or simply because of our tendency to seek meaning in all stimuli. Birdcalls can mark territory (like car horns), sound an alarm of a predator (like air raid or police sirens), or express pleasure (like music on the radio).

With the very broad-band noises like the wind, the sea, or a waterfall, our brain will pick out specific frequencies and imagine hearing voices or animal calls within. In designing the intention of the scene, actual voices or animal sounds can be mixed in very low, almost subliminally, to accentuate the desire we have to identify the unknown.

Man coming into the natural environment introduces sounds like footsteps, hunting (bow and arrow, gunshots, traps), and homesteading (digging, chopping, construction). Once the farm is established, the common sonic symbols appear — the dairy cow mooing to be milked, the alarm clock *cockle-doodle-doo*, and the defending watchdog bark.

The sounds of war have evolved over the eons, from hand-to-hand combat, clanking of metal, grunts, and battle cries. Drumming can serve to electrify an army, terrify the enemy, or instill terror (as in *Braveheart*). The introduction of gunpowder added explosions to the 14th century, and from that point the blasts gained in amplitude and dropped in frequency range until 20th-century bombings. Air flight added the dimension of whining dogfights that ultimately mutated into lethal jet fighters.

A curious note on the root of the word "bellicose," meaning "warlike," is that this word also is reflected in "bell" or "to make a loud noise" in Old English, perhaps because at that time the metal cannons were being melted into church bells, and vice versa. Bells symbolize the passage of time, reminding man of his mortality and fragility in the universe, just as war does.

As cities evolved in Europe and America throughout the 19th century, a distinction developed in the sounds due to the natural resources available for construction of roads and buildings. Europe had long since demolished its forests so the principal material was stone, creating the keynote of the chipping, scraping, and banging of rocks. America was carved out of vast virgin forests, so wood became the keynote element in so many walkways and planks, allowing each board to sound its own pitch and resonance under heel and wheel. But in the 20th century, all sounds became uniform between the continents and within the cities themselves when concrete and asphalt overtook all other materials.

As labor changed from the human rhythm of manual farming, ironsmithing, and handmade construction to the mechanization of all types of work, man and machine got out of sync. Singing ceased to create the pace, which instead became orchestrated by revolutions per minute. The sounds turned into hums and clatters of unchanging, uninterrupted flat lines, away from the melody of life. With the desire for speed came a keynote pitch of more than 20Hz, a level just audible to the human ear and practically impossible for the human body to create through its own movement. The drone ultimately creates an anti-intellectual narcotic for the human senses; if it becomes jerky and funky (like Han Solo's beat-up ship in *Star Wars*), it usually means the machine won't last much longer.

The level of noise has risen over the centuries, but more important has been the use (and abuse) of the loudest level of noise by those with authority. Descending from God (thunder) to the priest (church reverberation and bells) to the industrialist (factories, machines) to the rock'n'roll stars, the association of noise with power has never been broken in the human imagination. Within the context of a film, the louder environments usually will be associated with the seat of those in power as well. This is often challenged by a protagonist seeking transformation from an internal moral stand (in contrast very quiet) and/or an external physical action (which can become louder than the status quo power, as in *Braveheart* when the hero screams his refusal to submit under torture).

Locations can be distinguished through such subtleties as the kind of train whistles (Canadian, American, and British are all quite different in tone and timbre), police sirens, car horns, and even electrical hums (50Hz in Europe, 60Hz in America).

Within one location there can be variation of the soundscape as signals according to weather, time of day, or season. The acoustic activities of a town will change as people wake up, go to work, take a lunch break, settle at home, and go to sleep. A dry and wet period or hot and cold season will emphasize different environmental sounds like rain, wind, frogs, or cicadas. In a certain French fishing village on the tip of a peninsula, the wind shifts all day long so that, like a clock, the sounds that enter the village from afar rotate from north (church bells and farm sounds) to east (buoys off the coast) to south (boat motors at sea) to west (a blowhole), and finally back to the northern bells. Foggy weather calls for the signal of the distant foghorn, and so on.

Very special conditions can create what Schafer refers to as the "soniferous garden," in particular through water and wind sounds. In the Italian gardens of the Renaissance era, an extremely romantic relationship developed with water in endless fountains, streams, pools, and jets to form moving, organic sculptures that produced bird whistles, dragon roars, and fantastic rhythms. Bali's ingenious irrigation system of bamboo tubes tipping water into various rice fields creates a delicate symphony of bubbling and gurgling water sounds. Rain falling on all types of resonant objects like wood, metal, stones, glass, and shells will create extremely rich soundscapes as well.

The natural force of wind can put manmade chimes into motion; whether they are made of bamboo, metal, glass, or shells, their clatter or ethereal harmonies allow us to sense the invisible forces in the air. This energy can also activate what is known as an Aeolian or weather harp, which has strings that vibrate from the passing wind. As the atmosphere of a gale force plays lustily on the harp, it can howl like a giant harmonica, or drop to a breeze that murmurs like a somber distant bell. Even streaming through a crack in a door or window, the eerie howl can give life to the unseen strength of the wind.

The human voice is always raised outdoors, with no reverberation to augment the vocal energy. In a public place there is more of a tendency to be demonstrative, and people who live out of doors in hot climates tend to speak more loudly than those who live indoors in colder climates; the latter are more disturbed by loud noise. Inside an enclosure there can be a sense of privacy between lovers, family, boardroom scheming, or political plotting. So the type of human communication occurring will influence and be influenced by the environmental setting (see also Chapter 7, ***Spatial dimensions***).

The size of an indoor space will also influence the speed of information that can be conveyed. With a Gothic church, the music must play slowly to allow for the long reverberation time. As chamber music became more popular, the tempo accelerated along with clarity, until the 20th-century recording studios, which provide, if desired, no reverb at all. Contemporary office spaces are usually small, dry spaces suited for the frenzy of modern business and rapid communication.

The sounds of the spaces themselves can be characteristic of their era, function, and style. An older apartment building will have creaking wooden floors, cracking radiators, and groaning furnaces, while a modern building will have gusts of central heating or cooling, humming elevators, and electronic beeps and buzzes assuring that all is under some invisible cyber-control.

The fundamental resonance of a room, or **Eigentone**, will give emphasis to certain frequencies because of the reflection of sound waves between parallel surfaces. This can actually create a space conducive to a more male or female voice range, a bit like the sense of singing in a shower at certain pitches that sound wonderfully full. The notion of **room tone** as a basic level of sound below all specific voices or effects is related to this, although there can be other contributing factors, like electronic or mechanical hums, traffic background, or weather sounds.

Another form of orienting the audience to a specific geographical or cultural space is through the music style accompanying the scene. Historically, the influence of transportation has given different slants on the predominant music of the period. Examples include the clippity-clop of the horse for the hoe-down country square dance, the syncopation of the railroad for jazz, and the automobile with the surge of electronic, loud, driving contemporary music like rock'and'roll.

TRY THIS

Getting in touch with the soundscape can be both a passive and active pursuit. If you simply open your ears to what is happening as the audience, isolating as many separate sounds as you can within a given environment, you become more capable of creating rich ambiences for your soundtracks. Notice the changes as you move slightly in the space, then as you move more into an entirely different space, and whether these changes are abrupt or gradual.

A more active "soundwalk" involves paying attention to specific sounds and interacting with them as composer-performer. For example, compare the pitches of similar sounds like car motors or voices, or the duration of telephone rings or weight lifters' clanking iron. Then begin to interact with these sounds, like an improvisational musician. Beat out your own rhythm in sync or counterpoint to the soundscape. Sing in harmony with the refrigerator hum. Go into a store and listen to the variety of tones you can get by tapping on the different size jam jars and canned vegetables. Find a wooden bridge or pier and play it like a marimba with your feet. (Remember Tom Hanks in *Big* dancing on the huge keyboard?) With the sophistication of samplers, you can capture and play anything in rhythm, melody, or harmony on your soundtrack, but discovering this with your own body in a real environment can be one of the richest ways to liberate the essence of that location's soul and how it can be expressed in a filmic scene. You can get inside the skin of the actor/character through this interactivity, directly expressing the relationship and conflict in this way.

Convention has developed certain stock characterizations of time and place, seen in specific orchestrations and arrangements. Many of these themes are so overused that they serve more for comedy or historical references, yet their continued force on our subconscious cannot be denied.

TABLE 8-2
MUSICAL REFERENCES TO CULTURE/GEOGRAPHY

Geographic Location	Music Style
Middle Eastern	Minor key melody with much ornamentation
Indian territory	4/4 allegretto drumbeat with first beat accented, woodwinds with simple minor-modal tune
Latin America	Rumba rhythm and major melody with trumpet or marimba
Japan or China	Xylophones and woodblocks with simple minor melodies in 4/4, pentatonic scales
Turn-of-the-century Vienna	Strauss-like waltzes with strings
Rome and Paris	Accordions, harmonicas
Medieval, Renaissance	Harps, flutes
New York, big city	Jazzy or slightly discordant major theme with brass or strings
Pastoral location	Woodwinds in major key

While transitions between one environment and another can be marked by the change in sound, even a single soundscape may be composed of several elements that are mixed at different levels according to the dramatic moment. In *The Hunt for Red October* recordings were made above and below water on two tracks. By sound sculpting these perspectives with equalizing highs and lows, adding air elements, and recreating the rhythm with a synthesizer which could modify the attack-decay-sustain-release phases, a tremendous variety of sounds were created for the different dramatic needs of the scenes.

In the special circumstance of using reversed sounds, no natural reverberation is heard, but rather an expansion backwards to a bursting, echoless explosion. An anechoic chamber (the opposite of an echo chamber) gives this disconcerting effect as well, implying a world without boundaries, without air, without life. This deathlike acoustic experience can provide a soundscape for dream sequences or other non-ordinary states of reality.

Inventing sound objects

When creating sound effects for an event, movement, or impact on screen, very often a single realistic sound will not have the full effect necessary. Thus a **sound object** can be constructed from one or more elements, many of which may have nothing to do with the visual object they will be accompanying.

Some of the most inventive sounds have their history in Warner Bros. and Disney animation with masters Treg Brown and Jimmy MacDonald, while others came from Jack Foley's pioneering work that initiated the whole art based on his name. These men were geniuses at finding the emotional content of a sound, taking it out of context, and assigning it to a new one. An example is the sound of bowling pins crashing when people fall over in a cartoon.

While the composition of each sound object can be extremely expressive, keep in mind how these objects relate to one another throughout the story by building, contrasting, and transforming character and emotion.

TRY THIS

Free association and dream imagery can be keys to liberating new contexts of sound and image. By relaxing with a scene, closing your eyes and reviewing it in your mind, let the ideas link with the images. They may come in sounds, other images, verbal associations, or puns. They may be wild and wacky or subtle and mysterious. What does the story and emotion call for? Play with a sound library, mixing not-so-obvious audio files with the scene at hand.

Impact
A sock to the chin by John Wayne always carried a great sonic punch beyond any realism, accenting the fight scenes with visceral flesh-to-flesh experiences by using raw meat slaps and punches. Films like *Rocky*

established new levels of impressionism by using different combinations of sounds to compose a music-like score of pounding rhythms and timbres. *Raging Bull* fights start with the beef hits, then move into ripping, tearing, and stabbing. As the flesh gives way, water sounds are introduced to render the splatter sensation. Then animal sounds are woven in — and finally at the impactful climax, airplanes, jets, and slowed-down arrows are choreographed with the stunning action. In *Streets of Fire*, a pig carcass destined to become bacon was hit on the foley stage with everything imaginable — fists, rubber-gloved hands, two-by-fours, hammers, and a sedge hammer; and then they were added to sounds of crushed watermelons, green peppers, and wood. The alternating and mixing of the more cracky or thuddy sounds align with the different parts of the body being hit on screen.

Dane Davis describes how he creates fight sounds:

"We developed a whole library of sounds with a tight low-end component, like when you hit yourself you can hear, not so much of the reverberation, but defining the depth of penetration into the other person's body, whether it's playful or hurtful. I'd smash a pear with my bare hands to be more realistic, or use 2-inch diameter fire hose, wacking as hard as I can against a denim dummy we built out of sand, kitty litter, apples, and potatoes, giving a hard, painful kind of quality. There's always a combination of things, layers."

Firearms

The sound of a gunshot will often begin with the actual recorded firearm, but then much can be added to enhance the effect of the shot itself, the impact of the bullets and the ambience reverb. Sometimes the high timbre of a handgun may need to be reinforced with a bassier sound like slapping two-by-fours or a pitched-down version of the same gunshot. With larger weapons like torpedoes in *The Hunt for Red October*, the layering of animal growls and shrieks, a Ferrari engine, and a screeching screen door spring helps imbue the weapon with a vengeful purpose of its own.

There exists much more variation regarding how and where a bullet will hit, than for the shot itself. If it slams into metal, wood, concrete, glass, hollow, solid, or liquid, this will determine the timbre and resonance. The rhythm can also be played with (watch for other important sounds and build around them), since it is not necessary to see every firing or impact, especially when there are more than two or three guns in the scene, and if there are any automatic weapons with repeat firings. When a bullet hits a person, consider what kind of emotional involvement the scene calls for and how the sound can amplify that. For example, if it is a cold, silent assassination, there could be very subtle sounds of air stopping, a dry *thwack*, and a quiet sliding of the body down the wall. If it is a violent, raging murder, then we might hear bones being hit and splintered and blood splattering explosively against the wall. Counterpoint can be also used, as in *Terminator 2* with its massively destructive grenade launcher sweetened with cute little pipe sounds on loading, which contrasts image and sound. The aftermath of a shot can be dramatically descriptive of the environment, through ricochet, echo, or deadly muffled silence. If a gunshot occurs in a sacred church, the reverb could reach the denigrated corners of the saints' souls; in a rocky valley, the animals and nature spirits may be alerted to the hunter.

In the case of *Malcom X*, the sounds of gunshots are introduced gradually as a political statement; this is a perfect example of a sound object transforming with the development of the story line. The main character's social activism begins as a burst of fame, denoted by the popping photo flashes; as this fame grows it becomes more dangerous to the status quo. The sounds of flashes then become layered with more and more present gunshots, portending his assassination, a tragic result of his provocative politics.

Vehicles

Motorcycles can have a whole edge beyond just their typical sounds. In *Tron* the animated "lightcycles" used saw blades to turn the sharp corners, synthesized video-game–style sounds, and hundreds of types of recordings from the tops of the bikes. The Doppler effect was recorded as the bikes passed by, starting with high tones and dropping low as the machine zoomed close, then far away, at great speed.

Train sounds, even when they don't appear on screen, often lend an atmosphere of danger or tension to a scene, like in *American Graffiti* (hooking the cop car's axle), *The Godfather* (restaurant assassination), and *Bugsy* (Beatty shoots Gould). In the seduction scene of *The Hot Spot*, the sound of train cars hitting each other and brakes squealing accentuate the power play between the two characters. A long train is the kind of sound object that can be extended over several minutes, if need be, conducting the flow of a series of dramatic moments.

Jet fighters from *Star Wars* to *Top Gun* have benefited from intuitive sound designers who incorporated lion and tiger roars, monkey screams, and elephant blasts. The tracks of real jets have been combined or reversed, and the pitch manipulated to give a life to this dynamic sound object. Following a creative hunch, Walter Murch invited a group of women to scream in a resonant bathroom, overmodulated the recording, then took the resulting low-frequency pulsing from the distorted loudness and added a Doppler shift to give movement to the raging jets. Conversely, jet sounds have been employed by Cecelia Hall for wacky little pieces of machinery in a bakery scene.

Fire

Giving intelligence, mystery, and threat to fire, *Backdraft* uses an array of animal sounds like coyote howls to sweeten the visual moments of air being sucked out, with cougar growls and monkey screeches added to the fireball explosions. In a lighter moment for fire, the candelabra character in *Beauty and the Beast* gesticulates his arms and whips the candle flames with sound created by blowing on a lavaliere mike in a foley session.

More ideas and techniques

When an image goes beyond our everyday experience, the associated sounds often come from very familiar places, both because of their accessibility (kitchen, backyard, garage, playground) and their resonance in our subconscious. A case in point with *Terminator 2*: Sound designer Gary Rydstrom looked for a combination of liquid, metal, and gas sounds to portray the sci-fi morphing effects. He recorded dog food sliding out of cans, then injected compressed air into a flour-and-water goop. Together they form a sound object which has a beginning and an end, fitting perfectly with the visual transformation effects. At another moment in this film, a molten pit uses several tracks to give heat and density to the lava-like pool, including compressed air in mud modulated at various pitches, along with a high sizzle.

Rydstrom attributes a fresh and open approach to listening as an important part of creativity:

"Listening is certainly important because the world is full of opportunities for exotic sounds in very nonexotic locations, and you can make great sounds with things right around you. But I think the biggest talent you need if you're going to do sound design, is to be able to separate what the sound *is* from what it is being made *by*. It's a bit of a mind trick, and this makes it hard sometimes for me to remember where I got certain sounds from. But in an odd way, I don't care where they came from, because now the sound exists as an element for a T Rex roar or an interior tone for an isolation booth in a quiz show. I have no idea where I made that sound in *Quiz Show* because it doesn't matter anymore; I'm taking it from the real world and then splitting it from what it really is."

Moments of exaggeration of the sound object can be effective either explicitly to generate comedy or irony, or implicitly to focus our attention on an otherwise subtle event. In the black comedy *Raising Arizona* when a fly is tossed against the wall, we hear heightened sounds of a leather belt, chain, and block. In *Close Encounters of the Third Kind* when the aliens are unscrewing the basement vent, the sound that worked was much bigger than would be expected from the tiny screws; it was created by a string tied to a nail and pulled in a large circle.

TRY THIS

1) To become aware of the character distinctions between universally present sounds, place yourself next to a hard-surfaced stairway, close your eyes, and listen to the different footsteps. Can you tell the person's age, sex, dress style, urgency, or any abnormality like a limp, cane, or childlike hopping? The same exercise can be done on a street corner listening to vehicle engines, in a kennel listening to dog talk, in a video arcade, or next to a babbling creek. What does each isolated sound provoke in your visual imagination?
2) Discover how speed and pitch changes can affect normal sounds, creating totally different sound objects than the original source. For example, slowing down the recording of your breath will sound like an enormous steam engine, or biting into an apple will turn into a large tree falling in a reverberant forest. What can you find in your everyday soundscape that can be converted into different sound objects?

Auditory hierarchy

The way sound commands our attention in film can be described in three levels: 1) the immediate presence of something we are consciously listening to; 2) the support sounds for the event or environment that are heard but do not command direct attention; and 3) background sounds that we don't notice but that constitute the created reality and can influence our subconscious. This auditory hierarchy is founded upon Gestalt principles (described in Chapter 4, ***Gestalt principles and illusion***), specifically with the first level as **figure** and the second two levels as **background**. Focusing and unfocusing on different sounds at different moments allows them to make transitions between levels, jumping from figure to background and vice versa.

The distinction between levels and what is most appropriate at any given moment for any given sound (dialogue, effects, ambience, or music) is often handled in the mix, pulling up or dropping down (or out) the tracks as they play with the visuals. However, there are certain universal principles that can usually be applied effectively; preparing the sound design with these in mind can save time, money, and most importantly expand the creative use of multitrack sound.

Although exceptions exist, dialogue is usually the most significant sound, so all other tracks will work around the verbal information. Music typically lies low until the last word, then rises at a moment of decisive rhythmic or emotional change in the scene. To avoid conflict with simultaneous dialogue, music rarely uses woodwinds or pitches in the same voice range, unless an indistinguishable tone color is desirable for some reason.

Action also competes for attention with dialogue, so if a film musical calls for singing, this can stop the dramatic flow as well, becoming like a Greek chorus that comments on the temporarily frozen narrative. The entrance of music, action, or a specific sound effect can drown out the voice and detract from the understanding of dialogue. Conversely, the shifts in scenes, entrances and exits, or sound events (like a doorbell or phone) can be the introduction for a new ambience or the beginning of a nondiegetic musical accompaniment.

Gorbman analyzes René Clair's *Sous les toits* for its distinctive use of auditory hierarchy and how this can contribute to the narrative. This film establishes music as its primary audio level, then speech, and lastly effects. However, at its dramatic peak in a street fight, the hierarchy is toppled by dropping all music and allowing indistinguishable noise to predominate, consisting of shouts and gang mutterings. Nowhere else does the film allow stray voices, the very opposite of clarity — so this scene coincides with the transformation of the normally passive main character into an action fighter. At the climax of the fight, the sound of an approaching train and finally its consuming whistle in the auditory foreground serve to mask all other sounds, along with the visual masking of smoke in the visual foreground. Tension is displaced until the scene clears and music returns to restore narrative order.

Ben Burtt comments on the potential conflicts between dialogue, sound effects, and music, and how to be selective.

"I think of the sound as being literal and nonliteral. The literal side is like dialogue, when you see someone talking. On the other hand, you have music as the nonliteral — a very abstract thing, an artificiality, a style. Somewhere in between the two are the sound effects. Sometimes you want the effects to gravitate toward the literal side, but you've got to be very selective because you can't hear everything that's on the screen. You've got to help tell your story and enhance the drama. The most important factor for the sound designers is their choices, what they decide to put in and what they leave out. Looking at the equation, is it literal or nonliteral, what's the right direction to go? Do you want to hear any footsteps because you see it, or maybe no footsteps and just some kind of other sound that might be more interesting? Don't close your mind to making radical selections.

"It's important to always recognize this idea of orchestration, the loud and quiet, slow and fast contrasts. In *Always* we had to work with two steady-state sounds, one on the ground, one in the air, and with two people talking in the airplane. So we had to orchestrate by building with tension, suspense; and we made the drama build by raising the pitch of the airplane. The motors were used as transitional elements to get from one pitch up to the higher pitch, not too quickly, and letting the dialogue build.

"I think about how sound effects are the action and music is the reaction. For example, suddenly a spear flies out and hits the wall next to the character. Instead of scoring the spear with a *tah-dah*! let the sound effect do it, and then [the] emotional reaction is accompanied by music. With that you have a much better blend of things. There's no rule, but this has helped me orchestrate."

Within the context of auditory hierarchy, masking can be considered a tool for establishing levels. Noise in a bar may mask background music; conversely, the music may rise to mask the background noise. The determining factor should be what element plays the most important role in the narrative. Avoid the ambiguity of two or more levels collapsing and losing the dramatic impact because of lack of clarity.

Dramatic evolution

At the heart of storytelling is the classic structure of goal-conflict-resolution. In its most contributive form, sound design supports this dramatic evolution by developing themes and rhythms that underscore this narrative structure. Some examples in myth, music, and film will illustrate how this structure works. In Chapter 1 the techniques of creating visual and sound maps of a film offer practical applications.

As mentioned before, the great mythologist Joseph Campbell researched ancient stories of world cultures and found a universal blue-print for human transformation, calling it "The Hero's Journey." This is not the only narrative structure he found, but certainly it is one that remains valid in today's society and in our storytelling. We see it in films like *The Wizard of Oz*, *Star Wars*, and *Gandhi* (Chris Vogler's book *The Writer's Journey* splendidly elaborates this point), and it continues to give us hope against all odds that we will succeed in our quests. The structure consists of three basic acts: 1) discontentment or imbalance with the home community; 2) journey into the unknown in search of a treasure or solution, with many battles along the way; 3) return to the community with something of value, as well as an internal transformation of character and story resolution.

This three-act structure is also found in classical music, in particular the sonata form (see Chapter 5, ***The case of the sonata***), which has an equivalent to dramatic action using a beginning, middle, and end: a first theme which is countered by a second theme, development, and finally synthesis. The polarity created by the two contrasting themes can be seen as a reflection of life and society — with its contradictory emotional pressures and tensions that strive and struggle and ultimately reach a resolution.

On a more detailed level, music arouses expectation and heightens emotion using chord structures such as a minor seventh (see Chapter 5, ***Harmony and dissonance***) that demand resolution to the tonal center. This dynamic corresponds to the story development of a conflict demanding resolution.

Meaning in music, story, and film arises when expectation is contradicted. Setting up a joke with a 1-2-3 punch line is a classic twist of expectation, as with the satire of films like *Airplane* or *Scary Movie*. Similarly, Beethoven would develop his themes toward a logical point, then flip it toward a new direction, drawing the audience all the way to the end of a movement before resolving the structure. The contradiction occurs between the conventional expected structure based on genre (also considered the Gestalt background for the audience) and the individual story or musical structure that actually appears (the Gestalt foreground). The clearest tension is that which combines a maximum of contradiction with a maximum of unification between these background and foreground elements. In other words, arousing unfulfilled expectations, heightening suspense, and postponing resolution are all essential to build this tension so that the "all is well" ending has emotional value.

The pattern of arousal followed by relaxation is found in music, movies, sex, and competitive sports. In fact, this ubiquitous rhythm is found in all areas of human life, causing intense emotional sensations, followed by feelings of peace and satisfaction. This simple rise and fall of tension, when combined with the three-part synergy of thesis-antithesis-synthesis (and also modeled in chaos theory as the combining of two incompatible energies to make a new emerging form), provides the richness and stimulation that we hope for in a two-hour feature film.

When a sound element is repeated and associated with narrative themes at characters' transformational stages, they will be escorted with an accumulation of meanings that support the dramatic evolution. This is the creative process that occurs when the script or film is being analyzed and the sound designer discovers the perfect audio elements to convey the story as it unfolds (see Chapter 1, **Creating the Sound Design Step-by-Step**).

***Dane Davis developed a distinct dramatic evolution through the fight sequences in* The Matrix:**

"In that movie there are a bunch of fight scenes, all completely dramatically different in terms of what they mean. We didn't want them to sound the same — they had to evolve. And one of my goals was that I didn't want to use any sounds that had been used before for anything. So I had to create a completely new library for body punches, *wooshes*, etc. The first battle with Trinity could break certain rules of what people expect humans could do, like her jump in slow motion, but not with her karate hits. It couldn't be so outrageous that it would be questionable, because at that point people think they are in the real world. Then later when you realize you're not in the real world, all the usual hits could be exaggerated, augmented, an expanded reality, power that was not just derived from muscle structure. We did the very last scene in the subway and defined that that was where we were going to go, and it took weeks to figure out how powerful to make these guys, both Neo and Agent Smith. Then everything had to be between the first battle with Trinity and that last battle. For example, I really pictured that scene in the bathroom between Smith and Morpheus like two buffaloes ramming. From a craft point of view, we could do anything we wanted, but it had to be completely within those assumptions that the story led you to. We pushed the line of believability until Neo himself was seeing everything in code, breaking all the rules about what's real and what's not, but always maintaining a clear evolution of conflict between the good guys and the bad guys."

Earthquake effect

An earthquake is an example of a series of sound events that adds up to a dramatic narrative sequence rather than a simple boom and crash. One possibility is to portray it in four separate parts, with a few seconds' pause between each. First comes a low rumble, shuddering and growing for a second or two. Then make a couple of crashes of pottery mixed with a little louder rumbling. Next introduce a sudden sliding, crashing sound (which can be achieved by dropping a quantity of small stones on the sloping lid of a cardboard box with a glass jam jar at the bottom, and dropping the pitch an octave or two). And finally, bring in the rumbling noises again, then fade out to zero. An effective brooding sensation can be obtained in between the earthquake sounds with very faint distant voices, while panic noises like screaming and shouting can be laid behind the third "falling debris" section.

Production design and image analysis

Some people have a rare condition called **synesthesia**: they live in a world where one sensation (such as sound) conjures up one or more others (such as color). It is suggested in Dr. Richard Cytowic's book, *The Man Who Tasted Shapes*, that we may all have been synesthetic at one time during development. Our brains seem to be wired to be capable of perceiving the same elementary features in several of our sensory modalities.

What this implies is that production design and image can influence sound design, and generally in this direction because of standard scheduling of these tasks. However, in Chapter 1, **Creating the Sound Design Step-by-Step**, suggestions are made to have the sound design influence the production design as well, if there is time allotted for this fertile exchange.

The distinction in this chapter between production design and image analysis is based on the former being a planned strategy for the visual storytelling before the film is shot, and the latter being the actual result attained. Both will have the same relationship to the sound design with respect to their synesthetic influence.

The task of the production designer is to tell the story visually, as does the sound designer acoustically. The elements of image (brightness, hue, contrast, shape, space, texture, movement, framing) are different from those of sound (rhythm, intensity, pitch, timbre, speed, shape, organization) and music (melody, harmony, dissonance, tonal center), but they are related through the Gestalt principles. In both image and sound, the polarities or contrasts are what we perceive.

The choice of any of the image or sound elements, or their combination, should come from a master plan, namely the story and characters. If, for example, the protagonist starts off with the emotions shut down and life

TRY THIS

Our brains will easily make parallels between the contrasts in sound and image. For example, the polarity of light-dark brightness can be equated to loud-soft intensity, or rough-smooth texture with white noise-pure sine wave timbre. Innumerable comparisons can be drawn, but the most important step in doing so is that it be established within the context of the specific film on which you are working. Make a list of possible polarities in image, then see what you might come up with for corresponding sound polarities. Try switching around the sound-image pairs and look for unexpected alchemy.

possibilities seemingly stunted (think about *American Beauty*, *The Fight Club*, *Being John Malkovich*, *The Matrix*), it would be appropriate to show that character in an enclosed environment, framed into a colorless, static space. The sounds that would accompany such production design would have little perspective, directionality, or movement, and be unchanging (e.g., mechanical or electronic hums). At another moment in the story, when the protagonist explodes into new discoveries and ways of being, the production design would create spatial openings, depth, contrast, and dynamic movement. The sound design could mirror this with perspective in sound (near, middle, distant) and a variety of frequencies, timbre, and volume.

As music can have counterpoint between different instruments, so can production design and sound design. If the image shows constraint, like in the protagonist's stunted phase as described above, then perhaps another subconscious or fantasy level could begin to seep through on the audio track, indicating the desire to escape that particular reality. In this case, the image holds a certain dominance over the physicality of the scene, but the audio allows a subjective release. It could be the opposite in a carnival scene that explodes with visual activity, where the protagonist is hounded by a killer and the internal state is of complete paranoia and claustrophobia. In this case, the sound could contrast to the expected loud, joyful music by cutting out the music altogether and exaggerating the hoarse panting and frantic footsteps.

Performance analysis

For all the script structure, production design, and technical preparation to express the story on screen, nothing can really substitute for the spontaneity and authenticity of an actor's interpretation. This raw human energy is what binds the audience to the film more than any other element; it also can guide the sound design in new and subtle directions.

Walter Murch's book *In the Blink of an Eye* describes how he uses exactly that moment of an actor's eye blink to determine when to make a picture cut, because in fact this is usually a natural break point in the rhythm of the scene. By sensitizing to the actor's rhythm, the editor has choices of branch points in the storytelling. For example, the sequence of surprise, then recognition, can be extended or compressed by intercutting with a POV (point of view) shot, or the recognition component can be eliminated altogether to give the scene an entirely different meaning. The editor must identify these options and the meaning inherent in each, then decide which serves best for the film. The levels of anticipation, desire, excitement, and naturalness can be manipulated by minute adjustments of the in and out points of the cut. Good editing ultimately reflects the audience's own thoughts and feelings.

The performer's voice can give clues to the text and subtext of the scene, which can then be supported through other sounds. The prosody (see Chapter 6, ***Prosody — vocal melody and emotion***) can stimulate ideas for creating associated environmental sounds or subjective interior elements, either through reinforcement or counterpoint. For example, if the actor expresses a sentence broken by coughing and exudes a feeling of hesitation or timidity, then at the appropriate moment this could be paralleled by an off-screen sound of a car having difficulty in starting up, sputtering and backfiring.

Voice analysis can also be made on the level of identifying the formants and how these give clues to the character's inner emotional states (see Chapter 6, ***Voice personalities***). Knowing that a voice is lacking certain frequency bands or emphasizing others can provide clues as how best to modulate the frequencies of other sounds or music in the scene. For example, if the character has a hollow voice (nothing but the fundamental frequency) that contributes to the characteristic of depression or debility, then contrast and emphasis can be made with surrounding sounds that exhibit the higher frequencies. This is best done sequentially rather than simultaneously, otherwise the higher surrounding sounds might mask the voice's lack of higher formants. Using a different approach, the environmental sounds might resonate the same formants as the actor's voice, making the whole scene project the tone of the voice personality.

The actor's body and movement can also give stimulus for sound design. If the actor is aggressive and takes over the screen, then it is likely that the sounds will flow towards the character's presence as well. There may be an identifying piece of clinking jewelry or a swishing nylon jacket that will normally be foleyed in postproduction, which can also serve to identify the character's presence off screen or in the subjective memory or fantasy of another character. The movement of an actor might be languid, rigid, rhythmic, or spastic, which can lend a hint as to how the character's identifying sounds or musical themes might help emphasize a state of being. Furthermore, when the character undergoes a change in state of being as exhibited through movement or clothing (e.g., relaxed to tense, rigid to collapsed, fast to slow), this can be accompanied with the soundtrack elements as well.

Gary Rydstrom describes how his sound design is influenced by an actor's voice:

"There are times in movies that I love, when you go inside the mind of a character. In that case you could use the sound quality of their voice, the rhythm, as to how they are perceiving the world. In *Rush*, the cop character of Jennifer Jason Leigh starts doing drugs herself and has a bad trip, with her voice becoming very interior and slurred. We broke the soundtrack down as though it was losing coherence, even the Jimi Hendrix song was dropping away and turned into this point of view of mush. Some of these ideas came from her acting and the way her voice sounded, losing control."

If the film allows the extension of relating the characters with animal types, the actors' facial expression and body language can stimulate ideas in this area. This was used very explicitly for the wolf characters in *Wolfen*, *Wolf*, *The Tenth Kingdom*, and *X-Men*, but it can also be applied more subtly with straighter dramatic pieces. For example, a very sensual woman rubbing up to her partner affectionately might have a low-level cat purr mixed under her sigh. Or a glutton stuffing his dinner down might be accompanied by a few gleeful pig snuffles.

Sound references

Sounds have meanings to individuals or audiences depending on their context, and are considered symbolic when they stir in us emotions or thoughts beyond mechanical sensations or signaling functions. A significance or reverberation rings through the deeper recesses of the psyche with this type of sound event.

The acoustic symbol can come from four reference levels: **universal**, **cultural**, **historical**, or **film specific**. These levels also apply to musical meaning as pure musical structure/codes, cultural/social context, or cinematic relationships.

Universal

We are affected by sound since before birth; all cultures have a relationship to the universal aspects of our environment. Certain sounds resonate on an archetypal level for all people, like a lion growl, screeching fingernails on a blackboard, or a heartbeat. The more ancient portions of our brain respond to sound by helping us survive, provoking the flight-or-fight response, attraction to mother/food, sexual delights, or simply relaxation and a sense of wellbeing. Environmental sounds like water can produce a feeling of cleansing, change, and reawakening, while wind can provoke a sense of lack of direction, perhaps a place or moment not to be trusted. When glass is broken, it can tear at the heart like the sob of a woman, a forever-lost love.

These are potent types of sounds that transcend culture, yet by themselves can appear as clichés if not managed skillfully and in the right dosage.

Horror films play upon these physiological and archetypal references to the point of becoming genre stereotypes (see page 210, **Film specific**) and risking a laugh factor at the wrong place if not well choreographed.

Pure music originates with the percussive sounds of rain pelting on hollow logs, song birds, waves lapping on the shore, whistling wind, animal cries, stone and metallic tools, and human vocal sounds. As music becomes composed and performed it reflects the environment, eliciting the sense of being in a forest with a myriad of noises, or out on a barren desert with only a single drum. The mountains give opportunity to discover the very high and the very low frequencies, echoing the peaks and valleys.

Orchestral conventions play between universal and cultural references, having both a physiological and stereotypical aspect to the instrument sounds and musical genres (see Chapter 5, ***Emotional signifier*** and ***Genres***). Prokofiev's "Peter and the Wolf" played with this interface, portraying the duck with a quacky oboe, the hunters with courageous French horns, and the grandfather with the limping bassoon.

Cultural

Musical coding developed from our environmental background into culturally specific sounds. For example, ragas (see Chapter 5, ***Structure and function***, **World music**) reflect the sounds of nature, society at work, and the spiritual philosophy of the Indian people. For a Western ear though, it might be associated with "exotic," "India," or maybe even the Beatles, who were fundamental in introducing this type of music to the masses. The fact that twenty-two semitones exist in the Indian scale, recognizable to their ears but not to Westerners, points to a specific cultural learning of sound. On the other hand, a slinky saxophone solo might conjure up the image of a sexy blonde in a bar for American audiences, but the Indian audience might just hear "Western" music.

Each culture carries its soundmark through the environment, religion, work ethic, social life, language, and musical expression. The social symbolism of classical music (Haydn and Mozart in particular) becomes associated with the aristocracy, while rock'n'roll is for the masses, in defiance of the status quo and the older generation.

George Watters speaks of the importance of location sounds to establish an authentic cultural context:

"*The Thomas Crowne Affair* and *The Red Corner* were challenging in a different way than the big action films, which need lots and lots of sounds. These were filmed in New York and China. I enjoyed them because you focus somewhat on reality, contrasted with a film like *Armageddon* where nobody knows what an asteroid sounds like. They can't come to you and say, 'Hey, when I was on that asteroid it sounded this way.' As long as the audience believes what it hears in the film, you have done your job. For example, on *The Thomas Crowne Affair*, since people recognize what New York sounds like, it has to be recorded there. The film is shot on a sound stage, so you have to put in the traffic, horns, metallic brake squeals of taxicabs, etc. It is not like the sound of Los Angeles; people know the difference. In *The Red Corner* there were really small cars, higher pitched horn honks, which were totally different from the New York equivalents. I listed all the locations in this film and used wild track recordings from each Chinese city because of the different dialects in each region which contribute to the authenticity. You wouldn't be able to record in Chinatown in San Francisco, it wouldn't make sense or be believable."

If the name of the baseball team "Dodgers" is spoken, imagine how differently the context and relationship will be to listeners from Los Angeles (current home town), New York (Brooklyn, past home town), Tokyo (a foreign baseball legend), London (maybe heard about some American sports team), or Rio (no idea, no connection). The word travels from being an icon to nonsense, depending on the cultural association.

Technological sounds are generally disliked in industrial countries and often associated in film with bad guys or bad feelings, but are considered novel and amusing in places where they have never been heard. It was found that the whizzing of a dentist drill creates a phobic reaction in all countries polled except Jamaica, where there existed little if no dental care to create that cultural acoustic symbol.

Taboo sounds appear absurd to those outside their cultural context, but can be followed by banishment, destruction, and death if made inappropriately. Some tribes will not utter the names of enemies or dead ancestors out of sheer fright. Noises associated with the day, like the pounding of grain, are forbidden at night, lest they disturb the sleeping spirits in the depths of the forest near the village. The Christian habit of observing silence on the Sabbath exhibits similar social/religious precautions. In our contemporary world, the civil defense siren is reserved in silence for that fatal day when it might be sounded once and followed by disaster; but in a rock'n'roll concert or rave this same siren might elicit ecstatic cheers and trance dancing from the audience.

Another example of culturally based reactions to sounds is the expletives that surface for their shock value. Swearing by the names of "Christ," "God," and "Jesus" found its way into public conversation in 1960s North American lingo, converting previously sacred words into harshly spoken blasphemous slang.

Ultimately fear and intolerance of deviation from culturally defined standard ways to make sounds can cause a breakdown in communication across national boundaries. In real life, this is being shifted increasingly to a shared language (verbal and nonverbal) because of globalization through the media, especially in the upcoming years with the Internet streaming audio to all corners of the world. For now, this breakdown can be harnessed by the sound designer as a dramatic element in storytelling.

In *African Queen*, the opening sequences explicitly contrast the white and African cultures through the counterpoint of sounds and music. As the missionary's church organ pumps out Christian hymns accompanied by the overtly out-of-tune singing of the villagers, the scene is interrupted by the boisterous toot of Bogart's boat along with a playful *kalimba* (African thumb harp).

Once again the climax of *Air Force One* is a prime example of such a vivid cultural contrast: the American President and the Russian terrorists duke it out in a kind of battle of the bands. Piping over the plane's radio is the proud nationalistic Russian theme as their political leader is freed from maximum security. Slicing into this pomp and circumstance during the President's bold escape is a very American-style orchestral theme. This sequence is really a gem of mixing dialogue, screaming, rattling machine guns, and vivid foley, but the deepest current of emotion is carried by the two contrasting musical themes in a fight to the end. A similar situation occurs with the singing of the Nazi and French national anthems in *Casablanca*.

A special case applies to the genre of comedy, where references are intentionally broken in an unexpected way. Dane Davis compares his work in fight scenes like* The Matrix *with more light-hearted fare:

"There are completely different sets of rules for comedy than for drama. It makes it like a cartoon, like in the football scenes in *Romeo Must Die*, when everyone knows that you don't make those kinds of sounds playing football, and you get away with it because the audience is involved, rooting. Both the rules of film and the rules of football are being broken at the same time."

Historical

It is quite clear when you see a film with historical costumes, customs, transportation, and architecture that it is a historical piece. Less obvious, but as powerful in conveying this impression, are the appropriate sounds for that era.

As mentioned, within the Western culture the acceleration of change has reflected on the acoustic environment as well. Certain ideas expressed in sound have migrated from nature, to small town, to industrial city, to the information age. The "sacred noise" of thunder, the power of Zeus, was brought into the church, which became the sanctuary of the loudest sounds created by man (bells, reverberating pastors' sermons). Factories then took up the deafening roar of progress, materialism, and the sacredness of the big bucks, until this was grasped as a tool by the artists of the rock era and bumped up to ear-damaging levels on powered amplifiers.

Another migration occurred when the bird song was incorporated into thematic unity with the medieval garden and water sculptures (see page 182, ***Environments and the "soundscape,"***), an orchestration of romantic desires. In the 20th century, this was replaced by the radio and the Top 20 hits of love songs.

As touched upon earlier, the sounds of transportation in different epochs contributed to the musical expression of the times. Horse carriages with their clippity-clopping and horsemen's calls paralleled the development of opera. The clatter of mechanized industry introduced an element of percussion and multiphonic orchestration. The smooth rhythm and syncopation of modern trains laid the tracks for jazz.

Time also opens the way for extinction of certain sounds, which become historical artifacts, only appropriate for a period film or a memory device for a character's youth. Amongst the vanishing sound objects of our culture are the clanging of an ironsmith, an ice cream truck jingle, and a dial telephone ringing.

Music from another time can also jog the memory of a character and the audience toward the losses or joys of the past, propelling the story with powerful cultural currents (see page 212, ***Pleasantville — case study integrating story and music***). But also be cautious with the use of pre-existing music, as this association may provoke a loss of control in the storytelling process exactly because of the outside influence. Each audience member may bring a separate emotional memory with that music, and this may be contrary to what is desired by the film's narrative.

Film specific

Languages, metaphors, and clichés exist in the soundtrack of each film genre: the eerie whistle of the wind and echoing chain clanking in a horror film; the slide whistle and spring bonging in animation; the enormous rumble of a giant space ship in sci-fi; screeching tires and gunshots in cop movies. These serve as handles for the sound designer and audience to enter easily into known territory.

However, the inventive use of these genre sounds can push the experience into new and heightened directions. In *2001: A Space Odyssey* Kubrick took a Strauss waltz with its built-in lyrical, aristocratic qualities and juxtaposed this cultural reference with the space ships in a magnificent, memorable experience. To this day, many who hear this waltz automatically visualize those elegant floating architectures in the stars. For movie space ships, both the icons of subsonic force typical of the sci-fi genre (even if caricatured) and the brilliant inspiration of classical music can work. The decision should be based on what best serves the story and the emotions intended.

Within the realm of animated films, the references can take drastically different approaches. *Beauty and the Beast* strives to make the world as if you were there, using realistic effects and sweetening with precise ambient reverb for a naturalistic presence. *Aladdin* goes to the other extreme, with cartoon effects like a vaudeville slapstick act. The freedom is much greater and even Robin Williams' genie is full of adlib fun that became inspirational for sound designer Mark Mangini (who did both of these Disney films).

Once a sound is established within a film as a reference for that image-sound object or ambience, this should be adhered to unless a purposeful change takes place within the story. The ear is very keen on association, even when it is fabricated for the particular film, so something will feel different, maybe wrong, if it is shifted arbitrarily or unconsciously. On the other hand, if a sound is put in for convenience from the audio library at hand, this might upset a segment of the audience attuned to the accurate image-sound link. For example, in the 1970s TV series *Chips* a canned motorcycle noise was synced with a Harley-Davidson and drew the ire of many aficionado fans, persuading the producers to use the authentic sound.

The diegetic or nondiegetic source of the sound is another factor for referencing. If a character hears this sound inside the story, he or she may react viscerally to it, interpret it, respond to it, or try to ignore it. If it was a previously unheard sound, the reaction might be wonder, fear, or confusion, but if the sound has meaning and context, the reaction can be more subtle and integrated into the story line and character growth. If the sound was heard before but now has some modification or added element, then this change can well signify a direct change in the character's circumstances. When a sound is nondiegetic and not heard by any character in the story, then it falls upon the audience alone to register these references (see page 181, ***Primary and secondary emotions***).

Sound can serve as an emotional dictionary for any given film. As the audiovisual links are created in the story, they can be broken apart, recombined, amplified, and counterpointed. Once the film lexicon is established, the image and sound have the potential to stand alone and carry subliminal messages. Both the character's and the audience's memories can extract meaning in these fragments that is reinforced through the emotional context of the story. In *The English Patient*, for example, flashbacks are created using transitions of aural memory to fling us from the character's subjective experiences to the objective action on screen.

Pleasantville — *case study integrating story and music*

"The times they are a-changin'." Good drama is about change, confrontation of old and new — exposing the growing pains of a child, a relationship, a society. *Pleasantville* skewers all these levels and integrates the story with the evolving popular music of the '50s and '60s. The setting is a '50s black-and-white TV family drama (like *The Donna Reed Show*, referred to in the opening soundtrack) that is being viewed by a '90s teen ("Bud" in the TV show) who gets sucked into the TV world with his sexually precocious sister ("Muffy"). While the two participate in a sometimes hilarious, sometimes disturbing, emancipation, of this "perfect" society, the soundtrack begins with a happy, bustling "modern" city with strings and trombone orchestration as gallant firemen save Kitty in a tree — and everything's "gee, really keen." A bright post-WWII military anthem ushers the kids into school under the waving flag. (Muffy grimaces, "Stuck in Nerdville.") The fairytale romantic Pat Boone (Mom asks, "What's 'sex'?") croons as the kids hang out at Lover's Lane, inching up to holding hands.

Muffy introduces the handsome but naive basketball captain to what sex really is, and as the colors begin to appear in their blossoming black-and-white world, the music turns toward the hip-swiveling rock'n'roll of Elvis the Pelvis. The cultural gap begins forming both in the story and in the music, and Puritanical ethics are out the window.

When Bud is honored as a hero for getting the firemen to spray water over a burning tree (ignited by his mother's own sexual awakening), all the kids want to know where he learned about that. Wide-eyed with innocence, they hear him explain that outside of Pleasantville, "There are some places where the road doesn't go in a circle, some places where the road keeps going." The insidiously well-selected jazz tune of Dave Brubeck, "Take Five," beats in an edgy, non-Puritanical 5/4 rhythm, bursting the boundaries of these kids' traditional, cyclic 4/4 thoughts and lives.

But things go to yet another level when they find that the books, which up to now have been blank-paged props for the TV show, suddenly have text appearing. While Pleasantville teens find out about their new young hero Holden Caulfield, who discovers sexuality and more in the classic *The Catcher in the Rye*, Miles Davis' horn accompanies with sonic revelations from smoky jazz clubs, half-seen and half-thought bodies and shadows. And more and more kids transform into their full-color selves.

This is too far out for the establishment, and a grim crackdown results in book burning and outlawing lewd music. But Bud won't have it and plugs the juke box back in with that rockin' rebellious "...crazy feeling, I know it's got me reeling."

By now, the dam has burst and even the Gestapo-type mayor finds himself turning into Technicolor when he explodes with atypical, honest emotion. In the grand finale, the Beatles' lyrics of "Across the Universe" bring us solidly into the embattled, glorious, ironic '60s of change: "Pools of sorrow, waves of joy are drifting through my open mind, possessing and caressing me. Nothing's gonna change my world, nothing's gonna change my world..."

CHAPTER 9

THE FUTURE OF SOUND DESIGN

Where is sound design heading? The ability to make the finest, most supporting soundtrack possible depends to a large degree upon how soon the sound design work can begin in the production process. This important decision immerses the sound designer in a political and economic situation that is undergoing transformation in the world of cinema today. Other areas that can maximize sound design, such as Internet and interactive media, are developing new rules, thus offering brave new frontiers for structural and thematic exploration.

A word on sound politics — when can we start?

Traditionally the sound designer or supervising sound editor comes on board the production after the film has been shot, and often only after the picture has been edited. This unfortunately does not allow for much interactivity between the processes of editing image and sound. The music composer may not have much communication with the sound designer, and this too creates a gap between the elements, with a huge amount of energy and creativity wasted when it comes to the final mix.

My personal opinion is that the cost benefit of bringing on the sound designer early for consultation is greatly positive for the producer and the bottom line on the budget. If a consultation can be made before the film is shot, the sound designer can simultaneously help save money and increase the creativity in two major areas:

- **Script analysis** — Where can sound replace image to economize on costly shooting time? What image might open up a new possibility for the sound in order to increase its impact?
- **Preproduction planning** — In selecting locations and equipment, what might improve the production track to avoid having to "fix it in the mix," while taking maximum advantage of the sound crew?

Even the top sound designers in the industry have similar struggles to get on the production early and to have enough time to accomplish their creative tasks. Ben Burtt comments:

"A lot of what ends up in the mix depends on the personalities of the people involved and what their opinions are. As sound designer, I'm rarely given the opportunity to have final say. I can present alternatives, and if I can get the music before the final mix and I can play our material with it, we can make adjustments, and a big difference. That's only happened in one film I did, *Raiders of the Lost Ark*; just by a quirk in the schedule the music was recorded before I did a pre-mix of the sound effects. So I could adjust things so they orchestrated better. It just doesn't happen on a normal schedule. Usually everything arrives together and there's a collision at the mix. Then it's a matter of sorting things out, rather than polishing as it should be. You need to get your director, sound editor, and composer together to talk about these things, and obviously the best thing is if you can do some experiments. I think the key difference is a matter of scheduling and communication. The sound designer should get in there early with the director and composer, and experiment."

And George Watters adds:

"Films have become more complex both visually and in sound. This is a challenge creatively, which can be positive, except for the fact that the budgets and time schedules are decreasing. The average studio now spends a lot more money for what is seen on screen, but the budgets for sound have not increased. Personally, I wish this would change, because currently we have to basically beg, borrow, and steal for everything to do the job right. It is up to us to convince the director and/or producer to intervene, to enlarge a sound budget or to get us enough time in a schedule to give a film the detail it should have. For example, on a big-budget, action visual effects film, a studio will spend $30 million for visual effects which are seen in limited areas of the film. Sound, on the other hand, enhances the entire movie and we are given a tiny percentage of the resources at hand to do our work. Sound exists and supports the film from the opening to the end credits. We really take care of the whole movie."

It is not standard procedure for the production to hire a sound consultant in preproduction, so I suggest that you offer to read the script and give initial feedback free of charge. If you can prove your worth with this short investment of your time, then you have a better chance of getting contracted with a reasonable fee for the rest of the production. Consider the movie's whole budget as a parameter for determining how much you should charge for your services.

The bottom line is that sound has tremendous possibilities for expression and growth in the industry. As Gary Rydstrom says, "Sound is sometimes neglected, but I think it's a neglected powerhouse. People who are thinking of going into sound for film ask me, and I recommend it highly now, because of all the aspects of film I think it has the greatest possibility for improvement. So if you want to do something exciting and really shape how things are done, I think sound is an area to go in."

Internet and interactive media

The evolution of the computer industry and its market is so incredible that almost any comment in a book like this will be old news or maybe even inaccurate speculation by the time it reaches the reader's hands. Ideally this text would be accessible on a Web site with complete audio-visual accompaniment, interactive teaching tools, and constant updating for technological advances. But for now, let's consider a glimpse of the potential that this new media offers for the sound designer.

The development of both audio and video over the Internet and on CD-ROM and DVD to date (2001) has been constrained by the speed limits of the hardware. Short download times, lower resolution, small memory, little screens, repetitive loops, and basic simplicity have been the rules to follow in this area, but technical and market considerations will soon open up the field. This transitional phase will evolve so that no creative or technical boundaries will exist between conventional and "new" media.

There are indeed some aspects of the new media that go beyond what can be expected in cinema. For example, the separation of channels using headphones on the computer, rather than listening to sound through theater speakers, allows binaural effects to be used to their full potential. One example is binaural beating, which is similar to the beats created by close frequencies (see Chapter 4, ***Tone***, **Out of tune and beat phenomena**) but is occurring inside the brain in the absence of air molecules. The neurological connections create the beats, and in so doing also create an entrainment of brainwaves at the resonant beat frequency. For example, if the two tones are 400 and 408Hz, they create a beat of 8Hz, which will provoke an 8Hz brainwave, or alpha state. This does not occur readily in a theater because the pulse of the beat reaches both ears equally from the speakers.

The most profound difference between film and the new media is interactivity, the greatest leap that can be experienced by users (we used to call them the "audience," but that is too passive a position) and designers. Sound can either be **streaming** in a constant flow and often looped, or can be in the form of an **event** as a single audio object that is activated by some user control like pushing a button icon with the click of a mouse. The user has both the discovery and the decision to repeat or go forward along a variety of paths. Interactivity will take on unforeseen permutations and possibilities, a truly golden opportunity for sound designers to investigate.

Explore and share your discoveries!

APPENDIX

Classification of sounds

The purpose of classifying information is to discover similarities, contrasts, and patterns in the vast array of possibilities, to ultimately improve our perception, judgment, and creativity in designing the most impactful soundtrack we can imagine. Throughout this book different types of classifications of sounds have been made using characteristics of the physical (acoustics), subjective (psychoacoustics), meaning (verbal), emotional/aesthetic (music and storytelling), and technological (film processes).

Following is a classification of sounds based on their referential sources and functions. This is certainly not an all-inclusive listing, but is intended to serve as a further stimulus for perceiving relationships between sounds and their potential to help communicate in the audiovisual media.

NATURAL SOUNDS

WATER
Rain
Rivers
Oceans and lakes
Ice and snow
Fountains
Faucets
Steam

AIR
Wind (leaves, sand, window)
Storms and hurricanes
Thunder and lightning

EARTH
Rocks
Trees
Grass
Earthquakes
Landslides and avalanches
Mines, caves, and tunnels

FIRE
Forest fire
Building fire
Volcanoes
Camp fire
Matches and lighters
Gas lamps
Torches
Ritual fires

BIRDS
Hen
Rooster
Owl
Duck
Dove
Pigeon
Sparrow
Hawk

ANIMALS
Dogs
Cats
Horses
Cattle
Sheep
Wolves
Lions and other big cats
Bears
Monkeys
Gorillas and other apes
Frogs

INSECTS
Bees
Flies
Mosquitoes
Crickets
Cicadas

FISH AND SEA CREATURES
Whales
Dolphins
Fish

SEASONS
Spring
Summer
Fall
Winter

HUMAN SOUNDS

VOICE
Speaking
Calling
Whispering
Crying
Screaming
Coughing
Grunting
Groaning
Singing
Humming
Laughing

BODY
Breathing
Footsteps
Hands (clapping, rubbing, etc.)
Eating
Drinking
Evacuating
Lovemaking
Heartbeat

CLOTHING
Natural fibers
Leather
Synthetics
Shoes
Jewelry

CULTURAL SOUNDS

RURAL ENVIRONMENT
North America
Central and South America
Europe
Middle East
Africa
Central Asia
Far East
Arctic and Antarctic

CITY ENVIRONMENT
North America
Central and South America
Europe
Middle East
Africa
Central Asia
Far East

MARITIME ENVIRONMENT
Ships
Boats
Ports
Buoys
Beach
Seagulls

DOMESTIC ENVIRONMENT
Kitchen
Living room and fireplace
Dining room
Bedroom
Bathroom
Doors
Windows and shutters
Garage
Yard

PROFESSIONS
Computer programmer
Lab technician
Surgeon
Garbage collector
Butcher
Fisher
Teacher
Police officer
Tailor
Carpenter
Cook
Sculptor

FACTORIES AND OFFICES
Bakery
Stock market
Shipyard
Sawmill
Steel mill
Bank
Newspaper

ENTERTAINMENT
Movies
Television
Radio
Theater
Sports
Street performers

MUSIC
Singing
Acoustic instruments
Electric instruments
Electronic
Folk
Orchestra
Band

Pop
Ethnic

FESTIVALS/CEREMONIES
Parades
Carnival
Fireworks
Weddings
Baptism
Funerals

GARDENS/PARKS
Fountains
Concerts
Birds
Playground

RELIGIOUS CEREMONIES
Jewish
Catholic
Hindu
Moslem
Buddhist
Tibetan
Native American

MECHANICAL SOUNDS

LAND TRANSPORTATION
Cars
Buses
Trucks
Motorcycles
Bicycles
Skateboards
Rollerskates
Trains

OTHER TRANSPORTATION
Planes
Helicopters
Rockets
Boats

MECHANICAL TOOLS
Saws
Drills
Hammers
Chisels
Planes
Sanders

DEMOLITION
Compressors
Jackhammers
Bulldozers
Pile drivers

FARM MACHINERY
Binders
Tractors
Threshing machines
Combines

OFFICE MACHINERY
Air conditioner
Calculator
Telephone
Computer
Coffee maker

KITCHEN APPLIANCES
Toaster
Blender
Garbage disposal
Dishwasher

Refrigerator
Can opener
Chopping board
Cheese grater

WAR MACHINES
Guns
Rocket launchers
Bombs
Tanks
Fighter jets
Submarines

SIGNALS

BELLS
Church
Clock
Sports
Animals

HORNS/WHISTLES
Sports
Bicycle
Car
Traffic cop
Boats
Trains
Factory

WARNING SIGNALS
Curfew
Air raid
Alarm clock
Emergency vehicles
Contamination leak

QUIET AND SILENCE

TECHNICAL
Anachoic chamber
Physiological (only heart, breathing)
Film reproductive system (optical, electronic base noise)

SUBJECTIVE
Room tone
Countryside
Nighttime
Faraway animal calls
Isolated sounds (i.e., clock ticking)

FILMOGRAPHY

2001: A Space Odyssey........162, 210
African Queen....................208, 227
Air Force One.......31, 107, 208, 227
Airplane....................124, 199, 227
Alien...........125, 140, 146, 180, 227
All That Jazz....................162, 227
Alladin..127
Altered States..............................97
American Beauty........................ 201
American Graffiti.......................193
Amistad.................................... 158
Annie Hall..................................157
Apocalypse Now..............56, 80, 159
Apollo 13....................................127
Armageddon......................127, 216
As Good as It Gets........................10
Backdraft................45, 58, 126, 193
Bear, The....................................147
Beauty and the Beast..... 51, 147, 180, 193, 210
Being John Malkovich.................201
Blade Runner.............................163
Blair Witch Project, The.....126, 170
Braveheart........................184, 185
Bugsy..193
Casablanca..................................208
Casper... 57
Citizen Kane...............................113
Civil Action, A............................178
Clockwork Orange, A..............156
Close Encounters of the Third Kind 19, 194
Cocoon.......................................147
Conversation, The..............126, 135
Crimson Tide..............................177
Crossroads..................................112
Dances with Wolves......................158
Deliverance..................................112
Doctor Zhivago.............................180
Dreams..127
Drugstore Cowboy.........................179
Elephant Man, The..........................31
English Patient, The..............80, 211
E.T. 140, 147-148, 180
Face to Face..................................126
Farinelli...................................... 119
Fight Club, The............................201
Gandhi..198
Godfather, The.........25, 80, 118, 193
Gone in Sixty Seconds.....................37
Haunting, The..............................57
Hot Spot, The...............................193
House on Haunted Hill.................181
Hunt for Red October, The............ 177, 180, 189, 191
Jaws...78, 92
Jungle Fever.................................180
Life is Beautiful............................158
Malcom X.....................................192
Matrix, The...................17, 44, 143, 154, 179, 200, 201, 208
Mission to Mars..............................88
Mon Oncle....................................167
My Dinner With Andre..............163
Naked Gun......................................59
On the Waterfront........................118
Pearl Harbor.................................183
Platoon...182
Pleasantville................173, 210, 212
Quiz Show....................................194
Raging Bull..........................41, 191

Raiders of the Lost Ark........96, 162, 216
Raising Arizona..................159, 194
Red Corner, The....................37, 207
River Runs Through It, A...........126
Rock, The....................109, 183, 216
Rocky..190
Romeo Must Die..........................208
Rush.....................................56, 204
Saving Private Ryan............64, 162, 170, 178
Scary Movie................................ 199
Schindler's List............................158
Sous les toits................................196
Star Wars..................58, 60, 79, 89, 140, 147- 148, 169, 173, 179-180, 182, 185, 193, 198
Streets of Fire............................. 191
Super Xuxa.................................164
Teenage Mutant Ninja Turtles......58
Tenth Kingdom, The..................204
Terminator 2...............40, 128, 163, 192-193
Thomas Crowne Affair, The........207
THX 1138..........................34, 125
Top Gun.....................160, 193, 216
Tron...192
Twin Peaks.................................144
Who Framed Roger Rabbit?..........28
Witness.......................................180
Wizard of Oz, The.............153, 198
Wolf...........................175, 204, 206
Wolfen..204
X-Men.......................................204
Yellow Submarine..........................99
Zéro de Conduite.........................140

BIBLIOGRAPHY

FILM SOUND, MUSIC, AND EDITING

Audio Design: Sound Recording Techniques for Film and Video
Tony Zaza, Prentice-Hall, 1991, 408 pages

Audio-Vision: Sound on Screen
Michel Chion, Columbia University, 1994, 239 pages

In the Blink of an Eye: A Perspective on Film Editing
Walter Murch, Silman-James Press, 1995, 114 pages

Sound for Film and Television
Tomlinson Holman and Gerald Millerson, Butterworth-Heinemann, 1997, 368 pages

Sound for Picture: An Inside Look at Audio Production for Film and Television
Mix Pro Audio Series, Hal Leonard Publishing, 1993, 133 pages

Sound-on-Film: Interviews with Creators of Film Sound
Vincent LoBrutto, Praeger Publishers, 1994, 299 pages

Unheard Melodies: Narrative Film Music
Claudia Gorbman, Indiana University Press, 1987, 189 pages

NON-FILM SOUND

The Conscious Ear: My Life of Transformation through Listening
Alfred A. Tomatis, MD, Talman Company, 1992, 306 pages

A Course in Phonetics
Peter Ladefoged, Harcourt Brace Jovanovich, 1982, 300 pages

Ear Cleaning: Notes for an Experimental Music Course
R. Murray Schafer, BMI Canada Limited, 1967, 46 pages

An Introduction to the Psychology of Hearing
Brian C. J. Moore, Academic Press, 1997, 373 pages

The Mystery of the Seven Vowels: In Theory and Practice
Joscelyn Godwin, Phanes Press, 1991, 107 pages

The New Soundscape: A Handbook for the Modern Music Teacher
R. Murray Schafer, BMI Canada Limited, 1969, 71 pages

Sacred Sounds: Transformation through Music and Words
Ted Andrews, Llewellyn Publications, 1992, 232 pages

Soundmaking: The Acoustic Communication of Emotion
Peter F. Ostwald, MD, Charles C. Thomas Publisher, 1963, 185 pages

The Soundscape: Our Sonic Environment and the Tuning of the World
R. Murray Schafer, Inner Traditions Intl. Ltd., 1993, 301 pages

Sound Synthesis and Sampling
Martin Russ, Focal Press, 1996, 400 pages

Subliminal Communication: Emperor's Clothes of Panacea
Eldon Taylor, Just Another Reality, 1990, 131 pages

3-D Sound for Virtual Reality
Durand Begault, AP Professional, 1994, 293 pages

MUSIC

The Mozart Effect: Tapping the Power of Music to Heal the Body, Strengthen the Mind, and Unlock the Creative Spirit
Don Campbell, Avon Books, 1997, 332 pages

Music and the Mind
Anthony Storr, Ballantine Books, 1992, 212 pages

Music, Sound and Sensation: A Modern Exposition
Fritz Winckel, Dover Publications, 1967, 189 pages

Music, the Brain, and Ecstasy: How Music Captures Our Imagination
Robert Jourdain, Avon Books, 1997, 377 pages

Sound Medicine: Healing with Music, Voice, and Song
Leah Maggie Garfield, Ten Speed Press, 1987, 192 pages

Sounding the Inner Landscape: Music As Medicine
Kay Gardner, Elemente Books, 1997, 272 pages

The Sounds of Healing: A Physician Reveals the Therapeutic Power of Sound, Voice and Music
Mitchell L. Gaynor, Broadway Books, 1999, 288 pages

The Tao of Music: Sound Psychology
John M. Ortiz, PhD, Samuel Weiser, 1997, 390 pages

The World Is Sound: Nada Brahma Music and the Landscape of Consciousness
Joachim-Ernst Berendt, Inner Traditions Intl. Ltd., 1991, 258 pages

CREATIVITY

The Act of Creation: A Study of the Conscious and Unconscious in Science and Art
Arthur Koestler, Dell Publishing, 1967, 751 pages

The Artist's Way: A Spiritual Path to Higher Creativity
Julia Cameron, Jeremy P. Tarcher, 1992, 222 pages

Educating Psyche: Emotion, Imagination and the Unconscious in Learning
Bernie Neville, HarperCollins, 1989, 302 pages

Free Play: The Power of Improvisation in Life and the Arts
Stephen Nachmanovitch, Jeremy P. Tarcher, 1990, 208 pages

Go See the Movie in Your Head: Imagery — The Key to Awareness
Joseph E. Shorr, Ross-Erikson Publishers, 1983, 233 pages

The Man Who Tasted Shapes
Richard E. Cytowic, MD, A Bradford Book/Putnam, 1993, 234 pages

Personal Mythology: The Psychology of Your Evolving Self
David Feinstein and Stanley Krippner, Jeremy P. Tarcher, 1988, 268 pages

The Possible Human: A Course in Enhancing Your Physical, Mental and Creative Abilities
Jean Houston, Jeremy P. Tarcher, 1997, 256 pages

STORYTELLING AND SCREENPLAY STRUCTURE

The Art of Dramatic Writing
Lajos Egri, Simon & Schuster, 1977, 305 pages

Hamlet on the Holodeck: The Future of Narrative in Cyberspace
Janet Horowitz Murray, Free Press, 1997, 304 pages

Hero with a Thousand Faces
Joseph Campbell, Princeton University Press, 1972, 464 pages

Screenplay: The Foundations of Screenwriting
Syd Field, Dell, 1982, 272 pages

Screenwriting: The Art, Craft, and Business of Film and Television
Richard Walter, New American Library Trade, 1992, 240 pages

Story: Substance, Structure, Style, and the Principles of Screenwriting
Robert McKee, HarperCollins, 1997, 480 pages

The Writer's Journey: Mythic Structure for Storytellers and Screenwriters
Christopher Vogler, Michael Wiese Productions, 1992, 289 pages

MISCELLANEOUS

Freedom Chants from the Roof of the World, The Gyuto Monks
Rykodisc/Mickey Hart, Audio CD, 1989

Music for the Movies
Bernard Herrmann (Primary Contributor), Dir. Joshua Waletzky, VHS Tape, 1992

INDEX

3D space.................................. 160
accordion.................................. 189
acousmatic.......................... 29, 153
Across the Universe.................... 213
actions................................ 1, 2-3, 23, 25, 28, 37, 45, 78
actor's body, interpretation... 7, 202, 204
acuity....................................... 89
ad lib.. 157
adaptation......................... 94, 128
added value............................. 168
ADR (automated dialogue replacement)........ 33, 158, 159
Aeolian harp............................ 186
alarm................................. 55, 184
Alcatraz................................... 183
alien......................... 131, 147, 148
All Quiet on the Western Front.. 180
alpha brainwaves............. 110, 218
ambience.................. 1, 3, 6, 9, 14, 25, 29, 31- 33, 35-38, 42-43, 50, 55, 70, 73, 75, 80, 125, 158, 160-162, 165-167, 170, 177-178, 191, 195-196, 211
Ammons, Gene....................... 112
anechoic chamber............ 124, 189
anempathetic music......... 156, 169
animal(s)................. 31, 50, 53, 61, 84, 91, 102 104, 112, 115, 125, 131-133, 139-140, 142, 147-149, 156, 180- 181, 184, 191-193, 204-205
animation.................. 57, 190, 210
anticipation............. 115, 117-118, 123, 167, 203
Apollo.............................. 104, 127
approximants.......................... 132
archetypal sounds............. 182, 184
attacks....................... 39, 60-61, 66
auditory hierarchy................. 195
aural reflex............................. 75
Australian aboriginals............ 102
Bach.......................... 104, 109, 119
background.......... 5, 27-28, 32-34, 36-39, 50, 66, 69-70, 75, 80, 84, 97, 124-126, 139, 154,158, 166, 187, 195-196, 199, 206
bagpipe................................. 141
Bali.................................... 97, 186
balloon......................... 20, 40, 164
banjo...................................... 112
Baroque.................................. 109
bassoon............................. 68, 206
beat frequency, phenomena... 8,95, 218
Beatles........................ 39,206, 213
Beethoven.................. 22, 56, 114, 140, 199
bell(s)...................... 41,80, 82, 86, 96, 102, 183-186, 209
belongingness...................... 82, 83
Berendt, Joaquim-Ernst 122
beta brainwaves................ 54, 110
big band................................. 109
binaural beats..................... 96, 218
bipolar(ity).......................... 10-14
birds........................... 38, 83, 102, 153, 183-184, 205
blues................. 109, 111, 123-124
body temperature............... 54, 71
Bonny, Helen.......................... 105

Boone, Pat.............................. 212
brain hemispheres................. 138
brainwave(s).......... 54, 96-97, 110, 114- 115, 218
breathing............. 4, 8, 11, 19, 30, 33, 54- 65, 71, 74, 79, 94, 97, 109-110, 115, 116, 133-134
bridging................................ 165
Brown, Treg........................... 190
Brubeck, Dave.........................212
budget.................... 4, 48, 215, 217
bullet................................ 88,192
Burtt, Ben..............60,79, 89, 140, 146, 197, 216
Cage, John.................. 39, 58,124
Cage, Nicolas.......................... 159
call and response................... 112
Cameron, James.................... 170
Campbell, Joseph...... 114, 173, 198
Carroll, Lewis........................ 137
cartoon(s)............. 28, 57-58, 115, 164, 190, 208, 210
cat....................... 9, 41, 44-45, 61, 115, 133, 156, 179, 204
Catcher in the Rye,The............ 213
cathedral................................ 161
Caulfield, Holden................. 212
causal................................. 77-79
CD-ROM............................ 217
cello....................................... 59
chalk screech......................... 98
chamber music.................161, 187
chaos theory.......................... 199
Chewbakka............................. 147
chimes........................... 183, 186
China.............................. 189, 207
Chion, Michel.... 77, 153, 156, 171
Chips...................................... 211
Chladni forms....................... 121
Chopin.............................105, 109
church....... 184-187, 192, 208-209
circadian rhythm................... 111
city(ies).......... 28, 66, 96, 161, 180, 185, 189, 207, 209, 212
Clair, Rene............................ 196
clapping................................ 129
clarinet..............................59, 140
cliché.......... 8-9, 55, 107, 205, 210
clock........... 11, 14, 19-20, 29, 43, 55, 65, 84, 86, 90, 125-126, 154, 170, 183-186
closure.............................. 81, 114
cochlea.............................. 72-74
Cocteau, Jean......................... 56
comedy........... 5, 8, 29, 38, 41, 59, 61, 83, 117-118, 124, 143-144, 156, 158, 171, 174, 188, 194, 208
common fate......................... 82
completeness.................... 81, 121
composer........1, 15, 19-20, 23, 27, 29, 30, 39, 42-44, 101, 106, 111, 114, 123, 175-176, 182, 188, 215-216
computer............... 26, 39, 41, 97, 137, 154, 217
concrete sounds............ 19-20, 23, 27-28
conflict......... 11, 12-13, 44, 81, 95, 107, 110, 114, 122, 124, 140, 146, 157, 174-176, 179, 188, 196-198, 200
consonants.............. 67, 90-91, 93, 131-132, 136, 138
continuity................ 29, 101, 136, 155-166
contrast(s)..................... 55, 75, 84, 113, 128 154, 159, 180, 197, 201-202

counterpoint................ 6, 8-9, 15, 17-18, 22- 23, 31, 43, 71, 99, 101, 155-156, 188, 202-203, 208
country western.................... 109
creativity.......2,15,21,38,40,43,45, 53-54, 56, 57, 105, 194, 215
critical band.......................... 75,92
crowd......................... 7, 19, 82, 98, 106, 157, 180
cry(ing).............. 25, 27, 31, 61, 84, 92, 102, 133, 139, 149
cue sheet................................ 18,49
cymatics.................................. 121
Cytowic, Richard.................... 201
dakini...................................... 142
Davis, Dane.........17, 44, 115, 118, 143, 154, 165, 179, 181, 191, 200
Davis, Don.............................. 44
Davis, Miles............................ 213
de-acousmatizing.................... 153
dead bodies............................. 180
Debussy............................. 22, 109
decays................................. 39, 60
decibels.............................. 66,139
degree of expansiveness........... 162
dialogue...................... 3, 6, 10, 15, 17-19, 21, 24-25, 27, 29-30, 32-35, 38, 40, 43, 47-48, 50-52, 66, 81, 84, 90, 118-120, 125, 128, 131, 136, 137, 140, 144, 147-148, 151, 153, 156, 157-159, 161, 166-167, 169, 177, 182, 195-197, 208
dialogue recording.................. 159
diegesis........................ 14, 20, 23, 28, 152, 154, 166
diegetic................ 20, 25, 153-154, 157, 164, 211
Dionysus................................ 104
directionality............ 5, 73, 83, 85, 87- 88, 201
director..................... 1, 3, 6, 15-19, 23-25, 27, 31, 43, 45, 47, 51-52, 54, 55, 59, 147, 159, 162, 175-177, 179, 181, 216
Disney....................... 147, 190, 210
dissonance.............. 10, 18, 70, 95, 111, 120-122, 128, 152, 175-176, 198, 201
distance.................... 6, 31, 33, 57, 69, 77, 82-86, 87-88, 118, 131, 136, 157, 159, 160-162, 169
distortion................................ 32
distributor............................... 47
dixieland.......................... 109, 112
documentary.................... 43-44, 48
Dodgers................................. 206
Dolby........................... 46, 48, 124
Donna Reed Show, The............ 212
doorbell........................... 166, 196
Doppler................ 60, 88, 192-193
dramatic evolution................ 198
dream............ 15, 54-56, 105, 109, 144, 189, 190
Dreyfuss, Richard.................. 119
drone.................... 56, 71, 95, 123, 141, 179, 185
drum(ming).................... 141, 184
dubbing......................... 24, 32-34
DVD................................ 48, 217
E.T. 140, 147, 148, 180
ear canal................................. 72-73
eardrum.........................66, 72-73
earthquake........... 63, 67, 199-200
echo............ 10, 21, 24, 39, 49, 59, 69, 83-85, 160-161, 189, 192
echolalia................................ 132
Egri, Lajos............................. 173
Eigentone.............................. 187

Electric Night........................... 139
elimination.............. 126, 127, 157
ellipsis.................................... 166
Elvis the Pelvis...................... 212
emanation speech.................. 157
emotion........... 7-10, 29, 31, 42, 47, 104- 106, 107, 117, 122, 124, 133, 138, 144, 169, 173-174, 178, 182, 190, 198, 203, 208, 213
emotional signifier...........104, 155, 169, 206
emotions........ 1-3, 8, 22-23, 28-29, 59, 71, 101, 105-107, 134, 146, 156, 165, 173, 181-182, 201, 205, 210- 211
empathetic....................... 169,174
entrainment.................. 77, 97-98, 110-111, 115, 218
envelope......... 61, 68, 83, 104, 147
environments.... 1-3, 5, 23, 28, 38, 83, 159, 164, 182, 184-185
exaggeration... 41, 55, 61, 126, 194
exhibition............................. 1, 46
explosion............. 44, 88, 93, 128, 164, 168, 178, 184, 189
eye(s)........... 1-2, 6, 21-22, 45, 53, 72, 74, 78, 91, 114, 129, 145, 151, 152, 190, 195, 203
factories................................. 209
false sync point...................... 167
fantasy..................... 105, 110, 125, 155, 164, 179, 202, 204
Farinelli................................. 119
fatigue......................... 66, 94,145
Faulkner, William................... 180
feminine form........................ 113
Field, Syd............................... 173
fight................. 165, 190-191, 196, 200, 205, 208, 216
figure.......... 80, 117, 183, 195, 200
fire....................... 45, 58, 112, 126, 164, 191, 193
firearms.................................. 191
fission.................................... 119
flat voice................................ 145
flutes.......................... 59, 102, 189
foley......................... 34-36, 40-41, 57-58, 164, 208
folk music.......................... 43, 136
folk tales................................ 142
football........................... 208, 209
footsteps................................ 180
forced marriage..................... 171
foreground............. 124, 180, 183, 196, 199
foreign language............... 40, 158
formants............131-132, 144-145, 203-204
Four Seasons.......................... 175
frequency(ies).......... 5-6, 8, 11, 21, 30, 33, 36, 43-44, 47, 50, 59, 63-64, 67-68, 70, 71-75, 80, 83-86, 88, 91-92, 94-96, 98, 128, 132, 140, 144, 160, 163, 184, 187, 202-203, 205, 218
fricatives................................ 132
fundamental tone.............. 67, 95
fusion......... 89, 101, 104, 119, 120
genre(s) 5, 22, 27, 38, 41, 48, 101, 109-110, 124, 126, 155, 179, 199, 205-206, 208, 210
Gestalt.......................... 77, 79, 136, 183, 195, 199, 201
Ghiza-I-ruh............................ 102
Glass, Philip.................... 116, 142
glossolalia............................... 143
goals.... 17, 106, 114, 174-175, 200
Godwin, Joscelyn................... 146

gongs.. 102
good continuation.............. 81, 136
Gorbman, Claudia...... 44, 140, 182
gorilla.. 180
gospel... 109
Gray, Wardell............................ 112
Greek chorus............................ 196
Gregorian chants...... 109-110, 116
ground............. 31, 37, 80, 87, 147, 160, 169, 183, 197
grunge.. 109
Guided Imagery and Music (GIM)... 53, 105
guitar............ 16, 59, 112, 119, 124
gun(shots).... 63, 184, 192, 208, 210
habituation.............. 51, 55, 92, 94, 128-129
Hall, Cecelia.............................. 193
Hanks, Tom....................... 178,188
harmonic progressions............ 142
harmonic structure.................. 175
harmonicas................................ 189
harmonics.......... 59-60, 68, 95, 103, 120, 122, 124, 129, 131, 135
harmony................. 10, 30, 98, 101, 103-106, 108, 118, 120-122, 138, 140, 152, 156, 175-176, 188, 198, 201
harp..................... 41, 186, 189, 208
Haydn....... 104-105, 109, 114, 206
headphones.............. 37, 76, 86, 96, 137, 217
hearing loss................ 94, 170, 178
heartbeat............ 14, 17, 20, 54, 65, 74, 79, 94, 110, 115-117, 205
heavy metal............................... 109
Hendrix, Jimi..................... 56, 204
Hero with a Thousand Faces..... 173
Hero's Journey... 114, 173-174, 198
hertz.. 67
hi-fi.. 161
Hindemith............................... 106
hip hop.................................... 109
historical................... 144, 164, 173, 182, 188, 205, 209
Hitler....................................... 106
hollow voice............................. 145
Horn, Paul.......................... 87,161
horns.................... 28, 37, 102-103, 183-185, 206-207
horror............. 105, 118, 121, 155, 170, 181, 210
horse carriages......................... 209
Hunt, Helen............................... 10
Hutese...................................... 148
Huygens, Christian.................. 97
hypnogogic state.................... 54
identification music................ 182
impact.............................. 109, 190
Indian........ 95, 112, 138, 189, 206
infants...................... 104, 133, 139
infrasonic............................. 67, 98
inner ear.................. 2, 21, 23, 36, 38-39, 73, 88
integration time.................. 75, 89
interactive media............. 215, 217
interactivity.............. 116, 136, 149, 171, 188, 215, 218
internet................... 208, 215, 217
intonation...... 31, 33, 93, 140, 148
inverse sound spectrum.......... 129
ironsmith................................. 209
iso principle............................ 98
Jabba the Hut......................... 74
Jabberwocky.............................. 137
Jamaica................................... 207
Japan....................................... 189
jazz.................. 22, 101, 109-110, 112, 119, 187, 209, 212-213

jet fighters.............................. 193
Jourdain, Robert...... 110, 117, 156
kabuki theater......................... 136
kalimba............................ 41, 208
Kaye, Danny.....................140,148
Kenobi, Obiwan....................... 179
keynote sounds....................... 182
Kruger, Wilfried...................... 121
Kurasawa............................... 127
labyrinth................................ 161
Ladefoged, Peter..................... 132
language................ 16, 30, 43, 50, 55, 70, 72, 78, 80, 101, 120, 123, 125, 131-132, 137, 140, 142-143, 146, 148, 158, 204, 206, 208, 210
Latin America......................... 189
laughter................. 7, 61, 65, 102, 112, 133, 139, 141, 181
Lee, Jennifer Jason................. 204
Lévi-Strauss, Claude............... 103
Lievsay, Skip.......................... 159
lion...... 61, 78, 115, 180, 193, 205
listening modes...................... 77
loop track.............................. 38
loudness.......... 51, 63, 66, 74-75, 89-90, 92, 94, 98, 128, 193
love songs.............................. 209
low-fi.................................... 161
Lucas, George........................ 147
lullabies................................. 119
lute....................................... 141
MacDonald, Jimmy................. 190
Man Who Tasted Shapes, The... 201
Mangini, Mark................ 146, 210
mantra(s).......... 54, 102, 116, 142
Marpurg, Friederich.......... 107,108
Marsalis, Wynton.................. 110
masking............ 30, 40, 75-76, 80, 125, 139, 155, 196
McKee, Bob............................ 173
McTiernan, John..................... 177
meditation... 54, 80, 102, 127, 129
melody......... 30, 68, 81-82, 90-91, 101-102, 105-106, 108, 118-119, 138, 140, 144, 156, 175-176, 185, 188- 189, 201, 203
Menuhin, Yehudi.................... 101
metaphors.............................. 210
meter......................... 92, 116, 142
mickey-mousing..................... 156
microphone........ 7, 33, 35, 37, 41, 50, 60, 74, 76, 159, 163
Middle Eastern....................... 189
mix................ 1, 5, 18, 21, 28-29, 31-32, 34-36, 38-39, 43, 45-46, 48, 50-52, 74, 76, 80, 86-87, 94, 146, 149, 159-160, 163, 168-169, 195, 215- 216
monaural beats....................... 96
mood.................... 18, 20, 98, 107, 109-110, 129, 142, 166, 183
Moore, Brian........................... 160
Morpheus............................... 200
motifs................................ 21, 30
motorcycle....................... 192, 211
movement........................ 87, 111
Mozart............ 105, 109-110, 114, 138, 206
multilingualism...................... 158
multiple meanings........... 158, 168
Murch, Walter.............. 15, 56, 80, 125, 135, 193, 203

music.............. 1, 7, 14-15, 17-20, 22-23, 27, 29-31, 39-40, 42-44, 47, 50-52, 56, 66, 70-71, 74, 81, 87, 89, 90-91, 93, 95, 98-99, 101-107, 109-120, 122-123, 125, 128-129, 133, 136-138, 140, 142, 151-156, 161, 164-169, 171, 175-178, 182, 184, 187, 191, 195-199, 201-203, 205-206, 208, 210, 212-213, 215- 216
M&E (music and effects).... 40, 50
musical instruments........... 42, 53, 59, 68, 82
musical scale.................... 119-120
musique concrete.................... 58
Muzak.................................... 110
narrative analysis.................... 173
narrative cueing............. 155, 165
narrative unity........................ 155
nasals...................................... 132
Native Americans........... 112, 142
Neo.................................. 44, 200
new age..................... 90, 109, 110
Nicholson, Jack...................... 10
non-diegetic............. 23, 153-154, 196, 211
non-literal sound.................... 178
object............... 1, 3, 4, 10, 23-24, 28, 39, 55, 61, 78, 81-88, 116-117, 135, 152-153, 164, 166, 173, 177, 181, 186, 190, 192-195, 209, 211, 218
objective time......................... 90
oboe........................ 104, 131, 206
ocarina.................................. 131
octave.................................... 121
off screen.......... 28, 30-31, 33, 47, 125, 152-153, 160, 162, 166, 169-170
off track.................................. 154
on screen........... 3-4, 20, 24-25, 28, 44, 48, 50-51, 99, 110, 134, 153, 155-158, 162-163, 166, 168, 190-191, 193, 202, 211, 216
onomatopoeic................. 140, 143
onset transient distortions..... 69
on track.................................. 154
opera............... 113, 136, 175, 209
orchestra................... 97, 114, 119, 131, 163, 167
organization.......... 60, 63, 65, 70, 110, 201
orgasm............................. 11, 113
ossicles.............................. 72, 73
Ostwald, Peter.......... 139, 141, 144
out of tune............................ 95
overtone.................. 103, 124, 133
overtone singing.................... 103
oxygen atom.......................... 120
Pachelbel's *Canon in D*........... 116
Parsifal.................................. 175
percussion............... 103, 114, 209
performance............. 32, 159, 175
perspective........ 16, 23, 33, 50, 53, 57, 83-85, 96, 161, 163, 177, 201, 202
Peter and the Wolf............. 175, 206
phase shifting........................ 76
phone............... 2, 61, 78, 82, 119, 163-166, 196
phonemes........................ 134-135
phrasing........................... 116, 141
pianos.................................... 59
pig.................................. 191, 204
Pink Panther theme............... 156
pinna.................................. 72-73

pitch......... 6, 10-11, 20-21, 29-31, 36, 40, 43, 45, 49, 58, 60, 63, 65, 67-68, 71, 74-75, 82-83, 88, 90-95, 113, 117, 119, 124, 128, 139- 140, 147-148, 159-160, 168, 185, 193, 195, 197, 200-201
planets.................................... 120
Pleasantville.............. 173, 210, 212
plot.................... 9-10, 12, 18, 117, 122, 135, 142, 157, 174, 179
poetry..................................... 142
point of audition..................... 163
point of synchronization........ 167
polarity..................... 198, 201, 202
pop.................................. 109, 175
precedence............................. 86
pre-production planning........ 215
primary emotion..................... 182
print master.......................... 1, 51
producer.................. 19, 23-24, 47, 51-52, 215, 216
production design........ 4, 14, 173, 175, 201-202
programmatic music.............. 156
Prokofiev........................ 175, 206
proliferation........................... 158
prosody....... 30, 138, 140-143, 203
Proximity............................... 81
psychoacoustics...................... 7
pulsation threshold............... 116
punches.................. 177, 190, 200
punk....................................... 109
Pythagoras............................. 103
R2D2..................................... 148
radio......... 20, 34, 55, 73, 86, 101, 152- 153, 159, 184, 208-209
ragas....................... 112, 142, 206
Rakha, Alla...............................112
rap................................. 101, 109
Rapid Eye Movement (REM)... 111
Ravel................ 98, 103, 109, 116
recognition............................ 93
Redford, Robert..................... 126
reduced................... 52, 77, 79, 90
referential........................... 77, 79
reggae.................................... 109
Reich, Steve............................ 142
Renaissance..................... 186, 189
resolutions............................. 174
reverb(eration)......... 6, 24, 33, 37, 39, 47, 49, 51, 69, 83-84, 125, 136, 160-161, 163, 185-187, 189, 191-192, 205, 210
reverse................... 17, 26, 38, 80, 93, 144, 189
rhumba.................................. 109
rhythm............. 3, 8, 11, 14, 19-20, 22, 25- 26, 29-31, 33, 40, 56, 60, 63, 65, 67, 70, 77, 91, 94, 96, 97-98, 101, 106, 110-111, 113, 116-119, 128, 136, 138-140, 144, 156, 162, 164-166, 175-176, 185, 188-189, 192, 199, 201, 203-204, 209, 212
robust voice........................... 145
rock'n'roll................ 42, 109-110, 136, 185, 187, 206-207, 212
Rodgers, John........................ 120
rondo..................................... 113
Ruff, Willie............................ 120
Rydstrom, Gary..... 57-58, 64, 126, 128, 146-147, 162, 170, 193, 194, 204, 217
salsa....................................... 109
samba.................................... 109

samplers................ 41, 43, 60, 188
satire........................... 8, 141, 199
sax(ophone)................... 112, 206
Schoenberg............................ 106
Schumann resonance.............. 98
sci-fi (science fiction)..... 34, 39, 42, 105, 125, 155, 193, 210
Scott, Tony............................ 177
scream........... 11, 55, 92, 133, 193
script.......... 1, 2, 4-5, 9-12, 14, 18, 21-24, 26, 28, 37, 54, 126, 135, 148, 173-176, 179, 199, 202, 217
script analysis.......................... 215
secondary emotions................ 181
semantic...................... 77, 79, 138
semitones............................... 206
separation of channels............ 217
Serafine, Frank........................ 34
serial music............................ 106
shamanic drumming....... 109, 110
Shankar, Ravi......................... 112
shape........... 46, 60, 63, 65, 68, 69, 114, 120, 139, 161, 201, 217
sharp voice............................. 145
signals.................... 65, 70, 76, 85, 160, 182, 186
silence............... 5-6, 23, 36, 47, 52, 54- 66, 101, 117, 124-128, 135, 161, 164, 166, 180, 192, 207
similarity................. 55, 81-82, 90
sirens......................... 28, 183-185
sitar.. 112
size................... 27, 83-84, 86, 93, 161-163, 187-188
slang....................................... 208
slapstick.............................. 8, 210
snake................................ 56, 180
Solo, Han.............................. 185
sonata.............. 111, 114-115, 198
song............ 16, 30, 102-103, 116, 120, 123, 136, 138, 204-205, 209
soniferous garden.................. 186
sound arc............................... 170
sound editor............. 1, 15, 18-19, 25, 43, 75, 81, 215, 216
sound effects...... 1, 14, 20, 25, 28, 35, 39, 42, 44, 56-57, 115, 118-119, 143, 148, 154, 164-165, 168- 169, 178, 190, 197, 216
sound libraries..................... 36-37
sound map........... 1, 18-19, 21-23, 26-27, 31-32, 37, 42, 46, 49-50, 56
sound object.......................... 190
sound politics........................ 215
sound recordist.................... 24, 36
sound shadow......................... 85
soundmark(s).................... 182-183
soundscape.............. 80, 182, 184, 186, 188, 189, 195, 209
space ships............................. 210
spatial dimensions.......... 159, 187
spectacle music...................... 182
speech recognition................ 134
speed.......... 11, 36, 40, 45, 60, 63, 65, 68, 74-75, 79, 89-90, 94, 98, 139, 151, 161, 163-164, 167, 185, 187, 193, 195, 201, 217
Spielberg, Steven............ 148, 170
Stein, Gertrud 142
Stockhausen.......................... 58
story.................... 2-5, 7, 9, 12-15, 17, 19-20, 22-24, 26-27, 29, 38, 42-44, 48, 52-53, 64, 87, 101, 105, 113-114, 122, 124-125, 127-128, 137, 141, 151-154, 156-157, 163-166, 168, 170, 173-176, 190, 197-202, 210-212

storytelling......... 2, 11, 18, 21, 26, 29, 56, 83, 85, 112, 114-118, 122, 126, 128, 142, 151, 157, 167-168, 170, 173, 175, 179, 198, 201, 203, 208, 210
Strauss............................ 189, 210
Stravinski, Igor......... 103, 106, 113
streaming................ 186, 208, 218
stuttering............................ 8, 132
subjective time.......................... 90
subliminal........... 38, 80, 103, 211
subplots................................... 142
subsonic............................ 98, 210
subwoofer........................... 47, 60
summation.......................... 79, 89
suspension...................... 105, 127
synchrony....... 22-23, 97, 159, 166
synesthesia.............................. 201
synthesizers......................... 41-43
taboo sounds.......................... 207
Taj Mahal.......................... 87, 161
"Take Five"............................. 213
tala... 112
Tati, Jacques..................... 127,167
Tchaikovsky............................ 109
telephone............... 20, 21, 39, 49, 82, 91, 93, 139, 154-155, 163, 180, 188, 209
temporal delay........................ 85
temporal dimensions............. 164
temporal integration............. 89
temporal resolution............... 89
terror............................... 5, 38, 41
textual speech......................... 157
texture.................. 27-28, 90, 159, 164, 201- 202
theatrical speech.................... 156
thesis-antithesis-synthesis...... 199
theta brainwaves............... 97, 110
thunder.................. 29, 51, 59, 64, 153, 167, 185, 209
Tibetans............................ 72, 142
timbre.......... 6, 28-29, 31, 38, 43, 45, 60, 63, 65, 68, 80, 82-87, 90-93, 98, 128-129, 135-136, 140, 144, 166, 175, 185, 191-192, 201-202
tires............... 17, 88, 94, 115, 210
Tomatis, Alfred........................ 134
tonal center......... 95-96, 101, 106, 111, 123-124, 138, 175, 182, 198, 201
tones............. 8, 11, 39, 59, 61, 71, 73, 75, 89, 91-92, 96, 108, 112, 119- 120, 136, 138, 140, 152, 188, 192, 218
torpedoes........................ 177, 191
train(s)............. 25, 118, 152, 165, 179, 185, 193, 196, 207, 209
transformation........ 3, 25, 30, 115, 120, 129, 142, 185, 194, 196, 198, 215
transition(s)............ 1-3, 9-10, 12, 23, 28-30, 38, 49, 98, 102, 120, 166- 167, 189, 195, 211
transportation........... 37, 187, 209
Trinity.................................. 200
triplets.................................. 20
tripolar.................................. 12
Tristan and Isolde.................... 175
trumpet.................. 103, 110, 139, 141, 179, 189
tuning fork............................. 69
ultradian.......................... 22, 111
ultrasonic............................... 67
undertone............................... 124
underwater......................... 49, 64
Vader, Darth...................... 79,179

vaudeville................................ 210
vehicles................................... 192
violin........ 59-60, 68, 94, 141, 168
visual maps....... 1, 3, 12, 15, 22, 23
Vivaldi.............................. 109, 175
vocables.................................. 142
vocal............. 17, 46, 61, 102-103, 116, 119, 131-134, 138, 143, 147, 180, 186, 205
vocal chords............................ 131
Vogler, Chris.............114, 173, 198
voice(s).............. 1, 3, 7, 10, 13-14, 19, 21, 23, 25, 27, 29-35, 42-43, 47, 49-51, 59, 66-68, 70-71, 73-74, 79-82, 84, 91-93, 95, 104, 112, 123, 126, 129, 131-141, 143-149, 153-154, 156, 159-160, 162-163, 169, 173, 177, 180, 184-186, 187-188, 196, 200, 203, 204
voice acoustic stereotypes....... 145
voice personalities........... 144, 203
volume........... 6, 9, 29, 31-32, 45, 49, 51, 74-75, 80, 83-85, 88-89, 92, 94, 98, 117, 128, 140, 159, 163, 166, 202
vowels....... 131-133, 135-136, 146
Wagner.................... 105-106, 175
wailing........................ 57, 88, 139
walrus.............................. 147, 180
Walters, Richard.................... 173
waltz............................... 189, 210
war(fare)................ 103, 139, 162, 180, 184
Warner Bros.......................... 190
water........... 40, 54, 57-58, 63-64, 70, 73- 74, 88, 102, 112, 119, 126, 149, 162, 164, 178, 183, 186, 189, 191, 194, 205, 209, 212
Watters, George............ 25, 37, 51, 59, 177, 183, 207, 216
Wayne, John............. 133, 144, 190
weather harp.......................... 186
Web site................................ 217
Western culture...................... 209
whistles................ 63, 131-132, 137, 148, 183, 185-186
Wilde, Oscar.......................... 105
Williams, Robin..................... 211
wind......... 3, 38, 50-51, 59-60, 63, 68, 74, 80, 88, 93, 127, 131, 153, 181, 183-186, 205, 210
wolf..................... 31, 81, 154, 204
woodwinds.............. 114, 189, 196
world music............................ 111
worldizing.............................. 159
Writer's Journey, The......... 114, 198
xylophones............................. 189
Zeus...................................... 209

DAVID SONNENSCHEIN
SOUND DESIGNER

Photo by: Richard Ollis

David Sonnenschein offers seminars, lectures, and consultation in sound design for film, TV, and interactive media. He is co-founder and president of Sonic Strategies, a company specializing in sonification for interactive media and emerging technologies. His interests also focus upon the research and creation of sound for therapeutic uses.

For more information please contact:

Sonic Strategies
18212 Kingsport Drive
Malibu, CA 90265
Tel./fax: (310) 454-4377
E-mail: *dsonn@charter.net*

Web sites: *www.webpages.charter.net/sounddesign*
www.sonicstrategies.com

When you get some interesting results from the **TRY THIS** suggestions in the book, I'd like to hear from you about this, with the intention of expanding our creativity and understanding of how sound can affect ourselves and our world. E-mail me!

FILM & VIDEO BUDGETS

3rd Updated Edition

Deke Simon and Michael Wiese

For over 15 years *Film & Video Budgets* has been THE essential handbook for both beginning and professional filmmakers. Written by two pioneers of do-it-yourself filmmaking, this book outlines every element of production.

Updated and revised for digital video productions (and video-to-film transfers), this definitive book contains detailed formats and sample budgets for many different kinds of productions, from "no budget" digital movies to documentaries to a $5 million feature—along with all the crucial practical information that's made it an industry bible. Also includes new and highly useful materials, such as a comprehensive master list of line items for just about everything that could possibly be put into a production, and information-packed chapters on handling pre-production and setting up a production company. Also includes Excel sample budget templates downloadable for free from the Web.

Deke Simon and Michael Wiese are veteran filmmakers who have had extensive experience in film, TV, and video.

Budget samples include:

- $5 Million Feature Film
- Documentaries (both film and video)
- Industrial
- Music Video
- Student Film
- No-Budget Digital Feature
- Digital Video Feature
- Video-to-Film Transfer
- And more!

$26.95
Order # 9RLS
ISBN: 0-941188-34-5

DIGITAL FILMMAKING 101

An Essential Guide to Producing Low-Budget Movies

Dale Newton and John Gaspard

The Butch Cassidy and the Sundance Kid of do-it-yourself fiimmaking are back! Filmmakers Dale Newton and John Gaspard, co-authors of the classic how-to independent filmmaking manual *Persistence of Vision*, have updated their handbook for the digital age. *Digital Filmmaking 101* is your all-bases-covered guide to producing and shooting your own digital video films. It covers both technical and creative advice, from keys to writing a good script, to casting and location-securing, to lighting and low-budget visual effects. Also includes detailed information about how to shoot with digital cameras and how to use this new technology to your full advantage.

As indie veterans who have produced and directed three successful independent films, Gaspard and Newton are masters at achieving high-quality results for amazingly low production cost. They'll show you how to turn financial constraints into your creative advantage—and how to get the maximum mileage out of your production budget. You'll be amazed at the ways you can save money—and even get some things for free—without sacrificing any of your final product's quality.

Dale Newton and John Gaspard, who hail from Minneapolis, Minnesota, have produced three ultra-low-budget, feature-length movies and have lived to tell the tale.

$24.95
Order # 17RLS
ISBN: 0-941188-33-7

ORDER FORM

TO ORDER THESE PRODUCTS, PLEASE CALL 24 HOURS - 7 DAYS A WEEK
CREDIT CARD ORDERS 1-800-833-5738 OR FAX YOUR ORDER (818) 986-3408
OR MAIL THIS ORDER FORM TO:

MICHAEL WIESE PRODUCTIONS
11288 VENTURA BLVD., #621
STUDIO CITY, CA 91604
E-MAIL: MWPSALES@MWP.COM
WEB SITE: WWW.MWP.COM

WRITE OR FAX FOR A FREE CATALOG

PLEASE SEND ME THE FOLLOWING BOOKS:

TITLE	ORDER NUMBER (#RLS ____)	AMOUNT
	SHIPPING	
	CALIFORNIA TAX (8.00%)	
	TOTAL ENCLOSED	

SHIPPING:
ALL ORDERS MUST BE PREPAID, UPS GROUND SERVICE ONE ITEM - $3.95
EACH ADDITIONAL ITEM ADD $2.00
EXPRESS - 3 BUSINESS DAYS ADD $12.00 PER ORDER
OVERSEAS
SURFACE - $15.00 EACH ITEM AIRMAIL - $30.00 EACH ITEM

PLEASE MAKE CHECK OR MONEY ORDER PAYABLE TO:

MICHAEL WIESE PRODUCTIONS

(CHECK ONE) ___ MASTERCARD ___VISA ____AMEX

CREDIT CARD NUMBER ____________________

EXPIRATION DATE ____________________

CARDHOLDER'S NAME ____________________

CARDHOLDER'S SIGNATURE ____________________

SHIP TO:

NAME ____________________

ADDRESS ____________________

CITY ____________________ STATE ________ ZIP ________

COUNTRY ____________________ TELEPHONE ________

ORDER ONLINE FOR THE LOWEST PRICES

24 HOURS | 1.800.833.5738 | www.mwp.com

Printed in the United States
789500006B